COOPERATIVE WISDOM

COOPERATIVE WISDOM

Bringing People Together
When Things Fall Apart

Donald Scherer, PhD, and Carolyn Jabs

GREEN WAVE BOOKS

Published by Green Wave Books
3436 State Street, Suite 197, Santa Barbara, CA 93105
www.greenwavebooks.com

Editorial direction by Diana Landau, Parlandau Communications
Cover and book design by Glyph Publishing Arts, glyphpublishing.com

ISBN: 978-0-9971668-1-1

Printed in the United States of America

Distributed by Ingram and Amazon

Print books and the e-book may be ordered from cooperativewisdom.org

First edition

*We cannot solve our problems with the same
thinking we used when we created them.*
Albert Einstein

Alone we can do so little; together we can do so much.
Helen Keller

CONTENTS

Introduction   1
Five Virtues that Dissolve Conflict and Restore Cooperation

Chapter 1   11
Being Good Is Not Enough
Why We Need Social Virtues More than Ever

Chapter 2   32
Proactive Compassion
Anticipating and Responding to Vulnerabilities
   Practices:
   Respond to risks revealed by specialization
   Intercept harms triggered by change
   Address gaps between assigned responsibilities

Chapter 3   62
Deep Discernment
Discovering Bedrock Values
   Practices:
   Distinguish bedrock values from means
   Be vigilant about accumulating harms
   Honor multiple points of view

Chapter 4   93
Intentional Imagination
Expanding What's Possible
   Practices:
   Examine assumptions
   Extend known resources
   Excavate concealed resources

Chapter 5   122
Inclusive Integrity
Reworking Cooperation So Everyone Can Thrive
   Practices:
   Enlist flexible specialists
   Anticipate predictable weakness
   Treat every plan as a hypothesis

Chapter 6   157
Creative Courage
Embracing the Risks of Engagement
  Practices:
  Address the failing hypothesis
  Confront imbalanced benefits without undue blame
  Hold tight to the cooperative vision

Chapter 7   189
Cooperative Wisdom
The Social Virtues in Action

Acknowledgments   215

Appendix   217
Five Social Virtues and Fifteen Practices that Support Them

Index   218

About the Authors   223

Next Steps   227

Five Virtues that Dissolve Conflict and Restore Cooperation

The human race is challenged more than ever before to demonstrate our mastery — not over nature but of ourselves.
Rachel Carson

The only thing that will redeem mankind is cooperation.
Bertrand Russell

This book is for people who try to do the right thing. This includes most of us, most of the time. Even very young children prefer good actions that help others to bad actions that are hurtful, according to recent research. Such studies confirm what most of us know from experience. We want to do right by other people.

And that's the puzzle. Despite our good intentions we often find ourselves enmeshed in conflict, accused of causing harm to others. Here are just a few situations in which good intentions might result in unintended harm:

- An Internet company tries to improve its product by gathering information about its customers, but finds itself accused of violating privacy.
- An entrepreneur develops an alternative technology for collecting solar energy, but discovers it has devastating effects on migrating birds.
- A politician introduces a bill designed to help farmers in her district, but finds herself vilified by people who object to standard practices for raising livestock.
- An educator hopes to make history more vivid by encouraging students to share their family heritage, but causes unintended distress to some whose ancestors were either enslaved or slaveholders.
- International policymakers try to create a safe haven for persecuted people, but this sets the stage for generations of conflict with people displaced by the newcomers.

Even within families, fair-minded and well-intentioned people can find them-selves locked in disagreements over everything from how to allocate resources to how to discipline children.

How is it that people who aspire to lead ethical lives so often encounter and even become implicated in difficulties that distress and harm others? Why is it that people of goodwill find themselves at odds when they would be better served by cooperating? And what should good people do in the face of such conflicts?

This book answers these questions with a new approach to the old idea of virtue. *Virtue* is a term that may seem old-fashioned, even a little off-putting. It's gotten a bad rap because people who claim to be virtuous are more often smug and self-righteous. In this book we intend to reclaim the idea of virtues as prin-ciples that inspire and guide. What are the essential qualities of character that promote human well-being? What habits of mind make it more likely that peo-ple will enjoy the benefits of cooperation? What life skills reduce the risk of unin-tended harm? Our renovated understanding of virtue answers all these questions.

The book grew out of conversation, so it's written as a dialogue between two voices. One is a seasoned and engaging teacher, an applied philosopher who has spent a lifetime analyzing practices that help people cooperate for mutual benefit in the face of change and conflict, hardship and opposition. The other is an enthusiastic learner whose background in journalism has nurtured both skepticism and appreciation for a good story. The teacher con-sistently converts problems that are deeply frustrating to others into oppor-tunities for collaboration and growth. The learner wants to know how.

Exploring challenging ideas through conversation has a long tradition, starting with Socrates and Plato, and we've worked hard to replicate the energetic back-and-forth of a spirited discussion. We've also introduced structuring elements so readers can track where the conversation is going, but we decided not to burden the narrative with citations. Our examples are gleaned from per-sonal experience and from studies that can readily be found online.

The two voices in the book are composites that incorporate our own experiences, as well as people we've encountered and authors we've read. Still, the characters are rooted in our lives, so introductions seem to be in order.

Don: My father died unexpectedly when I was thirteen. As I struggled with my sense of isolation and abandonment, I found myself at the public library, where a compassionate librarian directed me to the 100s and 200s in the Dewey decimal system: works of philosophy, theology, and psychology. When I started to read them, I discovered I wasn't alone in asking a fundamental question: In the face of changes that are unanticipated, unintended, and apparently devastating, how can we carry on?

Eventually, in college, I committed myself to the study of philosophy and especially ethics. My thinking was deeply influenced by the work of several key environmentalists, including Rachel Carson. Like many other people, I found myself wrestling with the ethics of sustainability. It seemed natural to me that wherever human beings perceive something of worth, they try to defend it. Yet that response often puts them on a collision course with natural forces that are in constant motion, and with other people defending other values. In my research I saw this process play out again and again. As the founder of the Environmental Ethics program in the department of Applied Philosophy at Bowling Green State University, I reviewed thousands of case studies in which changes brought about through natural catastrophe and/or human actions imperiled flourishing environments.

Such reports can be demoralizing—but as I thought, taught, and wrote about these cases, I began to glimpse a hopeful possibility. Yes, human activity is often responsible for the degradation of once-healthy environments, but people also have played a pivotal role in sustaining and even restoring valuable environments. One example is Ohio's Cuyahoga River Valley, which in 1969 became infamous as the place where a river caught fire. People were responsible for the pollution that created this problem, but by the early twenty-first century the river valley had been restored, and Cuyahoga River National Park is now the eighth most visited of all United States national parks. People were responsible for that, too.

Through study and analysis of cases like this one, my concept of *environments* expanded to include the cooperative human networks and communities that are so deeply entwined with natural environments. These networks and communities are also dynamic environments: constantly in flux, flourishing under some circumstances and degraded by others. Gradually my understanding of sustainability shifted away from the goal of maintaining a place or continuing a behavior indefinitely. If humans and other living things are to survive and thrive, we must simultaneously preserve what has established value and adapt to the opportunities created by change. In rapidly changing environments, sustainability cannot simply enshrine what has worked in the past. Instead, it must encompass whatever has been made possible by ongoing changes in nature and in human society.

Eventually I began a systematic search for principles and practices that make this kind of sustainability more likely—because they encourage people to respond to threatened natural and social environments thoughtfully, co-operatively, creatively, and constructively. Those practices—the action component of our five renovated virtues—form the core of this book.

Over the years I've been fortunate to mentor scores of talented students, equipping them to intervene in troubled environments. They have used practices recommended in this book to achieve breakthroughs in a wide range of apparently insoluble problems. Before anyone knew the acronym AIDS, one student developed protocols for keeping blood supplies uncontaminated. Before insurance companies recognized hospice care as a reimbursable expense, another student developed influential materials on the legitimate goals of palliative care. When the Cuyahoga River Valley was still essentially a dumping ground for industrial waste, a third student intern argued that the costs of restoring degraded ecosystems could be justified by recreational as well as ecological benefits.

In my own career, practicing cooperative wisdom has helped me bridge the gap between theory and practice in facilitating partnerships among educational institutions, government agencies, progressive corporations, communities of faith, and nonprofits. Such partnerships have generated creative solutions to apparently intractable problems. In 2007 I advised NOAA on ethical questions surrounding remediation of oil spills. At Bowling Green State University I fostered a partnership among the local municipal utility, the Ohio Department of Development, and the Electric Vehicle Research Institute that led to installing solar cells at the university's ice arena, greatly reducing power costs. At Santa Clara University I consulted with groundskeepers about maintaining habitat on campus for the endangered burrowing owl. More recently I've explored the benefits of growing warm-season perennial grasses in northwestern Ohio—not only to produce energy but also as a cost-efficient way of handling water pollution and flooding problems.

After I retired from the classroom, my wife and I drew on the cooperative virtues when we designed and built a green home powered by a wind turbine. And as I continued to reflect on the practices that had proved so potent in my life and work—and for my students—I decided to distill what I had learned into a graduate-level seminar for advanced students in philosophy and other fields at Bowling Green State. I gave it the ambitious name Society, Sustainability and Wisdom, and hoped that the notes I prepared for the seminar might become the basis for a book.

Carolyn: I was one of seven students in that seminar. Although I studied philosophy as an undergraduate, I'd spent my professional life as an editor and writer. Early in my career as a journalist I wrote about environmental issues, notably in *The Heirloom Gardener*—a book that encouraged people to take responsibility for the genetic heritage growing quite literally in their own backyards. Over time I became discouraged because so many environmental problems morphed into endless conflicts. Serious, sometimes irreparable harms occurred while courts wrangled over competing claims. Like many others, I turned away from apparently irresolvable problems and stopped asking questions that didn't seem to have any answers. Instead I retreated into family life and wrote about the challenges of raising children, including one with special needs.

The world, of course, kept spinning. Changes, subtle or dramatic, threatened to disrupt the orderly world I kept trying to create. The writing skills I'd spent a lifetime acquiring seemed to be devalued by new technology. What I thought I'd learned about parenting wasn't working well with children who wanted out of the nest. Everywhere I looked I saw social problems that resisted solving, because no one was responsible and every potential solution seemed to create as much harm as good.

In search of better answers I went back to school at Bowling Green State University to pursue an MA in Applied Ethics. Even there, solid ideas about how to do good in a complicated world were elusive. For many professors of philosophy it seemed enough to set out a problem—and why it was insoluble. Then, quite by accident, I found myself in Dr. Don Scherer's seminar, a class that would prove to be life-changing in the best sense of the word.

The seven students in the seminar came from different disciplines and worked in different settings—what Dr. Scherer taught us to call "environments." Each was wrestling with serious problems: the erosion of moral consciousness in middle-school students, the devastation of Florida's manatee population because of boating practices, the implications of game theory for nuclear annihilation, the impact of a polluted creek on an inner-city neighborhood, the way white-collar crime was eviscerating businesses, and (my own topic) predation in online environments. I remember feeling skeptical at first about the premise of the class. What kind of advice could possibly be relevant to scholars engaged with such very different issues?

To Dr. Scherer the common thread was obvious. Every student was struggling with an environment destabilized by conflict or degraded by change. He saw the seminar as an opportunity to distill a lifetime of thinking, teaching, and activism into a set of teachable practices that embody a more robust understanding of sustainability. As the semester progressed, students began to see parallels between their concerns. Insights from one student stimulated productive ideas for others. Every student experienced aha moments that infused optimism into projects that had seemed hopeless. One by one, stubborn problems opened up under Dr. Scherer's patient inquiry.

When the semester ended, I remember feeling panic. I could see the power of these new ideas in the classroom, but I couldn't reliably put them into practice without Don's guidance. Lacking weekly doses of this new philosophy, I worried that I would drift back into old habits of pessimism and cynicism. I was also aware that Don was working on a manuscript growing out of lectures prepared for the seminar. He knew that the renovated virtues and the practices that promoted them were effective, because he and his students had used them to help people resolve political, professional, and personal conflicts. Now he wanted to develop a coherent way to present these tools, so people who were not trained as philosophers could master and deploy his new approach to cooperation.

■ ■ ■

And so we struck a bargain. We would meet biweekly. Don would develop a more systematic approach to the ideas that had been so transformative for his seminar students. Carolyn would ask questions, record the conversations, and translate them into a text. Don had always enjoyed working one on one with capable, motivated students. Carolyn had extensive experience interviewing academics and translating their ideas into prose congenial to lay readers. Over countless cups of coffee, the conversations and transcripts accumulated. Gradually we realized we were creating a guide that would help people use these proven principles and practices for cooperation in business, government, volunteer organizations, faith communities, schools, and families.

Is the urge to cooperate built into our DNA? People with better scientific credentials than ours are working to answer that hard question. We begin from a parallel observation, rooted in history: our survival, as individuals and as a species, rests on our ability to interact in ways that reliably create benefits for everyone involved. From families, neighborhoods, and schools to corporations, governments, and international NGOs, cooperation lies at the heart of every human success. The virtues we espouse in this book are deeply social, designed to promote cooperation that ensures widespread benefits and avoids unintended harm. Our goal is to introduce a code of conduct that makes cooperation for mutual benefit more regular and more fruitful.

When we look around, we see that a predisposition toward cooperation usually prevails. Neighborhood associations coordinate the efforts of residents to make communities more attractive and secure. Businesses promote innovation in response to the needs of customers. Social workers strive to restore a supportive environment for clients who have suffered misfortune or trauma. Government agencies create and enforce laws that facilitate cooperation and punish people who take advantage of trust. The list of successful enterprises in which people work hard, and effectively, to sustain productive forms of cooperation goes on and on.

Perhaps because cooperation is the norm, frustration quickly becomes acute when our efforts to work together create harms instead of benefits. Traditional ideas of morality are meant to make cooperation more reliable. But they also press us to assign blame: if something's gone wrong, someone must be at fault. In Chapter 1 we reveal the fallacy of that assumption by examining the many ways cooperative endeavors can misfire—even when everyone is trying to do what they see as right. When systems are complex and specialized, or when change disrupts familiar patterns of interaction, conflict can arise in any setting, with outcomes ranging from divorce, dysfunction, and bankruptcy to gridlocked legislatures, revolution, and war.

And so we come to the questions that are central to this book. In the face of change and conflict, how can we adapt, creating new and productive forms of cooperation without sacrificing what has true and lasting value? Finding good answers to this question is our central goal. More specifically, are there habits of thought and action that enable people to transcend conflict and cooperate in ways that reliably generate benefits for everyone? The answer to that second question is a resounding *yes!*

Those "habits of thought and action"—our renovated virtues—are described in the book's central chapters. We've chosen the word *virtue* deliberately for its resonance with timeless truths, but it's important to remember that virtue is never static. Ideas about what contributes to human flourishing evolve over time, and so they require periodic updating. Like traditional virtues, these new ideas about being good come to life when we make daily decisions to engage with them. Cooperative wisdom is the reward for appreciating, learning, and internalizing all five of these core virtues:

- *Proactive compassion* attunes us to the vulnerability of participants in our cooperative structures.
- *Deep discernment* distills and deepens our grasp of what matters and how it may be threatened when cooperation breaks down.
- *Intentional imagination* reconceives what is possible.
- *Inclusive integrity* is the work of renovating social structures to ensure that benefits and respect are mutual.
- *Creative courage* fortifies us so we willingly incur the risks that change entails and conflict exacerbates.

Cultivating these habits of mind equips us to recognize new opportunities for cooperation while preserving what's precious, even in the face of unexpected and disruptive change. Concepts like compassion and integrity may seem familiar, but our double-barreled terms reflect the dual character of the five virtues. Rooted in traditional ideas of what it means to be good, each has been renovated to make it responsive to complex contemporary problems. Our conversation will urge you to stretch your understanding of goodness. In our complicated, interconnected world an understanding of morality that focuses on the individual is no longer adequate. All of the renovated virtues are social, framed specifically to promote cooperation.

For each virtue, we introduce three proven practices that will help readers translate ideas into action. Using examples from history, current events, family life, and even scripture, we hope to deepen your understanding of why the well-being of the human community requires a set of virtues that promote cooperation. This approach to virtue creates a way into even the most resistant conflicts, opening a path to cooperative wisdom that starts where other ethical theories stop. Most readers will find some of the practices we recommend more intuitive and natural than others. But if applied consistently and conscientiously, these practices have the potential to untangle conflicts and strengthen cooperation in families, schools, corporations, nonprofits, communities of faith, and even governments.

These virtues and practices aren't hopelessly difficult, but they do require a change in orientation. People often see conflict as something that requires a referee, someone who can reliably decide what's right and what's wrong. Cooperative wisdom starts from the assumption that conflict arises because both parties are defending something that matters, and that sustainable solutions are possible only when all relevant values are taken into account.

This approach served us well in writing the book. As a philosopher Don was invariably drawn to abstraction, finding common themes in drastically different circumstances. As a writer Carolyn pressed for more specific examples and tried to ask questions a smart reader would want answered. This natural tension in our conversations created the potential for conflict, but we evaded it, using the principles we recommend here. Only by committing ourselves to long-term cooperation could we derive the benefits we've enjoyed from our interaction. Gradually we've become true collaborators, creating a book that neither of us could have written alone and that we believe is better for our interaction.

During the years of working together, each of us faced personal challenges. Don's house burned to the ground; Carolyn's beloved sister died from a virulent and relentless cancer. We also worked with others to resolve complicated community issues: Carolyn ran her local school foundation, and Don served as president of Green Energy Ohio. And, of course, we paid attention to conflicts unfolding in the world—a war rooted in unmet needs for energy, a housing market that imploded, a Congress that seemed unable to find common ground on any issue. In every one of these settings we found that practicing the virtues could open up opportunities for cooperative engagement.

If you've read this far, you're undoubtedly someone who wants to think of yourself as a good person. You've mostly tried to do the right thing in your life. You've done your best to be fair and honest in your dealings with other people. And still you find yourself entangled in conflicts that seem beyond resolution. Maybe you're the parent of a teenager who rebels against rules that seem essential for his safety. Maybe you're a journalist who uncovers facts that contradict the premise of the story assigned by your editor. Maybe you're a pharmaceutical sales rep who becomes aware of new data indicating that a popular and lucrative drug may have dangerous side effects. Maybe you're a public official whose efforts to make voting more accessible arouse the anger of an incumbent politician. Maybe you support a nonprofit accused of perpetuating the problems it's trying to solve. Or maybe you're simply a citizen discouraged by gridlock and incivility in government.

We believe this book will have value for anyone who has been tempted to turn away from personal, professional, or political problems because they seem impossible to resolve. The ideas we explore are likely to challenge much of what you think you know about being a good person. For those who work hard to apply them, the virtues and practices discussed in these pages have the capacity to transform lives shriveled by frustration and discouragement into lives filled with purpose and hope. It sounds like a tall order, perhaps, but we have witnessed the power of cooperative wisdom. We don't promise easy answers, but we do offer hope. There really is a better way to approach change and conflict.

CHAPTER I

Being Good Is Not Enough

Why We Need Social Virtues More than Ever

If we have no peace, it is because we have
forgotten that we belong to each other.
Mother Teresa

Friendship is born at that moment when one person says
to another: "What! You too? I thought I was the only one."
C. S. Lewis

NOTE TO OUR READERS: This book is written as a conversation, and we've used typography to distinguish between the speakers. The "learner" voice appears in italics; the "teacher," in standard roman type.

Society, Sustainability and Wisdom. That was the audacious name of the seminar where we met.

I came out of retirement to teach that seminar because I wanted to distill the practices that had emerged from a lifetime of teaching, thinking, and acting to support cooperation.

I was drawn by the idea of wisdom that would help me determine what to do in difficult circumstances. From the time I was a little girl, I've wanted to do the right thing—if only I could figure out what that was. So often my efforts to "be good" backfired and created conflict.

What you're describing is a very common problem. Traditional morality rests on the idea of responsibility. Within a community people are expected to follow moral principles and fulfill obligations. If things go wrong, it's assumed that someone came up short. So if you find those people and hold them responsible, you can restore order.

I've observed that it's not that simple. Many, if not most people sincerely try to be good. They work hard. They make themselves trustworthy by honoring commitments and keeping promises. They try to uphold their bargains. And yet problems, often serious problems, still occur. Think about income inequality, the rise of political and religious extremism, or climate change. The natural response to these ills is to look around for someone to hold accountable.

I often felt at fault when I was little, though I wasn't always sure exactly what I had done wrong. Even as an adult I sometimes feel I am implicated in causing harms, though I'm not sure what I was supposed to do to prevent them.

That feeling—of being responsible for problems you'd prevent if you could—can lead to apathy and even depression. It also makes people angry, and then they look for someone else to blame. If things have gone sideways and I've been trying hard to do the right thing, it must be the fault of . . . fill in the blank:

- Governments that make too many—or not enough—laws
- School systems that fail to educate kids properly
- Companies that seem to put profit ahead of other considerations
- People in other countries, or other parts of this country, who don't share my values
- In-laws who never appreciated my capabilities

The list of potential people to blame is endless. And yet, if you look more closely and without prejudice, you find a curious thing. Most of these people aren't very satisfying villains, because they too are bewildered and frustrated by harms they didn't intend to cause. They too set out to do the best they could in difficult circumstances.

That's what I find so frustrating. If most of us are trying to do the right thing, why do we face such stubborn problems in our schools, our companies, our country, even our families?

What Is an Environment?

From my point of view as an environmental ethicist, the kind of deep, recurring problems that seem to have no solution usually occur in settings—environments, if you will—that have become unstable because of change and increasing complexity. In a family, for example, the death of a beloved parent may trigger disruption of comfortable routines or disputes among siblings. In a community, immigration may lead to conflicts over housing or school systems. In business a merger may result in defensive and destructive turf wars. To understand this, let's consider what the word *environment* means.

Early in my career I thought about environments as the term is usually used—parts of the natural world that are threatened with dysfunction, often because of human actions. Over time, however, my definition of environment expanded to include any configuration, physical or social, that reliably enables a set of responses. Juveniles survive because a family protects and nurtures them before they can fend for themselves. A corporation thrives because it produces marketable products, income for employees, and dividends for investors. An organ functions properly because a particular gland secretes a particular chemical. Families, corporations, and bodily organs are all environments. So are cells and human bodies.

By your definition a household is an environment, and so is a town, a classroom, a hospital, a supermarket, a nation, and, for that matter, a planet.

Each of these is a complex system, developed in ways that support a set of beneficial processes. Each system operates well within certain parameters. When those parameters are stable, we tend think of such systems as fixed or even inevitable. But when parameters change—when a virus invades the cell or a household loses its breadwinner or a new technology disrupts a market—what has been predictable is called into question. The system must adapt to the new parameters or it will become unsustainable and perish.

Because change is the only constant in life, all environments grow unstable sooner or later. In the face of change or threat, the challenge is to preserve what's essential for the system to go on producing benefits while adapting to new circumstances. Sustainability means that we—our cells, our families, our networks, our communities, and our planet—have the ability to survive despite disruption, sometimes even catastrophic disruption, of once-stable circumstances and the beneficial processes they supported.

Specialization and Cooperation

All living systems adapt if they can. For people and the systems they create, adaptation almost always involves cooperation with other people. Because our social success depends on individuals fulfilling their particular responsibilities, we talk a lot about individualism. This sometimes obscures a larger truth: our ability to thrive as a social species depends upon creating mutual benefits by working together. The basic formula is simple: I do this. You do that. We are both better off.

I think every economist would agree that division of labor creates dramatic benefits.

From a biological point of view you can see the advantages in every species that has two sexes. One contributes sperm; another contributes an egg. Together they create new genetic possibilities that make a species more adaptable to changing environments. From there, humans and a few other species made the jump to further divisions of labor. I'll tend the house (or hive) while you go out and look for food.

Humans were able to establish highly complex divisions of effort because we developed language, accounting systems, and legal codes used to assign and enforce responsibilities. For example, I have grain. You have a boat. If we cooperate we can sell the grain at higher prices to people beyond our shores. Most social interactions involve this kind of exchange: I'll supply something that's available to me and valuable to you; you in turn supply something of value that I can't readily provide for myself. Individuals are less vulnerable when they are part of cooperative groups, if only because they don't have to try to think about everything. And groups flourish when individuals, protected by common moral understandings, devise new ways to produce benefits.

Every preschooler understands the benefits of cooperation in action. If everyone helps clean up the playroom, we get to go outside sooner. It's clear that cooperation enables people to avoid harms and enjoy benefits in ways they could never manage alone.

When we're sure we can count on others to do necessary tasks, each of us is free to pursue specialized labor that maximizes our value to the social unit. One kid picks up the blocks; another knows exactly where the plastic dinosaurs belong. As knowledge proliferates, people become experts about smaller and smaller slivers of what's known.

In modern, developed societies our cooperative structures have expanded into incredibly complex and specialized systems. Every day we depend on countless other people. Some we know very well because they are part of a nurturing community—a family, a church, a classroom—but we're also part of a network of people we will never know. Each of us depends on interlocking communities of specialists who do things we cannot, whether it's making pickles or reading CAT scans or training NBA defenders. We trust them to carry out their specialty because we really have no idea what it takes to make pickles, interpret a CAT scan, or run a crisscross defense. Today's networks can be very large and complex, often involving people on the other side of the planet.

The term social networks may have emerged to describe online communities, but it seems like an apt description of this greater phenomenon.

In both nurturing communities and anonymous networks the fundamental agreement is the same: I do this. You do that. We both benefit. And today more than ever, the well-being of individuals depends upon the *quality* of their cooperation. From childhood we learn that we're more likely to get what we want if we play nice with others. So we do. A basketball star can't win a championship without the other players on the team—plus a network of trainers, promoters, nutritionists, TV announcers, and so on. The success of the pickle manufacturer depends on the skill of farmers, brine makers, marketers, and truckers. The CAT scan wouldn't even exist without a highly sophisticated network of researchers, educators, and software designers.

Despite the romantic myth of the rugged individualist, almost no one chooses to live without the benefits created by cooperation—for good reason. Besides forgoing the opportunities cooperation creates, the lone wolf also runs the risk of failure without backup. Once you grasp how interconnected we are, you start to realize that your well-being is deeply implicated in that of other people. It really isn't enough for you to do your part well. You also need to be part of an environment that supports cooperative partners in doing their parts well.

Safeguarding Cooperative Systems

I can't help thinking that cooperation makes people more vulnerable. What if I do this but you don't do that? It seems like the trusting partners are more vulnerable.

They are. That risk must be taken very seriously, and we'll examine it closely in Chapter 6—after we describe practices that promote trustworthiness in all parties. The crucial point is that cooperation rests on the idea that benefits will be mutual. *Both* of us are better off when we fulfill our individual commitments. If people can't count on each other to do as they've promised, cooperative agreements become chancy. Then we all risk losing the benefits of specialization.

Further, an arrangement that creates disproportionate benefits for one partner or group of partners is exploitive. Autonomous individuals—those who are truly free to choose in their own best interests—won't make such an agreement unless they're deceived or coerced. Any sustainable social network must have a code of responsibility with rewards for cooperators and sanctions for those who break faith with their cooperative partners, or try to appropriate an unfair share of the benefits created by cooperation.

From my point of view traditional morality and the virtues it promotes are primarily a way to protect the cooperation on which human systems depend. A person who grasps the imperative of cooperation is more likely to value and practice traditional virtues; conversely, a person who values and tries to act with justice, fairness, and honesty is more likely to be a reliable cooperative partner. Traditional morality is especially effective in communities where people have direct contact with and knowledge of others. Standard ideas about ethics help extend a system of responsibility by making it easier to spot fellow cooperators, structure agreements that work for both parties, and discipline those who misappropriate benefits.

Let me make sure I understand this. You're saying that moral codes are attempts to identify and promote what's good. For intelligent, social creatures, like human beings, cooperation is good because it creates benefits no one could achieve alone. So a functional moral code has to promote cooperation.

Cooperative specialization, supported by traditional ethics, has been hugely successful for human beings. Voluntary agreements, facilitated by moral codes, undergird successful marriages, functional families, quality schools, healthy faith communities, productive businesses, and responsive governments. The benefits of such cooperation are so conspicuous that western civilization has placed few restrictions on voluntary agreements and lots of emphasis on ethical behavior.

From childhood, people learn that the benefits of cooperation are very real, so they cultivate dispositions that make them more desirable cooperative partners. It's not just Boy Scouts who are honest, fair, thrifty, loyal, and the rest. These characteristics strengthen the community of cooperators, so we all learn in varying degrees to practice them and to recognize them in others. Therefore we regularly make cooperative agreements that really do result in mutual benefits. Most of what parents teach children boils down to this: Be reliable in doing your part so you will be welcomed and affirmed in communities of mutual benefit.

The Cheating Problem

Children also figure out that if everyone else is following the rules, you have a big individual advantage if you cheat.

So true. Having cooperation as the norm leaves an opening for freeloaders, crooks, and even predators. Despite our best efforts to trust only the trustworthy, people sometimes take benefits at the expense of others. In those cases, traditional morality looks for a responsible party and imposes sanctions. The sanctions are strongest for those who deliberately exploit others, but we also hold people accountable when they fail to fulfill obligations clearly assigned to them. They may not have intended to take advantage, but through laziness or inattention or some other failing they caused an imbalance in the distribution of benefits. That's when courts get involved to sort out who agreed to what and whether the disputants did as they promised.

The penalty for taking advantage of trust is quite clear: other people won't want to cooperate with you in the future. It's a fact every five-year-old understands. You may win one game by cheating, but as soon as the other kids catch on, they won't want to play with you. If you enjoy playing the game with your buddies, it's to your advantage not to cheat—even though you could.

Adults make the same calculation. Predators get a lot of attention, but they are not the norm. We isolate them in prisons or we refuse to do business with them. The consequences of being excluded from cooperative arrangements are drastic, so most people don't consciously take advantage of each other. They don't cheat, steal, or lie even in situations where they could probably get away with it. Without thinking much about it, most of us realize that true self-interest is not a matter of maximizing our own advantage. Instead, we develop habits that allow us to enjoy the benefits of ongoing cooperation with other people.

It all sounds very utopian. So why do we find ourselves with stubborn and apparently insoluble problems like contaminated food supplies or workers who can't pay their bills, no matter how many minimum-wage jobs they work?

There are so many examples of bad outcomes caused by people who thought they were cooperating. Although their intentions were good, they created harms. Such outcomes belie the assumption that undergirds all cooperative systems, including global capitalism. When agreements are voluntary and consensual, they are supposed to create mutual benefits. But in a complex, interconnected, highly specialized system, this hypothesis may turn out to be false. People may think they are cooperating for mutual benefit, but harm occurs anyway. Because the problems were unanticipated—maybe unforseeable—and unintended, no one is to blame.

Looking for Villains

Recognizing this makes most people extremely uncomfortable. Traditional morality tells us that when harm occurs, someone must be at fault. When we find ourselves enmeshed in a stubborn problem, we automatically look for someone to blame. Aha! Greedy coal extractors must be responsible for global warming. Greedy bankers must have precipitated the college debt crisis. Greedy health insurance companies cause runaway healthcare costs.

In each case we say "greedy" to imply that people have appropriated an unfair share of benefits. They've violated the assumption about benefits being mutual that makes cooperation work. But many complex problems don't result from predation. Those who cause them may be unwitting, unwilling, unsuspecting, unprepared, or simply unfortunate. So traditional morality is turned on its head, because the "villains" turn out to be people who were trying to do the right thing.

So people who perform their specialized roles as prescribed, and who practice the traditional virtues, can still cause harms that jeopardize human well-being—or even survival?

Sad but true. Hard as we look, we can't find a villain or even a set of villains responsible for global warming or the housing bubble or inner-city blight. These problems are byproducts of activities that were in themselves perfectly legitimate. It's not fanciful to imagine that each of the specialists involved was trying to do the right thing. Being able to blame someone for such outcomes would certainly make life easier, but in general these ills weren't the result of bad intentions. When you look closely, it's clear that most of those implicated think of themselves as decent people. They wanted to cooperate. They knew the rules of traditional morality and followed them more often than not.

How is that possible? I thought honesty and fairness were supposed to ensure that cooperation would produce mutual benefits!

When communities become complex and networks become very large, we can no longer be sure we'll all come out ahead even if I do X, you do Y, and millions of others do their part. Even when people cooperate under voluntary agreements, bad things can happen. It's not that one group wants to hurt another. Things just go wrong—often terribly wrong.

Driven to Distraction

Let's look at an extremely common example. The typical highway is a model of cooperative interaction. People follow rules about speeding, passing, merging, and so on without thinking much about it. If pressed to analyze their behavior, they might agree that everyone benefits when traffic moves smoothly. So even if they're occasionally inconvenienced by these rules, it makes sense to follow them, and most drivers are perfectly willing to cooperate.

Yet traffic congestion and even accidents regularly occur. Sometimes a road wasn't designed to handle much traffic, but once it was built, people discovered its convenience for getting from here to there, so it's being used more than expected. Or maybe the road is used more because its very existence encourages social or commercial developments that draw more traffic. In some situations, researchers tell us, slowdowns result from nothing more than one driver tapping his brakes, which causes the driver behind to tap her brakes, which causes the driver behind . . . and so on.

No one—neither the drivers nor the engineers nor the taxpayers who funded the highway—intended to cause oppressive traffic or dangerous accidents.

This pattern of unintended harms recurs over and over. Pollution is another example. No one wakes up in the morning and says, "I'm going to foul the earth today." Instead, a company agrees to supply customers with products they want and need. As a byproduct, emissions begin to accumulate, eventually harming people downwind or fish downstream. The people and the fish don't deserve to be harmed, but that harm was never the intention of the company or its customers.

People who cause such problems may be entirely unaware of the harm they have created in performing their specialized roles. In some cases they may even be victims of their own actions. The loyal worker in the coal company may have an asthmatic child. The honest bank employee may lose her house to foreclosure. The trustworthy representative of the insurance company may have a medical condition that isn't covered by his policy. These situations are frustrating because traditional morality was supposed to protect us. But in our highly specialized world it doesn't always turn out that way.

People are trying to do the right thing, but harms occur anyway. Why does that happen?

Cooperative systems that are very large, very complex, or very specialized predictably breed unhappy results for three reasons:

1. Specialists feel uncomfortable outside their specialties.
2. Scale creates unanticipated difficulties.
3. Variations from the norm become problematic.

These effects regularly disrupt cooperative environments and require some kind of adaptive response. So they deserve our close attention.

How Specialization Creates Tunnel Vision

Let's talk about focus first. Anyone who has used a camera understands that if you narrow your focus to a particular subject, other things go out of focus. Similarly, when we agree that you'll do this and I'll do that, we also agree that neither of us will try to think about every aspect of our cooperative endeavors. Some people may try to micromanage every detail, but they are rarely successful.

The likely result is that each of us loses track of part of the picture, especially when the picture is large and complicated. The unspoken assumption is that someone else will focus on concerns that fall outside my assigned area of specialization. In many cases this is true. On a construction project the carpenter concentrates on woodwork because he can count on the electrician to install the wiring and the plumber to lay the pipes. During surgery the anesthesiologist focuses on keeping the patient sedated so the surgeon can pay attention to what needs to be repaired.

Even in a marriage the husband may balance the checkbook while the wife supervises investments.

Now multiply these agreements millions of times. As systems such as healthcare, education, or commerce grow very large and very complex, specialists concentrate on smaller and smaller slivers of what needs to be done. Consequently they lose their sense of how their actions connect to what others are doing. One electrician wires the lights and another hooks up the heating system. Neither talks to the plumbers, who have their own zones of specialization.

The more specialized you become, the more likely you are to work in an environment and use vocabulary that are incomprehensible to anyone who doesn't work in the same field. This often interferes with cooperation for mutual benefit. Before the development of computer-aided design and manufacturing software, work would come to a halt on big construction projects while electricians tried to reconcile their needs with those of the plumbers. Cutting wires to make room for pipes simply won't do!

Specialists talk about working in silos. Within your silo everyone understands what you're doing and why it's important. You may even have effective ways of coordinating with specialists in adjacent silos. But what if there are spaces between silos? Who pays attention to them?

I witnessed this phenomenon when a family member was being treated for cancer. The surgeon focused on recovery from surgery. The oncologist focused on getting the right combination of drugs for chemo. Neither paid attention to the patient's diabetes.

Often the spaces between specialties become a no-man's-land. What occurs there falls outside of everyone's focus. No one feels responsible, so things just happen. We use the term *unintended consequences* to capture the idea that no one anticipated—or wanted—a particular result. Economists use the term *externalities* to describe costs (and sometimes benefits) that weren't part of the cooperative bargain.

Some externalities are positive: happy accidents that create unintended benefits. If the local utility installs a power-generating dam upriver from my property, the dam may protect me from flooding. Even though I didn't participate in the process or pay for the construction, the changed environment protects me. Lucky me!

More often we become aware of externalities when they are negative. Maybe the dam restricts water flow so I can't float my boat or irrigate my crops. I never agreed to *that*. To be fair, that's not what the utility or its customers had in mind either. They were focused on producing an adequate supply of inexpensive power, a perfectly legitimate and beneficial goal. Because externalities are outside the scope of the cooperative plan, clear lines of accountability are lacking. People don't necessarily take credit for positive externalities, because they may not even be aware of them, and they certainly don't expect to be blamed for negative externalities.

It sounds like specialized roles make it harder for people to see negative externalities, and easier for them to ignore them.

To illustrate, let's go back to highways. The automobile was invented to satisfy the very basic human desire to get from here to there. Like other new technologies, it opened up tremendous new opportunities. Suddenly people could easily travel longer distances in search of employment or goods or adventure — if they could find paved roads.

Ideas about how to create the infrastructure required by gas-powered vehicles proliferated rapidly. At the 1939 New York World's Fair, a mere thirty-one years after the Ford Model T was introduced, a model of an interstate highway system was displayed in the Pavilion of Tomorrow. Amazingly, it featured much of what we currently know about handling traffic efficiently without traffic signals. Specialists had already figured out, for example, that braking was inefficient, so they designed the cloverleaf to manage traffic with nothing more than a yield sign.

The engineers who eventually built the interstate system were focused on a genuine benefit: traveling long distances quickly and efficiently. Other issues inevitably fell outside their focus. As it turned out, some of the externalities created by highways were positive. The cost of trucking declined and overnight delivery services became feasible. Other externalities were negative: small towns unlucky enough to be bypassed by the interstate saw their commercial areas shrivel.

The highway designers didn't intend to create ghost towns.

It's crucial to understand that the people who designed and built this system were making a bona fide effort to create benefits. In the process they also created new environments in which some cooperative enterprises thrived and others became obsolete. Think of the network of services available at every interstate exit. Restaurants evolved to get customers in and out quickly; after all, the exit ramp wasn't their final destination. Eager to get back on the road, people wanted food that was familiar and fast.

For designers of the interstate system, what happened at the exits was an externality, outside their focus. At first it was probably assumed that motorists would use exits to get to existing developed areas. Instead the exits themselves became commercial zones, crowded with motels, service stations, fast-food outlets, and eventually malls. No one anticipated the way some cities would thus be eviscerated. No one gave much thought to the jumbled ugliness created by businesses vying for the attention of travelers. No one could have foreseen the sense of national restlessness created by the feeling that this exit complex is not our destination—just a stop on the way. These consequences weren't any part of the highway designers' intention.

I guess that was true of the restaurants, too. Their focus was on hungry customers who were in a hurry. The waistlines and cholesterol levels of those customers were outside their focus.

The Impact of Scale

Those expanding waistlines are an example of scale problems—the second vulnerability endemic to complex, specialized systems. When a new technology or practice produces genuine benefits, people adopt it. If enough people alter their habits to incorporate the new idea, environments that seem well established will change, sometimes rapidly. When I was a boy, families ate meals at home. Then Ray Kroc, the founder of McDonald's, literally changed both physical and dietary environments with all those golden arches. When people ate an occasional hamburger with fries while traveling, the impact of those extra calories was minimal. But people enjoyed hamburgers, and eating them more often brought changes in their bodies as well as in their kitchens and neighborhoods. Today fast food is ubiquitous—and so are people with weight-related illnesses.

This double whammy is likely to occur whenever the scale of human action changes an environment. First, negative externalities that were insignificant when things were done on a small scale become significant. Second, the infrastructure that grows up around the popular new activity reinforces the newly created problems.

I think the wait staff of every restaurant understands that first phenomenon. If one dissatisfied customer doesn't leave a tip, it's annoying but no big deal. If the kitchen gets behind on orders and many customers protest by leaving smaller tips, the entire wait staff suffers.

As individuals we tend to assume that the scale on which we operate will not undermine the environment in which we act. If I hike in a forest today, I won't substantially affect the forest—or other people's ability to hike in it—tomorrow. For much of human history this was pretty much true. When human beings had to depend on physical strength, our ability to change environments was limited. But as we have tapped into sources of energy beyond our own brawn, our ability to alter environments has increased exponentially.

Think about cars again. At the beginning of the automobile era, the supply of oil in the United States seemed boundless. The very fact of abundance shaped what people wanted to do. Soon families were taking Sunday drives just for fun, going on road trips for vacation, buying suburban houses that required a commute, and shopping in malls that could be reached only by driving. None of this was the sinister work of unethical people.

When I was a kid, we always piled into the car for a Sunday drive. My parents would have been shocked to think that a family outing was creating problems beyond backseat bickering.

Our awareness of externalities often lags behind their importance, especially as they accumulate. Whenever people implement a new practice, unanticipated consequences occur. At first the impact may seem too minuscule to matter. One family enjoying a Sunday drive really doesn't have much impact on anything but that family. But increase the scale of activity, and up goes the risk of externalities. When everyone heads out for the weekend, highways get clogged, fuel prices rise, roads need more repairs.

At one scale harms may be truly insignificant. We can ignore or work around any problem that arises. But eventually things reach a tipping point. It's been raining for forty days. The first thirty-nine days were tolerable; now the house is afloat.

It seems perfectly natural for people to adopt new practices that seem to be working for others. Success inspires imitation.

The impact of scale is something specialists should consider whenever they introduce new practices or technologies. The more popular an innovation becomes, the more likely it is to disrupt the environment in which it thrives. We've seen this over and over with the Internet. When a few college kids started swapping audio files of their favorite bands, nobody paid much attention. When millions of people started sharing files, they endangered the entire recording industry and the artists it supports.

The scale factor often comes as a surprise—especially in America, where we started with the premise that land, resources, and opportunity were limitless. I remember, when I was about seven, seeing the Detroit Edison smokestacks puffing black smoke into the air. Being a curious lad, I asked my mother where the smoke went. And she said, "Away. The sky is big. It goes away." My mother wasn't stupid or uninformed. Her explanation was generally plausible if there are only a few smokestacks.

Scale problems are hard to spot because they often develop gradually. When only a few travelers make arrangements through an online lodging service like Airbnb, it's no big deal. When many people did it, communities that depended on tourism found themselves scrambling to make up revenue from hotel taxes they weren't collecting.

Such problems can also be hard to correct because by the time you see what's happening, an infrastructure has grown up around the practices that caused disruption. By the time we realized that fast food was creating health problems, vast networks of franchises and their supply chains had proliferated. Lots of people were implicated in this cooperative system, from farmers who grew potatoes suitable for making french fries to families that liked to throw birthday parties in the play area of the local burger place. When the farmer or the parent of an eight-year-old asks, "What am I doing wrong?" the honest answer is, "Nothing, but look what happens when everybody's doing it!" Scale matters.

Keep in mind that more isn't necessarily better or worse. Bigger cooperative systems may create benefits because they allow more specialization as well as economies of scale. Consider the U.S. Postal Service. For many years it was able to service people in out-of-the-way places because the volume of mail in big cities was great enough to generate the necessary revenue. But such large systems also create risk, because eventually the environment will change. When people started using e-mail, the Postal Service sold fewer stamps but still had a massive infrastructure to maintain. Now people in very remote locations may find that they no longer have a local post office—and they can't get Wi-Fi either! When scale changes, externalities may accumulate and interact in ways that harm people who weren't involved in the decision making.

I see how some externalities occur because everyone thinks someone else is taking care of a problem. And how others emerge because something becomes too popular, or falls out of fashion. What's the third glitch in big, complex, specialized systems?

Outside the Mold

Every social environment evolves to meet the needs of people who share certain characteristics. When individuals vary from that norm, harms may occur even if that was never anyone's intention. Sometimes the harm is negligible. In the supermarket I regularly encounter women who are too short to reach the top shelf. The management added more shelves to offer more choices, and the environment works well for people above a certain height. The extra-high shelves, however, put some products literally out of reach for some shoppers—who tend to solve the problem by asking someone like me to hand them the product they want.

Sometimes the harm is more serious. Consider what makes something "toxic." For generations scientists have used the word to describe the "median lethal dose": a quantity that causes death in 50 percent of cases. Our rules about how much of various chemicals are acceptable in food, air, or water all derive in one way or another from that definition. However we define "not toxic," some people will nevertheless be harmed by a smaller dosage. Peanuts, for example, are considered not toxic because most of the population can consume them at will. For the few who are allergic, though, even the residue from peanuts may be lethal.

Some schools have actually banned peanut butter sandwiches because a few students have allergies. That's the kind of situation that can lead to conflict between a majority that feels comfortable with existing norms and a minority that is at a disadvantage.

In general, norms emerge because they work for many if not most people. Those who benefit from the status quo may be oblivious to or even resentful about problems caused for others: Why should I have to change what's working for me and for many? But this question imperils the cooperative bargain. Yes, we need to preserve the advantages enjoyed by the majority—and we also need to give serious attention to harms created for the minority.

Whenever you aim to create a satisfactory cooperative environment, you have to ask, satisfactory for whom? When girls started playing soccer, it was assumed that anatomical differences wouldn't be significant. That assumption turned out to be mistaken. Consider the serious knee injuries doctors diagnose as tears to the anterior cruciate ligament. Female players suffer four to ten times as many of these knee injuries as males. What's the proper response to this harm? Should the game be changed so it puts less stress on the joints of female athletes? Should girls be trained so their bodies are less vulnerable to those stresses? Or should women be discouraged from playing soccer at all because it's not suited to their bodies?

This story has no villain, yet the consequences for female athletes playing soccer are quite serious.

You see such challenges in other arenas too. The typical home, for example, is designed for adults, and we often need to make adjustments for family members who are at the margins. A bathtub is a perfectly safe environment for most people, but it presents one set of risks for young children and different risks for seniors. Entire industries have sprung up to provide adaptive equipment that compensates for risks built into standard home design. There are plugs to protect curious toddlers from electrical outlets and stools for young cooks who can't reach kitchen counters. At the other end of the spectrum we find grab bars, ramps, and automated lifts for elders who aren't steady on stairs.

In fact, we all find ourselves in the outlier group more often than we care to admit. Property taxes seem like a reasonable way to fund public schools but may force senior citizens on fixed incomes to sell their homes. Flashing fire alarms installed to protect people with impaired hearing may trigger seizures in people with epilepsy. Corporate security systems that require longer passwords may become vulnerable if employees with less nimble memories must write down their passwords. In all such cases cooperative projects create genuine benefits for some, but give rise to equally genuine (albeit unintended) harms for others who fall outside the target group.

The Art of Adaptive Cooperation

Let me try to recap. When cooperative systems are large and complex, three built-in phenomena often lead to unintended problems. First, the focus required by specialization may mean that problems emerge in places that fall out of focus. Second, cooperative systems that create clear benefits at one scale may become problematic if they grow larger or smaller. Third, systems designed to benefit most people may create harms for outliers. In all three cases harms occur even though people have conscientiously tried to do the right thing.

Scrupulous individual morality will not save us from these unfortunate consequences of our social nature. Every cooperative social unit, from the family to the United Nations, faces such liabilities. Pursuing our own often worthy projects, willing cooperators may be oblivious to the ways in which focus, scale, and variation in tolerance undermine the benefits we are trying to create.

Even after serious problems come to our attention, we are often reluctant to consider changes in what we are doing. Sometimes we don't have the knowledge, authority, or technology to do things differently. Sometimes we're heavily invested in the status quo. And sometimes we aren't even willing to acknowledge the harm because we know we've played by the rules. We practiced the traditional virtues, worked hard, and were honest in our dealings. We are understandably attached to the cooperative organizations we've created. It's simply not our fault that shortcomings arise in social systems.

Discovering unintended consequences can be very demoralizing. It's discouraging to find that, in the process of trying to generate benefits or solve problems, I may have undermined benefits for others or harmed an innocent bystander.

We see this again and again in so many realms. The medication that was supposed to help relieve the symptoms of menopause increases women's risk of cancer. The factory exhaust that creates jobs and products in one state causes acid rain that kills trees in another. The subprime loans that were supposed to encourage home ownership result in millions of loan foreclosures and the collapse of investment banks. The sanitation system that treats waste for one community creates toxic algae blooms elsewhere.

Discovering these unintended consequences makes people defensive, especially when they are part of a network trying to do something constructive. After all, pharmaceutical companies, factories, banks, and sanitation systems create genuine benefits. It's hard to persuade ourselves to set all that aside because of unintended harms. But the hard fact is that harms are occurring. Women are diagnosed with cancer. Trees succumb to acid rain. Families fall behind on their mortgages. Asthmatic children wheeze in hospital emergency rooms.

In each of these situations people on both sides have legitimate claims. And when each of us correctly believes "I've done my part," it's easy to conclude that the fault lies with some other guy. Instead of trying to figure out new ways in which cooperation could produce mutual benefits, we draw battle lines and consult attorneys.

Adversarial situations like these make my head ache and my stomach clench. They don't seem to have that effect on you, and I'd like to know why.

I start from the premise that, no matter how well intended a plan may be, it's likely to create unintended consequences. Over and over I've seen serious problems caused by people acting with only goodwill. Human systems are contributing to climate change, creating conflict over resources, exposing people to toxins, exhausting the power of our medicines, endangering habitats, degrading neighborhoods, and generating other apparently insoluble problems. The idea that humans can put together cooperative structures without unintended consequences is naïve, or arrogant.

Relying on traditional morality, essential as this is, hasn't prevented or resolved the most serious problems we face today—in part because it pushes us to assess responsibility and assign blame. This isn't helpful when harms are unanticipated and unintended. Instead we need a new, more social approach to virtue, one that will help us assess what has happened and make beneficial adjustments. Acknowledging harms we never intended to create is no defeat. It's not a reason for shame or blame, discouragement or judgment. It's just a necessary first step toward *adaptive* cooperation.

Traditional moral codes evolved in smaller, tribal societies where labor was far less specialized, the impact of human activity was much smaller, and the consequences of human systems for outliers were less significant. Today what we do and consume can have significant impacts on cooperative partners and innocent bystanders we will never know directly. Our system of ethics must address the global reach of our human networks. Our understanding of cooperation must be refocused to affirm and expand the original cooperative bargain: I do this. You do that. Millions of other people play their parts. And we all benefit.

Sounds great, but what exactly are we supposed to do?

As a scholar of social ethics I've pored over many case studies in which people successfully corrected difficult problems and restored cooperation for genuine and widespread benefit. I've worked to analyze the dispositions shared by humans who cooperate successfully, and to articulate what has been central to their success. Gradually I've come to see that human communities are most likely to thrive when people can sensitize themselves to harms, discern the sources and nature of those harms, imagine alternatives, devise better ways to integrate the components of a cooperative system, and embrace the risks of engaging in cooperation, even at its most challenging.

People have all these capacities, but complex cooperative systems become more resilient, durable, and mutually beneficial when we exercise them deliberately until they become habits of interacting with each other. In my experience *cooperative wisdom* emerges as we study and refine five social dispositions. As noted in the Introduction, I call them

- Proactive compassion
- Deep discernment
- Intentional imagination
- Inclusive integrity
- Creative courage

I use the term *virtue* to describe these dispositions because I think they have an ethical dimension. But you could also call them competencies, life skills, or habits of mind. Each is rooted in an ancient understanding of what it means to be a good person, and I extend each to account for the complex social circumstances in which we operate today.

I can't imagine that anyone is opposed to compassion, discernment, imagination, integrity, or courage. But I don't know how to apply these virtues to the kinds of problems we've been discussing.

I'm not surprised. Mastering the cooperative virtues isn't simply a matter of deciding to do it. You learn any sophisticated skill—cooking, neurosurgery, classroom management—by breaking it down into smaller parts and exercising discipline to practice the components until they become second nature.

I propose to guide readers in this learning. For each of the five virtues I've identified three specific practices that will help people explore and adopt this new approach to change and conflict. These practices are nothing more (or less) than skillful habits that enable people to recognize harm, reconcile conflicting values, and reorganize cooperative systems so that mutual benefits can flourish.

Mastering the social virtues and practices helps people create healthier, more sustainable environments of every kind—including stronger marriages and resilient families, robust associations and responsive companies, progressive communities and effective governments. The more we practice the virtues, the more likely we are to transcend inadvertent harms and restore cooperation that yields benefits for everyone who aspires to be a responsible cooperator.

CHAPTER 2

Proactive Compassion

Anticipating and Responding to Vulnerabilities

Kindness is the language the deaf can hear and the blind can see.
Mark Twain

*When will our consciences grow so tender that we will act
to prevent human misery rather than avenge it?*
Eleanor Roosevelt

I'm definitely one of the people you described in the first chapter. Much as I try to practice the virtues I learned as a young person, I find myself implicated in problems that cause harms for others. I drive a hybrid to save fuel, but it puts pedestrians and bicyclists at risk because it's too quiet. When I flush expired meds to keep them out of the hands of kids, I'm contaminating the water we drink. Even the diamond in my wedding ring may have caused suffering for people halfway around the world.

When you have feelings of regret about problems you didn't intend to cause, you're at the edge of the first of the cooperative virtues: proactive compassion.

But compassion doesn't sound like a new virtue. Doesn't every moral code call for people to feed the poor, tend the sick, and comfort the afflicted?

Absolutely. Every culture praises people who care for the vulnerable and judges those who exploit them. But adding *proactive* makes a difference. The compassion I'm talking about is an active response to problems that sneak up on us because of gaps in focus, distortion of scale, and/or inattention to differences. If we hope to be effective in dealing with conflict and wise about responding to change, we must expand our concept of compassion to anticipate harms that may arise from each of these three sources.

The Empathic Roots of Compassion

Even though the traditional understanding of compassion fails to address some predicaments in which we find ourselves, it is the soil from which proactive compassion grows. Traditional compassion grows out of empathy. You see someone in distress. You can imagine how he or she must feel. You experience a surge of compassion that makes you want to help.

When the distress of others is made visible to us — after an earthquake or at a funeral, for instance — most of us feel that impulse to help, and we try to do what we can. Compassion is an almost universal response to demonstrated human vulnerability. In many ways that compassionate response is the glue that holds human communities together.

At first glance this seems to contradict the idea that cooperation should create mutual benefit. When we respond compassionately to people in distress, we don't assume they'll be able to reciprocate.

Compassion addresses the weakest links in the cooperative network. Often those who inspire compassion aren't in a position to offer anything in exchange for what they need. Traditionally compassion motivates us to support people who for various reasons are unable to care for themselves, much less others. We sacrifice time, money, or other resources, knowing that in the short term we won't share in the benefits we create.

Still, we feel good about caring for the vulnerable, partly because we hope our response will help them resume their place as reciprocating members of the cooperative community. Also, it's easy to imagine ourselves similarly overwhelmed by some unexpected misfortune. We know that circumstances and roles can change over the course of time. When we practice compassion, we affirm our long-term interest in being part of a supportive community that responds to adversity and suffering by doing whatever it can to restore capacities for cooperation. The idea that we can alleviate harms for each other through cooperative effort is at the root of all the other virtues.

I read somewhere that compassion develops very early in children. Even an eighteen-month-old will pat another child who is crying.

A child who tries to comfort another child shows a caring response to vulnerability that echoes what loving parents do from the time an infant is born. Humans are born with huge capacities for development but almost no ability for self-protection. A species with such helpless infants will survive *only* if adults sense their vulnerability and respond by protecting and nurturing them. Human adults typically do both.

In this respect humans are quite different from some species, for whom parenthood ends as soon as the next generation is birthed or hatched. Sea turtles, for example, bury hundreds of eggs in sand. The babies hatch and instinctively head toward water, but most are picked off by birds of prey. Adults don't protect the juveniles; if there's going to be a new generation of turtles, it's because the females produce so many eggs that at least some of the young will elude their predators. In other species the birth rate may be lower, but the young are still expected to fend for themselves almost immediately after birth. A mare will nudge her foal to stand within minutes, because if the foal cannot move along at its mother's side it may well become food for some predator. In contrast, human parents protect their young for years.

I remember feeling overwhelmed by everything that needed to be done after my first child was born. Like most new parents, I learned quickly because I had such strong feelings about protecting this very helpless creature.

A huge part of parenthood is exercising compassion, activated by the infant's tremendous vulnerability. At first, of course, it's all pretty straightforward. The baby cries and parents respond. Is he hungry? Does he need a diaper change? Does she need to burp? Most parents learn to read cues so they can respond effectively to their infant's distress. The parent has the ability to respond—*response-ability*, if you will—and so he or she does what the child cannot yet do for itself.

Anticipating Harms on Behalf of Others

What you've been describing seems like traditional compassion. I see someone who is vulnerable. Their distress makes me uncomfortable. I do what I can to provide relief because it makes them—and me—feel better.

Right, but good parents don't stop there. They also anticipate situations in which a child might be harmed and do their best to avoid or modify those situations. For an infant even something as simple as bath time is fraught with risk: Is the water the right temperature? Is there a draft in the room? Can he grab the hot-water tap or knock his head against it? Will the soap make her so slippery that the parent can't hold on?

This part of child-rearing gives us insight into how we need to expand our concept of compassion. Parents respond to such risks by being proactive and making changes in the environment. Close the door to the room and raise the thermostat. Check the bathwater to be sure it's a safe temperature. Put a towel at the bottom of the sink, or purchase a special tub with a cushion that makes it less likely the child will slip. Clothing is another way parents modify the environment to minimize a child's vulnerability. We bundle kids up when it's cold and remove clothing when they're at risk of overheating. Snowsuits and onesies create microenvironments, making wearers less vulnerable to fluctuations of temperature outdoors.

Parents have been making modifications like this for a long time. For our distant ancestors, ensuring safety might have involved finding dry caves for shelter and seeing that a child didn't stumble into the fire. For contemporary parents it means installing child-proof locks on kitchen cabinets and monitoring use of social media. In both cases parents are reconfiguring the environment to remove harms that are obvious to adults but not to children.

Notice the shift we've made. We've traditionally thought of compassion as something we practice *after* harm occurs—the outpouring of generosity for victims of earthquakes and hurricanes or for a child who needs an operation. But because people are interconnected in such complicated ways today, compassion after the fact simply isn't enough. By then the damage has been done, and it's likely to be extensive, harming our cooperative partners as well as others outside our local cooperative arrangement. The kind of compassion we need today develops out of our ability to anticipate harm. We improve our complex, specialized world by being alert for externalities that result from gaps in focus, changes in scale, and variations from the norm.

As an example, consider the people who lost homes to a 2014 landslide in Washington State. When they built their homes, they were focused on the beauty of the natural environment and couldn't see certain dangers that were obvious to people with experience and specialized knowledge. Geologists knew that the underlying structure of the mountains was unstable; forestry experts understood how logging might change runoff patterns during downpours; local officials had been around long enough to remember other landslides. These experts, however, failed to exercise proactive compassion. Because they didn't cooperate in making the risks known, people built houses they presumed were safe, and an entire community was put in jeopardy.

I wonder if those officials would have handled things differently if a friend or relative was planning to build a house in that area. Often we find it natural to look out for people we know personally.

True. Proactive compassion is most easily learned and practiced in small social units that give people direct knowledge of each other. Most of us find it rewarding to participate in a variety of small communities that may or may not overlap. We feel committed to our extended family. We get to know other parents with kids who play the same sport or are the same age as ours. We form connections with colleagues and with those who share our interests. Social scientists argue a bit about how many people such networks can hold and still maintain intimacy, but the limit is probably around 120. Within these groups we're often quick to respond to vulnerability, providing encouragement and sometimes more tangible forms of support.

Such face-to-face ties are important. But in our highly specialized world, small social groups that connect people directly are only part of the story. The cooperative units that enable humans to flourish today are much larger and more complex. School districts. Medical complexes. Media conglomerates. City, state, and federal bureaucracies. Multinational corporations and NGOs.

In settings like these, people can't possibly know everyone in the organization, much less all the people they are trying to serve.

All these social structures start from the premise that benefits can be created through cooperation. And all find themselves creating inadvertent harms, in part because they can't keep track of all the people who are affected by their actions. A program that tries to empower girls may unintentionally undermine achievement in boys. Efforts to sanitize surfaces in hospitals promote the evolution of superbugs that resist antibiotics. Regulations intended to enhance public safety may bankrupt small businesses. A technology that extracts gas from shale pollutes groundwater. A company that tries to save money by manufacturing products overseas discovers that its subcontractors are employing school-age children.

Interdependence on a large scale creates enormous opportunities, but the benefits created by cooperation must always be distributed fairly. This is a bedrock principle of cooperation. If some suffer while others reap the benefits, even if the harms are unintended, the social bond on which we all depend is threatened. To address the inadvertent problems created by immense, intricate social systems, we need to expand our practice of compassion beyond the spontaneous empathy that makes us want to help children and people we know. Proactive compassion anticipates and responds to potential vulnerabilities, even for people we may never know directly.

Three Domains of Vulnerability

So how can we practice proactive compassion in the cooperative networks we're all part of today?

A social virtue is a habit of mind — a way of approaching things that becomes reflexive if you cultivate it. The best way to learn a new approach to anything is to break it down into components that can be mastered with diligence and patience. Think of an elite athlete trying to reach a new level of performance. He or she may have to replace old habits by focusing on particular movements and repeating them over and over until the new way of doing things becomes automatic. Similarly, anyone can learn the cooperative virtues, but it doesn't happen instantly. That's why I've identified three practices for each virtue: exercises, if you will, that expand our moral range of motion.

With regard to proactive compassion there are three domains in which we're likely to be ambushed by vulnerability. First, vulnerabilities emerge in environments that have been framed by specialists with experience and training that others don't share. Second, an environment in flux creates the potential for harms not present when the environment was stable. Third, in places where no one has clear responsibility, new vulnerabilities emerge.

Three practices help us become attuned to these domains of vulnerability, so we can respond before harms occur or become serious:

1. Respond to risks revealed by specialized knowledge.
2. Intercept harms triggered by change.
3. Address gaps between assigned responsibilities.

Each of these practices has roots in traditional compassion, and each expands our understanding of responsibility. Along with the practices recommended for the other virtues, they equip us to work proactively toward strengthening arrangements that help cooperative communities thrive.

1. Respond to risks revealed by specialized knowledge

Each of us knows things that other people don't know. We acquire this specialized knowledge through training or through experience. The epidemiologist can predict which hospitals should be prepared for outbreaks of the flu. The teacher sees that a child labeled a troublemaker has capabilities that could be cultivated with the right lessons. The busboy who notices which foods restaurant patrons leave on their plates has insights into waste reduction. Our unique perspectives let us spot vulnerabilities that people who lack our experience or expertise simply can't see.

Again, think about parents who use their own experience to anticipate and, whenever possible, prevent accidents that may harm their oblivious children. If a child is about to be hit by a swinging door, his vulnerability motivates us to grab the door or shout a warning. And once we become aware of the risks posed by the door, we look for ways to prevent harm even in our absence—perhaps by propping it open or installing a slow-closing hinge or getting rid of the door altogether.

Sometimes there's a tight link between the person who sees the incipient harm—in this case the parent—and the response, such as fixing the door. But people unacquainted with this parent and child also have a role to play, if they have certain expertise. Childcare workers, carpenters, public health officials, even the manufacturers of hinges may have insight into minimizing the risks of swinging doors. Each has an opportunity to practice proactive compassion, by anticipating harm and translating anxiety about what could happen into a response that mitigates vulnerability.

Expanding the number of specialists who take an interest in the health and safety of children seems like a very effective way of preventing unnecessary harm.

Today an enormous network of people beyond family members coordinate efforts to promote the well-being of children they do not know. Medical researchers investigate vaccines to prevent childhood illnesses, and pediatricians see that children get those vaccines at the proper time. Specialists in design, nutrition, and engineering scrutinize the safety of sippy cups and food and playgrounds. A cadre of educators teaches skills and concepts that help children become productive and self-protective in a world so complex their parents can't possibly know about more than a sliver of it. So specialized is this network that parents can find experts to help a child with distinctive talents, like an aptitude for chess, or unusual challenges, like an allergy to sunlight.

Something similar has happened in the field of gerontology. As the proportion of older people in the population increases, there's been a proliferation of specialists who help families cope with everything from estate planning to dementia.

The training and experience of specialists enable them to negotiate certain environments more adeptly than those who don't share their expertise. The researcher who studies dementia has insight into the predictable progress of the disease. The nursing home administrator knows how to train staff so they can apply new techniques that promise to slow cognitive decline; the nursing home aide knows which techniques work best with specific patients. And the occupational therapist teaches techniques that help keep the elderly safe in their own homes.

All such specialists tend to become aware of vulnerabilities earlier than people who lack their background. Instead of applying a band-aid after the fact, specialists can practice proactive compassion by looking for ways to prevent problems before they occur or, failing that, before they become serious.

I've seen this over and over online, where so many of us proceed with childlike faith in the safety of the environment. We've become very dependent on experts to warn us about phishing and malware and gaps in security.

Medicine is another field where people consciously practice proactive compassion, even if they don't call it that. Mortality and morbidity committees in hospitals analyze cases in which patients were harmed and recommend revised practices to prevent such outcomes. One of the most common is redundancy: when I had a cataract removed, the anesthesiologist asked which eye would be involved in surgery. Then the head nurse asked the same question, as did the surgeon, who made a big black X with indelible marker over the eye that was to be treated—all part of a deliberate effort to minimize the risk that they might operate on the wrong eye.

When you think about it, many specialized fields have developed in response to human needs and vulnerabilities. Consider law, agriculture, education, and even occupations like auto repair or dishwashing. All are motivated to some degree by compassion: if I don't do my job, people will be at risk, either because they will suffer harm or because they'll miss out on enabling prospects.

The Heart of Specialization

I think specialization sometimes makes people feel like cogs in a machine. But you're saying that, regardless of your occupation, you can practice proactive compassion by being alert for vulnerabilities within your areas of expertise.

We aren't necessarily aware of the compassionate underpinnings of our work because we are taught practices out of context. Most of us decide on a career because we have an aptitude for the work, we've mastered the tools required, or we're pleased to get paid for doing something we enjoy. Typically we don't think deeply about ends. Why did this specialty develop? Who benefits? Who is protected?

Even people who want to consider those questions may have trouble locating compassion at the root of what they do. Their profession's original goal may have been to reduce a particular vulnerability. Yet, as the environment changes and specialization intensifies, they may lose sight of how compassion motivates their specialty. For example, a company might develop a new navigation app that makes driving safer because it steers people away from vulnerabilities created by heavy traffic. But a programmer, focused on developing special features, may lose sight of the original goal and make drivers more vulnerable because the app is too distracting.

Cooperative networks are strengthened when each of us consciously uses our specialized knowledge to anticipate and mitigate risk on behalf of others. In today's world we all must depend on specialists, who in turn count on us to do our part. These interlocking systems suffer whenever anyone with specialized understanding fails to practice proactive compassion. We must be looking out for vulnerabilities all the time, especially where our specialized experience and training allows us to see what others can't.

Most people don't think about what they do in these terms. But it occurs to me that I'm more engaged in my work when I feel as though I'm writing about something people really need to know. I guess you're saying that the accuracy of my information and the clarity of my communication may stand between my reader and the fast-swinging doors of contemporary society.

Whenever our expertise allows us to see harms that others don't, we have an obligation to make use of specialized skills, procedures, and tools that protect them. Put a brightly colored strip of nonskid tape on a stair to prevent falls. Sterilize instruments to avoid infection. Make packaging for dangerous products child-proof. Many problems that have plagued humankind in the past have been minimized or even eradicated because specialists reworked a risky environment by improving standard practices.

This kind of compassion sounds very much like the child-proofing parents do for young children.

And, like children, we may not even know what's been done to minimize our vulnerability. For example, by studying statistics about where traffic accidents occur, highway engineers have learned to design roadways that simply preclude many accidents. Think about the barriers that separate lanes of cars going in opposite directions, or rotaries that force people to slow down and watch for traffic instead of speeding through an intersection.

Specialists can modify social as well as physical environments to prevent harms. Whenever there's a campus disturbance such as a bomb threat or a shooting, security specialists at other colleges and universities review their standard procedures with the aim of preventing similar situations. They may develop protocols that make it easier to identify and help troubled students. They may train specialists who can detect and disarm explosives, or install security systems that allow them to monitor and if necessary lock down buildings. Because these preventive measures are often highly effective, they may be invisible to students and faculty.

On an even larger scale, proactive compassion is built into the mission of regulatory agencies like the Food Safety and Inspection Service of the U.S. Department of Agriculture. People unknown to us process most of our food, and ordinary people cannot detect contaminants such as E. coli and salmonella. We depend on a network of food safety specialists to discover and issue warnings about such dangers *before* lots of people get sick.

To practice proactive compassion we need to reconnect with the compassionate premise at the heart of everything we do. This includes our activities outside of work, where we may also have specialized knowledge that can promote safer environments in the causes we support and the passions we pursue. A walker who regularly takes the same route through a park may be the first to spot a dead branch that's likely to fall. A volunteer coach may be the one who notices that children in one family don't have warm clothes for the winter. As we get into the habit of practicing proactive compassion it becomes easier to spot risks early, when harms are minor and can be addressed through relatively modest changes.

Sharing What We Know to Prevent Harm

As parents know, child-proofing goes only so far. What about harms that can't be prevented by making changes in practices or in the environment?

When specialists can't prevent harms, it's their responsibility to warn the rest of us about dangers they foresee. Parents do this as soon as children understand language. When children encounter environments that parents can't modify, they get lots of advice about how to avoid harms: When you go for a walk, stay on the sidewalk and don't run into the street. When it snows, wear mittens. When you ride the carousel, hold on tight.

In successful societies experts create signals that make citizens aware of known harms. Highway engineers know that water freezes sooner on bridges because the road surface is colder than on highways. They can't engineer around this problem, so they warn: "Bridge surface freezes before highway!" to alert the rest of us to a danger we might otherwise overlook. Such warnings regularly save lives.

Some people worry that our society has become too protective. We hear complaints about "helicopter parents" who protect kids from every setback and the "nanny state" that curtails freedom by imposing too many regulations.

In a healthy cooperative system we want everyone to be a full-fledged cooperator. That means encouraging people to be responsible for their own well-being whenever possible. In stable and familiar environments people are generally quite good at doing their part. They contribute benefits and sidestep harms without much difficulty. The challenge arises when we encounter environments that are unfamiliar or highly complex. Driving safely in your own neighborhood is no problem, but if you're navigating in a city you don't know, you'll be grateful for clear signs that show up well before the exit! In unfamiliar environments, risks multiply, and we benefit enormously from guidance by someone who knows the ropes.

The idea that those who know should guide those who don't is rooted in antiquity. In the ancient world travel was rare because it was so risky. Only kings could afford the kind of entourage that made travel a little safer, and even kings were vulnerable in a strange place. The traveler needed a host, someone familiar with the environment, to point out risks and steer him away from dangers. Sure enough, the ancients considered hospitality to strangers a privilege and a virtue. Homer mentions it repeatedly. At bottom hospitality means seeing to it that strangers aren't overwhelmed by the strangeness of a strange land.

Hospitality sounds like a form of compassion. Hosts imagine the ways in which ignorance of the environment could harm their guests and respond with guidance that helps guests avoid those risks. Even at home you put a night-light in the guestroom so visitors won't trip in the dark.

When we travel today, a battalion of specialists works to minimize risk. A computer programmer makes the reservation website user-friendly. Security experts screen out predators. Baggage handlers make sure that belongings arrive at a destination when their owners do. A fraud expert at a credit company checks to make sure the traveler really charged that meal in London. The hotel concierge advises guests about the best local restaurants and how to get there safely. All these people practice proactive compassion, first by anticipating vulnerability and then by following procedures and issuing warnings that minimize risk and steer travelers toward benefits in unfamiliar environments.

As environments become more complex and specialized, we can feel as though we are in strange lands and in need of hospitality even when we're close to home. The first time we find ourselves in a government office, a medical center, a school system, or even on a social networking site, we enter a foreign environment. Even when we return to environments we once knew well, we may find them altered in ways that make us uncertain—the supermarket has rearranged the produce, or a favorite website has redesigned its homepage.

Whenever you understand an environment better than others do, you can practice proactive compassion by pointing out risks that are obvious to you but not to them.

Both the people who designed a particular environment and those who use it routinely can navigate that environment comfortably, so they can and should function as hosts, providing tools and cues that will keep newbies from making predictable and potentially costly mistakes. In physical environments, GPS systems, directories, event programs, and orientation sessions are just a few standard devices that ease the discomfort of unfamiliar settings and the vulnerability of those newly encountering them.

In social environments, too, we benefit from structures that link those who know with those who don't. Realtors often put new homeowners in touch with the local welcome wagon or newcomers club. Companies develop human resource teams to coach employees when they need additional training or support in their personal lives. Service organizations like Rotary, Kiwanis, and Lions have traditionally encouraged seasoned businesspeople to mentor the less experienced.

It sounds as though any kind of teaching or mentorship can be a form of proactive compassion—if it's motivated by an understanding of vulnerability.

Every specialist has such opportunities. As a professor I practiced compassionate hospitality with my students. The concepts of ethics were foreign to many of them when they walked into my classroom, and I took it as my job to guide them through terrain I understood very well. I did this in part because it had been done for me.

When I was a brash young graduate student I attended a lecture about perception given by the renowned professor Max Black. I naïvely thought I had discovered a huge hole in his argument, and as we were leaving the lecture hall I was explaining the "error" to another grad student—without realizing that Professor Black was walking behind me. He could have mocked my inexperience, which certainly goes on in some classrooms. Instead he recognized my vulnerability and practiced compassion by asking a gentle question: "How would you explain the idea that blue seems closer to green than it is to yellow?" Rather than letting me waste my time on an intellectual dead end, he pointed me toward a more subtle understanding of concepts deeply familiar to him.

I guess I did something similar when I helped organize a support group for families with deaf children. I remembered how vulnerable I'd felt when my daughter was first diagnosed, and I thought that some of what I'd learned about audiology and IEPs (Individualized Education Programs) might be useful to other parents. Eventually I wrote a column about techniques that were helpful when my daughter was first learning language.

Once we start thinking this way, we see opportunities for proactive compassion everywhere. We can practice it whenever we have access to specialized skills, procedures, and tools. We can practice it on behalf of family, friends, and neighbors, or people we don't know. We can practice it by modifying social and physical environments or by helping people navigate those environments more easily.

Thinking of our specialized roles as opportunities to practice compassion brings new meaning to work that might otherwise seem routine. What's the second way to practice proactive compassion?

2. Intercept harms triggered by change

Proactive compassion becomes especially important when circumstances are changing. For example, when the first Ebola patient died in the United States, many people felt an acute sense of vulnerability. Suddenly they saw risk in environments that had seemed stable. Were airplanes safe? What about hospitals? Public health officials had to mobilize quickly, tracking and sometimes quarantining people who'd had contact with infected patients. They had to revise procedures for screening and processing incoming patients as well as safety protocols for nursing staff.

Change of this kind is increasingly common because it's so easy today for people— and pathogens—to travel from place to place. People are on the move, sometimes to flee from war or political instability but often in pursuit of new opportunities on the other side of the country or the other side of the world.

Of course, change of any kind challenges structures predicated on a certain degree of stability. We organize things to avoid known risks. When circumstances change, we cannot necessarily depend on what's been reliable in the past, and we cannot possibly foresee all of the implications. We *will* be taken by surprise, and for many this is an unsettling experience. We want to believe that if we arrange things carefully, we'll be able to live happily ever after. Get the right education. Choose the right partner. Find the right job. Discover the right medication. Pass the right legislation.

The truth, of course, is that "right" cannot possibly be permanent. What we've learned will become obsolete. Our partner will grow in unpredictable ways. Technology may make our job irrelevant. Germs will mutate to evade our medications. Loopholes will subvert the good intentions of our laws. Change may sneak up on us or it may arrive in an instant. Either way we'll do better if we start with the understanding that we can't step in the same river twice.

This seems like another place where the experience of parenthood is illuminating. A newborn may be perfectly safe in the middle of a big bed, but as soon as that child learns to roll over, the bed is not a safe environment. In my experience parents often feel as though they are playing catch-up. As soon as you figure out Facebook, the kids move to Instagram and Vine.

Anyone who hopes to practice proactive compassion must embrace this reality. Sometimes the environment will change just when we think we've gotten things settled once and for all. In other cases the solution that seems so clever will carry within it the seeds of new problems. If we practice proactive compassion we'll constantly be alert for changes and for emerging externalities. The goal is always to spot germinating problems before they take root.

The Compassionate Chain Reaction

Let's be clear: when environments are in flux, we won't be able to predict all the ways in which people might be vulnerable. The goal of proactive compassion is to be alert and responsive, recognizing harms early, when they are relatively insignificant, and then revising cooperative structures so the harms don't become more serious.

To better understand this process, let's look back in history. Ancient people organized themselves into clans, around 120 people you could know well through firsthand experience. You were tied to members of your clan by genetics, tradition, and proximity. You'd grown up with them and knew them intimately, so you could predict how they would behave. But the prospect of trusting people outside the clan—much less cooperating with them—was a very big deal.

At some point, however, people saw that creating alliances with other clans might bring significant benefits and reduce certain risks. Those people might have different skills or access to needed resources. They might also be willing to band together to fend off threats. Of course, cooperating with outsiders brought considerable risks. Their customs and language weren't necessarily familiar. Even when communication was possible, what would show that they were trustworthy?

Just seeing another clan from a distance would change the social environment. People would wonder about those others. Some would see them as a threat. Others would be curious about new ways of cooperating.

For ancient people the solution to this predicament was often a formal code of rules. Unspoken assumptions within each clan were made explicit so that everyone could agree on them. Very early norms such as Hammurabi's Code and the Ten Commandments emerged among tribes that were trying to broaden cooperation beyond the clan. These norms minimized potential conflicts, rewarding cooperation and punishing defections from a written, shared standard of responsibility.

That makes sense. If I don't know you directly, I'll have more confidence in you if I know you subscribe to the same laws. If we both agree on the Ten Commandments, I can assume you won't kill me, steal my stuff, or have sex with my spouse. And vice versa. But how does this relate to proactive compassion?

Each adjustment in the social environment—reaching out to another clan, then setting up mutual guidelines for behavior—was a compassionate response to anticipated vulnerability. People always embark on cooperative efforts because they see potential benefits. But whenever we do things differently, potential harms await. Anticipating and addressing those harms is one way to prevent conflict.

In the ancient world having a set of simple rules seemed at first to create a more stable environment. But it also created a new set of problems as people started to ask how a rule applied in specific circumstances. The rule may state clearly that a man is not allowed to have sex with his partner's wife, but is he allowed to see her face, talk to her, or engage in commerce with her? Within the clan everyone depended on the patriarch to rule on such matters. But between clans some other authority was needed. Even with a common set of rules, you're going to need impartial people to interpret them when their application isn't clear.

Again, the question is how to preserve the benefits of more elaborate cooperation without incurring unnecessary risk.

Historically the solution was a new kind of specialist who could interpret the law and apply it to varied circumstances. It's probably no accident that in the Bible the book of Judges follows closely after the Ten Commandments. In the ancient world judges were circuit riders who arbitrated inter-clan disputes.

From our vantage point in history it's pretty easy to see the next complication: like any other kind of specialist, judges have to be compensated. At first it seems obvious that the people embroiled in the dispute should pay because, after all, they benefit directly from the judges' services. That solution, however, raises an interesting question: What's the difference between compensating a judge and bribing one? Not much. And that being the case, how can you be sure the judge is impartial? It seems perfectly natural for a judge to favor the party that pays more.

Let's see if I have this straight. Isaac and Joseph are neighbors who get along because they both agree stealing is wrong. A pumpkin vine planted by Isaac sneaks under the fence and produces a pumpkin in Joseph's yard. When Joseph picks the pumpkin, Isaac accuses him of stealing. The law doesn't address wandering pumpkins, so they call for a judge. The judge needs a place to stay for the night, and Joseph puts him up. If the judge gives Joseph the pumpkin, it looks like payback.

Exactly. You've got a situation in which rules are established to facilitate cooperation. To preserve the benefits of cooperation, conflicts over the rules must be resolved peaceably. The judge is a specialist in conflict resolution, but his judgment is likely to be corrupted if either of the disputants pays for his services. An evolving system of cooperation has solved some problems but created others. In such cases the usual solution is that the community—which is the ultimate beneficiary—takes up a collection to pay for the judge. Voila! We are on our way to some form of taxation that underwrites the benefits created by peaceful resolution of legal disputes.

At every stage of this story people could—and probably did—become discouraged, because a development that was supposed to solve problems created new problems. And at every stage some people practiced proactive compassion, recognizing and responding to vulnerabilities that emerged because the social environment had changed in response to new forms of cooperation. With the introduction of taxation, again benefits are created and old vulnerabilities resolved, but—

Let me guess—new vulnerabilities are created!!

This progression is extremely important. Each social configuration—from interacting clans through codes, judges, bribery issues, and taxation—is a sincere effort to mitigate known risks and longstanding difficulties. Invariably, however, changes in the social environment give rise to new social difficulties. Vulnerabilities emerge that didn't exist before the new configuration went into place. People practice proactive compassion by being alert to this dynamic.

Compassion in a Dynamic Community

Let's turn to a more contemporary example: in the 1970s laws in many places changed to permit a right turn at a red light. Benefits were created, because less idling at red lights saves time and fuel. But the new law also produced an unhappy externality. Pedestrians used to taking safety cues from traffic lights were suffering increased injuries and even fatalities. Not surprisingly, children, the elderly, and people who had been drinking alcohol were most vulnerable.

Soon, though, both drivers and pedestrians began to practice proactive compassion by watching out for each other in the changed environment. Pedestrians learned to look over their shoulders before crossing the street. Drivers learned to check the curb as well as the light before making their turns. New instruction emerged for schoolchildren, and public service announcements on television targeted the elderly. Around the same time, tavern owners became more proactive about cutting off patrons who seemed impaired, and encouraging them to take taxis. Once these compassionate adjustments were made, this harm subsided.

New regulations weren't required. Pedestrians and drivers, bartenders and cab drivers all spotted harms created by this change in the environment. Then they adapted to the situation in ways that preserved the benefits of right-turn-on-red while minimizing the risks.

What we're describing is a dynamic community that responds to changes in the social environment by evolving to provide new opportunities and prevent or significantly reduce new dangers. At each stage of the process, unexpected vulnerabilities engage our compassion. When changing circumstances exacerbate vulnerabilities, especially in ways we didn't anticipate, people practice proactive compassion by asking, What can we do?

Here's another example: when teenagers learn to drive, the risks are huge. They have to master a complicated set of skills and adapt them to varying circumstances. A teen may have demonstrated that he is capable of driving in the neighborhood, but what about merging onto a highway? At night? When it's raining? With music on the radio? With other teens in the vehicle? In many states legislators have tried to create a series of graduated steps so that adolescents move gradually into the more complex responsibilities of driving.

Now change the environment by adding a new technology—cellphones with texting capabilities and internet access. Again, specialists have practiced proactive compassion by coming up with various ways to prevent emerging harms. States have enacted laws with penalties for texting while driving. Programmers have created apps that shut down the phone (or its texting capacity) if it's in a moving vehicle.

And parents—who are specialists in the capabilities of the teenagers in their household—make rules about when and how vehicles and phones are to be used.

Notice what's required here. People must be aware that the environment is changing, and willing to respond quickly to emerging harms. This can be especially difficult for specialists, who have learned to use specific techniques to achieve specific goals shaped by the environment as it was. Specialists become comfortable with and even attached to particular ways of doing things, and they may be reluctant to modify, much less abandon, specialized knowledge.

When environments are in flux, practices that once created benefits may start to create problems. As more students depend on smartphones and tablets for note-taking, research, and collaboration, school administrators have to reconsider policies banning them from the classroom. Now that password-cracking software has become readily available online, website administrators must investigate other techniques, such as two-step verification, for keeping information secure. When members of a congregation become dispersed, trustees have to consider other ways of making church buildings vital to the life of the congregation and the neighborhood. In every case, people with specialized responsibilities must be alert enough to recognize a change in the environment and flexible enough to modify what had been regarded as appropriate practice.

By this way of thinking, I practiced proactive compassion when I wrote an early column about Snapchat, an app that was being used to distribute racy photos. By then parents had warned kids about sexting, but Snapchat changed the environment because images were supposed to disappear in ten seconds. Unfortunately, the pictures didn't go away if someone grabbed a screen shot! Kids were vulnerable in a new way, and parents needed information so they could at least talk to them about the risks created by this new environment. In areas like technology, where change is rapid and disruptive, proactive compassion seems especially important.

When we don't anticipate vulnerabilities created when environments change, the consequences may spiral out of control. Think about the financial crisis of 2008. Most people, including many financial advisers, simply didn't understand how investments like derivatives were changing the economic landscape, and they certainly didn't understand how a bubble in the housing market could jeopardize their pensions. People who weren't financial experts simply saw that housing prices were rising. In that environment buying a second home made sense because you could "flip" it in a year or two and make a lot of money.

I remember that people acted as though rising real estate prices were a permanent feature of the environment. They were genuinely shocked when the housing market started to crumble.

The scale of the problem wasn't readily detected by nonspecialists. Most people had no insight into the credit market and no way to understand how extensively credit practices had been compromised by the sale of derivative financial instruments. The system could handle a few overextended homeowners, but there came a tipping point when the downside got out of hand. When huge numbers of people lost their homes, investors lost their investments, the housing market was flooded, and the construction industry was undermined. Soon bankers, pensioners, hedge fund managers, small business owners, and taxpayers were implicated—not only in this country but around the world.

In the middle of that crisis a CEO at Fannie Mae said, "Almost no one expected what was coming. It's not fair to blame us for not predicting the unthinkable." To me that comment reveals a failure of compassion. It *is* the job of the CEO—and every other specialist—to exercise proactive compassion in the face of change. Specialists must pay closer than usual attention when the environment they know best is in flux. We all have to be alert to indications that things aren't going as well as we hoped they would. We need to imagine worst-case scenarios on behalf of each other. And we should be especially alert if a "small" problem begins to grow or spread.

To recap, specialists should use their expertise to prevent harms that aren't obvious to the rest of us. And all of us should be alert for harms when environments are changing. What's the third way of practicing proactive compassion?

3. Address gaps between assigned responsibilities

Under traditional ideas of morality, we respond to harm by asking who failed to fulfill their responsibilities. As we've discussed, our justice system penalizes people who take advantage of the trust required for cooperation: The corporation that knowingly sells dangerous products. The investment advisor who profits by steering clients into pump-and-dump schemes. The politician who accepts bribes in exchange for legislation that benefits some constituents at the expense of others. The thief who breaks into someone's home or steals someone's identity. Predators like these imperil the cooperative structures on which we all depend, so they must be identified and isolated, or rehabilitated if possible.

We should also impose sanctions on people who create harms by shirking duties assigned to them. The hospital worker who takes shortcuts in hand-washing may be responsible for spreading pathogens. The teacher who doesn't assign essays because it takes too long to grade them puts students at a disadvantage. The factory supervisor who lets quality control slide may be responsible for product defects. These people may not intend harm, but in failing to be conscientious about their responsibilities they put others at risk.

For cooperation to work, we have to hold each other accountable so benefits continue to be mutual.

That's good as far as it goes. But the problems we're talking about often occur in the gaps where no one has clear responsibility. A 2014 cover headline on the *New York Times Magazine* read: "Every hour, an acre of Louisiana sinks into the sea. Who is to blame?" The article told the story of a man who sued oil companies to force them to pay for their part in destroying the Mississippi delta. True, the oil companies bear some responsibility, through building a porous network of tunnels and canals that drain the region's fragile wetlands. But the destruction is also an unintended consequence of levees built to keep the Mississippi from flooding New Orleans and dams built as far away as Montana to control rivers and create reservoirs.

This definitely seems like a case where things have gotten out of control because specialists didn't see what lay outside their areas of specialization. Scale seems like an issue too, because changes that produced benefits at one level became problematic when they were more widely implemented. And tolerances also come into play. Wetlands are resilient up to a point, but that point was passed.

In such situations, we understandably want to hold someone accountable, but often that's a distraction. People may have been oblivious to the value of wetlands without intending to destroy them, or to put New Orleans and its surroundings in peril. Whatever the decisions that contributed to the severity of those problems, they were made by well-intentioned people aiming at other goals.

Moving Beyond Blame

With many such complex problems, breakdowns can't be attributed to any-one in particular. All parties were sincerely trying to do their parts, yet harm has occurred anyway. There isn't a clear culprit, so our standard ways of assigning responsibility break down. We can get hung up on doggedly trying to assign responsibility. Or we can be motivated by the idea that, in a dynamic society, unanticipated harms will occur in the spaces where responsibility is unclear or unassigned.

The third practice for proactive compassion involves recognizing these gaps and stepping in to fill them whenever possible. Riders on London's

Underground are warned to "mind the gap" between train and platform: a space that's neither train nor station. In the context of proactive compassion, minding the gap mean spotting spaces, often between specializations, where no one has direct responsibility. Sometimes this means taking personal initiative to mitigate vulnerability. Or it may involve connecting people with responsive networks. The essential point is that we go above and beyond the duties assigned to us. Instead of trying to find a villain, asking who failed to do what they were supposed to do, we prevent further harm by asking who has response-ability—the capacity to respond in a compassionate way that mitigates vulnerability.

So if I'm able to address a problem, I should act even if I'm not responsible in the usual sense of the word?

Most of us do this spontaneously when we see people overwhelmed by forces clearly beyond their control. We respond viscerally to the plight of abandoned or abused children. We try to assist those harmed by accidents that can't be prevented or illnesses that can't be cured. We aren't responsible for natural disasters, but we do what we can to help the victims. In all these cases we didn't cause the problem, so we don't have direct responsibility. But we can see that no one intended or consented to this harm, so if we are able to respond, we do. We should respond similarly whenever we discover inadvertent and unpredicted harms in our cooperative enterprises.

Exercising Personal Response-Ability

Again, we can learn a lot by noticing what parents do spontaneously with children. Initially parents anticipate harms on behalf of the child, but as soon as the child begins to understand language, parents begin to transfer response-ability to the child. Through parental instruction as well as their own experience, children learn to recognize threats. As they begin to appraise risk for themselves and respond in ways that minimize vulnerability, they are able to recognize gaps and take initiative to prevent harms even when they haven't been asked.

When my children were young, we spent a lot of time at the playground. Some parents warned their kids constantly about the risks of swings and slides. But it seemed to me that children really needed only a little initial coaching. After that they were highly motivated to avoid falls.

Taking initiative to protect oneself from harm is a very basic way of practicing proactive compassion on behalf of a larger group. Because we are all connected, harms are rarely limited to one person. You could say that a child who takes care not to fall off the playground equipment is protecting not only himself and potentially his playmates but also his family members, who would be distressed if he were injured, and even the medical personnel that might be involved in his care.

As adults, we have frequent opportunities to minimize vulnerability by exercising personal response-ability. For example, I ride my bicycle wherever I can — enough to know that environments organized primarily to accommodate automobiles create risks for cyclists. I can and regularly do mitigate those risks by doing things that aren't technically required of cyclists. Even though it's not mandated in my community, I always wear a helmet. I listen for cars coming up from behind and watch for driver-side doors that might open as well as cars that might turn in front of me without signaling. More than once I've straight-armed a right-turning car that otherwise would have knocked me to the curb. And I inform myself about routes that have been modified to reduce bicycling risks. Much of this might seem like common sense, and it is. But it's also a deliberate effort to spot gaps where harm might occur and respond constructively.

Interesting. I wouldn't have thought about taking care of oneself as a form of compassion, but I can see the point. If you're involved in a collision with a car, the circle of harm will ripple out to the driver, the bystanders, your family, your employer. Being proactive about your own well-being protects all of them.

Further, becoming aware of gaps in the safety net equips us to respond to the vulnerability of others. Because of my own bike-safety awareness, I also make sure my grandkids have and wear helmets; I tell other cyclists about safer routes, promote safe cycling, and help regional authorities plan and connect bike routes. When I drive with other people, I can raise their awareness by pointing out situations in which cyclists are vulnerable. Whenever I find a situation in which no one in particular is responsible for preventing harms, I want to exercise response-ability if I can. Institutions also can take such initiatives: a university situated along a busy state route made cycling safer by offering some of its buffer land as a bicycle route.

Again parents have a role to play. Yes, we want children to be responsible for tasks assigned to them. We also want them to actively look for ways to mitigate vulnerability—first for themselves and then for others. That's why we praise children who go out of their way to help a sibling. And we encourage three- or four-year-olds to "help," even though their participation almost always makes the job take longer. When children get this kind of support from an early age, they start to learn the skills and develop the mindset that will allow them to anticipate vulnerability and respond effectively.

This makes me think about a four-year-old named Hannah who saw a homeless man who had no socks. She wanted to give the man her own socks, but her mother suggested that instead they donate socks to him and other people at a local shelter. That first donation grew into Hannah's Socks, a nonprofit that has collected and distributed over half a million pairs of socks to people in need.

Good Samaritans in a Complex World

That's a wonderful example. It illustrates how one person can fill a gap, as well as how her efforts become more powerful with the help of a network. To understand this intersection better, let's revisit the story of the Good Samaritan, a parable that beautifully captures the idea of response-ability. As Jesus tells it, a man falls among thieves and is left for dead at the side of the road. Two men with religious affiliations pass him by without helping. Then a Samaritan comes along. Even though he's a member of an outcast group widely despised by the people Jesus was addressing, the Samaritan demonstrates compassion for the injured man. He treats his wounds, helps him to safety, and pays for his care.

By the time Jesus asks, "Who proved neighbor?" there's no question about the answer: "The man who showed compassion to him." The Samaritan wasn't in any way responsible for the man's predicament. He hadn't caused his wounds, and he wasn't in charge of public safety. He did have the ability to respond, though, so he did.

It seems like that story would unfold quite differently today.

In our complex, specialized world, individuals don't always have the ability to respond constructively, even if they may wish to. If you pass someone in trouble on the highway, you aren't likely to have the skills they need. Usually the motorist is best served by a network of specialists in public safety. The most compassionate thing may be to alert the highway patrol of a problem at mile marker 89, and maybe wait nearby until help arrives. The emergency operator can deploy a specialist who can repair or tow the car and specialists who can manage medical emergencies if someone has been hurt. The EMRs in turn will use a siren to alert drivers and clear the road, and they'll call ahead so specialists at the hospital are prepared to respond swiftly when the patient arrives. En route those specialists advise the EMR how to stabilize the patient by taking advantage of capacities built into the environment of an emergency vehicle. Response-ability is built into this network, along with the training, tools, and procedures to aid the unfortunate motorist.

If I were stuck at the side of the road, I'd be anxious about accepting help from another motorist, no matter how well intentioned. I'd rather get help from paramedics who have the equipment to treat my injuries or a mechanic who understands my car.

Your reaction is evidence of how well our cooperative systems work. And it reveals the dual nature of response-ability: sometimes I am in a position to address vulnerabilities, and sometimes the best thing I can do is to connect people with a specialized network that can address their needs. We need to cultivate our ability to respond on both levels. Here's an example: a year or so ago a woman drove several hours to meet with me because she was upset about wind prospecting in her county. I'm not a specialist in this field, but I have a little expertise. In addition to installing a wind turbine to produce power at my home, I've consulted with the state of Ohio about how to develop wind resources in the state.

The woman who came to visit me—let's call her Joyce—had decided she was adamantly opposed to the construction of turbines, in part because she'd gotten information from a coal lobbyist who was paid to be anti-wind. Also, back then officials in her county were struggling to master the basics. They didn't have a good grasp of externalities such as noise levels, the flicker caused by turning turbine blades, or the impact on wildlife.

Joyce had acquired a reputation for being abrasive because she insisted on asking difficult questions. It would have been easy to dismiss her, but I could tell that her anger sprang directly from her vulnerability. No one seemed to care that wind turbines might threaten the qualities she valued in her community. Her apprehension was palpable and justified. The environment she cared about was changing rapidly, and she was in a responsibility gap.

In such situations it's very easy for those in charge to respond to anger with anger. It takes discipline not to be caught up by her anger and to focus instead on her underlying vulnerability.

Joyce had become abrasive because she felt things were getting out of control. And her concerns fell into the gaps, outside the focus of the specialists involved in the project. The wind developers were focused on producing clean, affordable power. The farmers were focused on the money they would get from leasing their land. No one was focused on quality-of-life issues like noise and flicker and harm to wildlife. Joyce wasn't opposed to benefits for the farmers or the developers. She just didn't want those benefits to come at the expense of things that mattered to her.

I was an individual bystander with no direct responsibility for the problems Joyce was facing. But I had the ability to respond to her concerns because I'm familiar with some of the issues. And so I took time to help her think through the situation and clarify her questions. Are all wind turbines noisy? How does the sound at the base of the turbine compare to the sound of traffic or a home air conditioner or a power lawnmower? Under what circumstances does flicker occur? How many birds or bats do turbines kill each year, and how does this compare to the number killed by hitting a skyscraper or by cars on the highway? If Joyce had better information, she would be able to intervene quickly and effectively while plans were still in development.

So even though you had no assigned duty to respond to Joyce, you stepped into the gap and helped her figure out how to reduce her vulnerability.

Identify Who Can Help

I was also very aware of the limits of what I could do as an individual. Although I could offer a general understanding of the issues related to wind energy, I'm not an expert on the technology of turbines or the political realities in Joyce's county. Instead I pointed her to existing networks of specialists who could provide reliable, nonpartisan answers to her questions. Part of Joyce's vulnerability came from her feeling that she was alone in her misgivings. Connecting her to knowledgeable experts who shared her misgivings reduced her isolation and gave her the confidence to have calm and civil conversations with local officials. As part of an informed network, she was more likely to play a meaningful role in creating a cooperative plan that would protect what mattered to her, while allowing others to pursue benefits important to them.

You're saying that individuals should get in the habit of asking, "Who can help?" even when they aren't directly implicated in a problem. The answer to that question may be, "I can! I'm in a position to respond!" Or it may be, "We can! I'm part of or know of a network that can address the problem."

Human societies are still learning how to practice response-ability in environments that require coordination and cooperation. Even when it's clear that massive harm is occurring, we tend to look for one person or group to take charge and solve the problem. If only the president would do this or Congress would do that. In our complex, interconnected social systems, that mindset is ineffective. The serious harms to which we are vulnerable have many dimensions, addressed by specialists who may not always communicate with, much less understand each other. So when we become aware of gaps in accountability, we should look beyond our usual roles to consider how we might minimize vulnerability.

As an example, think about respiratory problems like asthma. The doctors who treat this condition are understandably focused on medical tests and procedures. In another dimension experts in air chemistry and pollution understand the kinds of airborne particles that are likely to be present in residences and workplaces and how those particles can create and aggravate respiratory problems. The patient with asthma is vulnerable because there is a gap between these specialists. Instead of just offering patients medication, physicians could reach beyond their assigned responsibilities to ask about air quality in the environment where a patient lives and works. For their part, air quality specialists could try to share what they know with medical professionals. Both could thereby practice proactive compassion. When an unexpected vulnerability arises in complex, interconnected networks, response-ability is likely to depend on the coordinated efforts of people with a variety of specialized skills.

When we feel unable to exercise response-ability as individuals, we need to make ourselves part of a responsive community.

One person with limited expertise, acting alone, isn't likely to solve a problem that has many dimensions. In such situations, we practice proactive compassion by identifying, engaging with, and sometimes creating responsive networks. You can see this clearly with volunteer organizations: the most successful ones skillfully coordinate the specialized expertise that volunteers contribute. For instance, when residents of the Shenandoah Valley saw suburban Washington, D.C., sprawling toward them, local leaders who perceived the perils of unrestrained development mobilized volunteers with expertise in architecture, banking, conservation, farming, regional planning, and law. In 1990 they created a land trust, the Valley Conservation Council (VCC), which has established and maintained regional land use policies that take community concerns into account. Today the VCC is an oft-cited exemplar of the land conservancy movement, which continues to improve the sustainability of natural and social environments nationwide.

The members of the VCC practice proactive compassion by participating in a network that anticipates problems on behalf of the larger community, actively looking for gaps in the planning routinely done by developers and government agencies.

Precisely. In our complex, interdependent world, even our best efforts at cooperation can create vulnerabilities. Proactive compassion is the deliberate effort to recognize and address them before they become serious harms. We can cultivate this capacity by engaging in the three practices I've described: Pay special attention to risks that are obvious to you because of your specialized point of view. Be alert to vulnerabilities that grow out of changing environments. Notice the gaps where responsibility is unassigned, and encourage engagement by individuals and networks that have response-ability.

Compassion Is Not a Cure-All

I can see how compassion is motivating. I think most people really do want to prevent harm when they can, but harm often seems unavoidable. No matter how you respond to a problem, somebody is going to get hurt.

When we realize that things have reached this point, it's tempting to walk away. To some extent that's what happened in the environmental movement between 1970 and 2000. The vulnerabilities were clear. Species were being driven to extinction by pollution and loss of habitat, caused by voluntary agreements between companies that produced products and consumers who exercised their freedom of choice in purchasing them.

Companies pointed to all the benefits they were creating: workers were employed, shareholders were profiting, and consumers enjoyed the benefits of convenience and low costs. None of these groups intended to impose harms, so they resented the increased costs created by regulations intended to protect people they didn't know and wildlife they couldn't see. On the other hand, people who cared deeply about woodlands, wetlands, and other natural habitats were alarmed by serious and in some cases irreversible damage.

I remember that feeling of discouragement. For me it all came to a head over spotted owls. I have family in Oregon, and when the owl went on the endangered species list it seemed as though the choice was between preserving owls and preserving jobs. Both sides were vulnerable. If I took action on behalf of one group, it seemed others would be harmed. Practicing compassion seemed to put me in a situation where I was going to be miserable no matter how things worked out.

Proactive compassion alone is not enough when we find ourselves in such lose-lose predicaments. Standard practices evolve over time in response to specific interests. They create benefits for certain parties in certain environments. But the environment changes, sometimes because of the practices themselves; unintended costs are generated, sometimes for parties who were never involved in the original cooperative arrangement. Beneficiaries of the original arrangement may be understandably attached to that system, but a system that creates benefits for some at the expense of others jeopardizes the promise of sociality.

So where does that leave us?

When standard ways of doing things produce unacceptable results, we have no choice but to rethink our cooperative arrangements. Such change always introduces new vulnerabilities for one or another party in the arrangement. To make real progress in reworking the cooperative system, we need to look beyond the compassionate response to discern what each of the affected parties values and will defend. If our goal is cooperation for mutual benefit, we must learn to perceive what what risks and benefits look like for all willing cooperators.

CHAPTER 3

Deep Discernment
Discovering Bedrock Values

When we try to pick out anything by itself,
we find it hitched to everything else in the Universe.
John Muir

Let us not look back in anger, nor forward
in fear, but around us in awareness.
James Thurber

Practicing compassion seems essential. Cooperation thrives on mutual benefits,
and proactive compassion helps us spot the places where harms, rather than ben-
efits, are being created. We become more adept at proactive compassion by using
specialized skills, tools, and procedures to prevent harms or warn others about
risks that may not be obvious to them. We pay special attention when environments
are in flux, and we look out for gaps between specialized realms, cultivating the
ability—in ourselves and others—to respond to foreseeable harms.

And even after we do all that, we may find ourselves in conflict, as you point
out. The loggers may very well care about wildlife, but they need paychecks
so they can feed their families. The conservationists may be sympathetic to
the problems of the unemployed, but without habitat the owls die.

People who aren't directly involved often throw up their hands in despair. It's very
uncomfortable to choose between adversaries when either party will suffer signif-
icant loss if the other prevails.

This unhappy predicament cries out for deep discernment. Traditionally
theologians have thought of discernment as the process of divining and coming to terms with God's will. I see this virtue a little differently. If we want the

62

considerable benefits that cooperation can create, we have to make sure those benefits are mutual. Conflict is stirred up whenever some feel that they have to sacrifice what matters to them so others can get what they want.

Deep discernment is the habit of trying to understand precisely what is at stake for everyone who is significantly affected by cooperative agreements. We practice deep discernment when we distinguish between values and means, watch out for accumulating harms, and honor multiple points of view. These three practices can go a long way toward defusing conflict.

When you think about it, conflict generally occurs because people feel that something they care about enormously is at risk because of something other people are doing. Often the parties don't know or can't articulate exactly what is at stake, but they feel threatened: "If you get what matters to you, I have to give up on what matters to me, and I'm not about to do that!" So, like the woman who was worried about wind turbines in her neighborhood, they respond aggressively to defend what matters to them.

It's perfectly understandable that people become self-protective and even angry if others seem to be benefiting at their expense. This is as basic as two children squabbling because they want to play with the same toy.

The Real Wisdom of Solomon

It's sometimes said that parents need the wisdom of Solomon to resolve such disputes, and Solomon is one of my favorite examples of discernment. In the story that won him his reputation, two women claimed to be the mother of the same child. Both had recently given birth, but one baby died and now each mother wanted the living child. Solomon would have benefited from genetic testing, but that option was centuries away. At the time all he knew was that the physiological evidence was inadequate, and both women seemed genuinely distraught.

One of them would suffer no matter what Solomon did, it seemed. The well-being of an innocent child was also at stake. And the coherence of the whole community would suffer if the king's decisions appeared arbitrary or unfair, even if his information was scanty.

Given the circumstances, conflict seemed inevitable. In that unhappy context Solomon announced a startling decision. The only fair way to resolve the question was to cut the child in half, and he called for a sword. In a flash he changed the environment. One woman sprang back in horror and relinquished her claim. Solomon then awarded custody to her.

Her response revealed that she must be the child's biological mother.

That's what people usually think, but there's really no textual evidence for this assumption. Solomon discerned something deeper: the woman who put the infant's needs ahead of her own would be the better parent, regardless of whether she was the biological mother. "Mother love" notwithstanding, there are various reasons a mother might not want or be able to care for a child. Perhaps she was depressed. Perhaps she despised the child's father. Perhaps she feared that caring for the child would interfere with her livelihood. Solomon didn't get into any of that. He discerned that the child needed a mother who would make the baby's well-being paramount. By threatening to cut the child in half, he identified that woman.

I could have used something like that kind of discernment when we discovered my daughter's deafness. One group of specialists said we should teach her to sign because she would be happiest in the deaf community. Another group insisted we teach her to speak because she'd have more options in life if she could participate in the hearing community. I often felt as though two conflicting groups were staking a claim to my child.

After a while I began to see that one side prized community and the other valued achievement. But this was my daughter. I wanted her to have both friends and accomplishments and didn't see how I could choose. The Solomon story suggests that this wrench in the stomach—I'm going to be forced to do something I don't want to do—signals the need for discernment.

No one wants to compromise fundamental values. No one should need to do so. When it seems like that's what the current environment requires, it's time to dig deeper to uncover the core values of each disputing party. Deep discernment is crucial because it lays the groundwork for practicing other virtues. We can't begin to practice imagination or integrity unless we know what values need to be taken seriously.

Aren't important values obvious?

Figuring Out What Really Matters

Not necessarily. We aren't talking about a set of abstract principles determined by philosophers or policy makers. When I speak of values I'm talking about what people truly care about, what gives their lives meaning and purpose. Sometimes these values are quite clear and then conflict can often be avoided. In healthy families, for example, parents often practice discernment spontaneously. They know intuitively that for a family to be happy and sustainable, everyone's needs must be met.

Let's take a very simple example. Winter is coming. Three kids need new coats. The parents usually shop at a high-end department store, but this year their economic situation is different, and they have only enough money in the budget for one department store coat. Do the parents buy a coat for one child and let the others shiver through the winter? Absolutely not. They grasp that the fancy department store coat is merely one way to keep the kids warm and healthy. Without a moment's hesitation they reallocate resources, shopping at a discount store or dressing the kids in layers.

Or going to thrift shops or swapping coats with a neighbor who has kids of different ages or wearing last year's coat until after Christmas, when coats go on sale.

Or . . . or . . . or. That kind of imagination is made possible by deep discernment. Once parents are clear about the underlying values—keeping kids warm, spending only what they have—they realize they can't buy three brand-new coats on this year's budget. Bingo: they start coming up with creative alternatives and rearranging resources to provide warm winter clothing for all their kids.

But if what these family members value is unclear, there's plenty of room for conflict. Maybe Mom has unexpressed anxieties about going into debt. Or Dad is attached to the idea that his kids should have nothing but the best. They won't be able to enjoy the benefits of cooperation unless they can get to the bedrock values—keeping the kids warm and staying within budget. Once those are clear, there's plenty of room for thinking about how to achieve both goals. Where they shop—or whether they swap—are secondary matters of means.

Parents who don't exercise that kind of flexibility on behalf of their kids are considered dysfunctional.

Unfortunately we tolerate such dysfunction in other arenas of life. We make it seem as though we cannot respect multiple values simultaneously, calling it "inevitable" that something we or others care about must be sacrificed to achieve goals that someone else deems paramount. You hear this sort of thing all the time. We can't have both security *and* respect for human rights. We can't have quality healthcare *and* a balanced budget. We can't have environmental protection *and* a strong economy.

All these dichotomies are dangerously wrongheaded. In a truly sustainable system all essential values are respected. You can't ask parents to choose between their children. It's just as unreasonable to ask people to choose between security and liberty, medical care and bankruptcy, pollution and employment. So many of our deepest and most damaging conflicts occur because people feel as though they have to choose between values that seem on the surface to be incompatible. Deep discernment means grasping all the values that must be honored in an adequate solution.

That sounds like a lot to ask.

Perhaps, but the rewards of practicing deep discernment are significant. Here's an example. Many communities are riven by chronic battles between people who favor development and those who favor preservation of open space. If you push them, people in both camps say they want to make their community a viable, desirable place to live. In other words, they actually agree on the end point. They just disagree about how to get there. And when you look closely at communities that regularly show up in the "best places to live" lists, they are invariably places that have integrated open spaces with mindful development. These conflicts may look like a case of either/or, but with some deep discernment it's clear that what's really needed is both/and.

It sounds like deep discernment will be helpful whenever we feel as though we have to give up on value A to secure value B. But I don't really understand how to practice this virtue.

Deep discernment pushes us to dig deeper so we fully understand what is at risk—not only for people who thought they were cooperating but also for those who are affected by their agreements, often accidentally. In my experience, three practices help people appreciate and master deep discernment:

1. Distinguish bedrock values from means.
2. Be vigilant about accumulating harms.
3. Honor multiple points of view.

Each practice encourages us to move beyond our biases and fears to inquire about what really matters: to us, to our cooperative partners, and to those who seem to be adversaries. After all, we want our cooperation to be durable, and that will happen only if everyone is convinced that benefits and burdens are being shared fairly.

1. Distinguish bedrock values from means

Problems often look insoluble because we confuse ends—goals linked to values we should not have to compromise—with means: operating procedures, protocols, and technologies, which can be adjusted or revised without compromising essential values.

In the family we described earlier, keeping a child warm in the winter seems like a value. Buying new coats at a department store is a means.

Precisely. We make these distinctions easily in some settings. And when we gain clarity about multiple values—keep the kids warm, stay in budget—we can be flexible about achieving our goals. Over time, though, people become attached to the means and lose track of what they were trying to achieve when they adopted them. And this exacerbates problems that arise when environments are complex or changing.

Standard ways of doing things evolve because they solve problems or provide benefits for cooperating parties. If circumstances change, different harms emerge, or the original benefits may no longer be relevant. A young family stops at a convenience store because one of the kids needs a diaper change. While there they happen to buy ice cream. A few years later, when none of the children wear diapers, the original reason for the stop is no longer relevant, but the kids may still assume that every road trip should include an ice cream stop. A company may institute a mandatory retirement policy to ensure that its workforce stays up to date with developments in technology—but years later, when the pace of technological change is much faster, that policy edges out experienced workers without guaranteeing technological competence.

People figure out ways to cooperate that create benefits or reduce harms. But later, in different circumstances, those forms of cooperation generate vulnerabilities that weren't anticipated. Parents would rather have healthier and less messy snacks on road trips. Companies find that recruiting and training new workers costs more than bringing experienced workers up to speed with new technology.

In such situations proactive compassion pulls us in two directions. On one hand it makes sense to retain existing practices because we know their benefits. They were put into place because they resolved obvious problems or created opportunities not available before. They are familiar and comfortable, and seem less risky because we know what to expect. On the other hand we're aware of new vulnerabilities, either because they've emerged from a changing environment or because they've been brought to our attention for the first time.

To understand this better, let's revisit the parents who need coats for the kids. Perhaps when the parents were children they wore coats made at home on a sewing machine. At some point, though, buying clothes in a department store created benefits: it freed up time for other pursuits or took advantage of materials, such as down linings, that wouldn't readily be available to someone making clothes at home. Yet that practice introduced new vulnerabilities because money spent on coats couldn't be used for other family necessities. When budgets tightened, the parents might actually have thought about returning to the old way — only to find that no one in the household knew how to sew anymore.

Also, in a social environment that includes fewer people who sew for themselves, fabric may actually cost more than readymade clothing!

When environments change and conflicts emerge, it's crucial to see that *how* things have always been done isn't the bedrock value — it's only standard procedure. It's *one way* to enact a value, nothing more. Admittedly, if we change standard practices, some people may feel vulnerable and we may create harms we don't fully understand. Still, we can't ignore vulnerabilities that come to our attention. Instead of defending operating procedures that now cause harms, we must clarify the values at the root of those procedures.

Many Paths to the Same End

Think for a minute about healthcare in the United States. Over the last forty to fifty years we've extended the average lifespan by twelve or thirteen years.

That's nothing to sneeze at, but the costs have been enormous. About one-third of Medicare's annual multibillion-dollar budget goes to patient care in the final year of life. In contrast, Japan has also extended life expectancy but with much less medical cost. The Japanese share the same value—longer life—but they've achieved it more economically.

Aikido instead of blood pressure pills.

That's an oversimplification, of course, but the two countries' traditional modes of operation have been quite different. In the United States policy makers decided many years ago that they could ensure an abundant food supply by subsidizing corn production. Extra corn was used to fatten animals and produce corn syrup, and today the typical American diet includes plenty of meat and lots of syrup-sweetened products. Japan is an island, an environment that encouraged people to look to the sea for nourishment. Their diet includes lots of fish and seaweed; as an externality they have fewer of the costs associated with high blood pressure and cholesterol.

Now let's not kid ourselves: no matter how people decide to live together, costs are generated. American subsidies to corn farmers may have inadvertently contributed to the epidemic of diabetes, but the fishing fleets that satisfy the Japanese appetite for fresh seafood have put pressure on fisheries and ecosystems. Long life itself is a widely appreciated benefit, but it too involves externalities such as higher costs for Social Security and larger numbers of people with dementia. In practicing deep discernment we are trying to identify core values: longer life and better health, abundant food and resilient ecosystems. When we do that, we're more likely to recognize means that create serious negative externalities or have outlived their usefulness.

We practice proactive compassion so we can avoid vulnerability whenever possible. When harms and costs can't be avoided, we want to be sure they are distributed fairly and reasonably.

When we can't, or don't, accurately predict vulnerabilities, harms, and costs, they get handled willy-nilly as they arise. Conflict is likely to result because different segments of society dig in to make sure they won't be the ones to pay. That's what's happening with Medicare. As boomers age, the costs of extending life are increasing tremendously, and younger people are understandably worried about where the money will come from.

Often the wrench of perceived conflict makes us feel as though we need to choose sides or rank our priorities. I'm proposing that we resist such moves and discern what's really at stake. Multiple values deserve our attention. In the case of Medicare it helps to remember that benefit X (longer life) doesn't necessarily carry cost Y (exorbitant end-of-life medical expenses). Getting a good grasp on the fundamental values makes it easier to separate them from means, so we can think more clearly about forms of cooperation that really will produce benefits for all.

Many people face that wrench personally every time they try to decide what to eat. Everyone wants the kind of healthy old age that's more likely if we eat lots of vegetables and whole grains. Yet preparing foods from scratch takes time, which is in short supply in many households. And foods to which folks are culturally attached seem more satisfying, as do many foods that are high in fat and sugar. There's a reason we call some meals "comfort food."

When people persist in behavior that causes harm, it's usually because something they value is at stake. Discernment is about uncovering that value. The person who prefers takeout from the local fast-food place seems to face a lose-lose conundrum: give up convenient, tasty foods or risk health consequences. Good health is a readily understood value, but having a quick meal that everyone will eat with enthusiasm also has benefits. We need to recognize that the takeout meal is a means and not an end. If we figure out why that meal appeals, we're more likely to find alternatives that embody this value—along with healthiness.

So if convenience is what you're after, you might look for a place that does takeout salads. Or if you want the feeling of good times that you associate with a burger, you might experiment with turkey or veggie burgers, loaded with the toppings family members love.

Discerning About Ditches

Once we extricate the value from the habits, it's much easier to see alternatives that accommodate all the relevant values. To understand this better, let's work through a more complicated example. In Ohio's Wood County, where I live, people perceive water as a problem. In the spring or after a storm, water stands in farm fields. Farmers can't use their machinery, and seed that's been planted in the fields rots. Meanwhile water rises beyond riverbanks, wreaking havoc in downstream towns.

None of this is surprising. Northwest Ohio was originally a swamp; when the region was first settled not many people wanted to live here. The few who came noticed oil bubbling to the surface of the water. Even then extracting oil was a priority, but getting at it required equipment too heavy to operate in a swamp. To stabilize the ground enough for oil extraction, settlers had to drain water from the land. The solution was to dig ditches.

Even today you can see ditches along every country road.

From the beginning, digging ditches produced unintended consequences. At least one of them was positive: once the land was drained, it turned out to be very fertile. Farmers started plowing and discovered one of the richest agricultural regions in the nation. So even after the oil was gone, people kept digging ditches to drain more cropland. Farmers also began installing drainage tile: perforated pipelines that collect water from the fields. Of course, the tiles directed more water into the ditches.

As any ditch digger knows, the most efficient way to get the job done is to dig straight ditches. That too led to unintended consequences. In flat country the topography doesn't encourage rivers to flow in straight lines. Instead they meander, making large loops across the countryside. During the rainy season, straight ditches drain water off the land very efficiently, creating a rapid influx of water those meandering rivers can't easily handle. In the past a raindrop that fell on Wood County took about two and a half weeks to get to the nearest river. Today, thanks to those efficient ditches, the same raindrop makes the journey in three hours.

No wonder there's flooding!

We think of floods as natural occurrences, but that's not an accurate description of what's happening. Contemporary floods are triggered or intensified by the ways people have changed the environment. Farmers install drainage pipe in their fields. Towns pave roads and parking lots. Homeowners and businesses build roofed structures that keep rain from soaking into the earth. The result is heavy runoff that rushes through pipes, sewers, drainage tile, and ditches into a meandering river, which moves slowly and is more likely to overflow when the surrounding terrain is flat.

Some folks talk about how strange it is that so-called hundred-year floods now seem to be happening every few years, but the big change isn't annual rainfall. It's the amount and speed of runoff—inadvertent byproducts of how we have redesigned the world. Humans have changed our environment in ways that promote some values and undermine others, and this demands our attention. We may value the convenience of parking, for example, but it has a cost. Water isn't soaking into the asphalt; it's running into an efficient ditch that speeds it to a nearby river. The floods that result put other values—dry homes and businesses—at risk. Every time you're in a parking lot, discern!

I see how this problem becomes gut-wrenching really fast. The farmers want tax dollars to maintain the ditches. Storeowners want the same dollars spent on roads and parking lots. And townspeople demand levees and other structures that will protect them from rising rivers. This is one of those situations where I simply don't see how everyone can get what they want.

And that's precisely the predicament in Wood County. County engineers have devised expensive solutions for the problem of too much water. Plans have assumed lots of engineering and oodles of cost for taxpayers to absorb, one way or another. The ditches, the levees, and the parking lots all seem necessary because they solve real problems, but remember: these standard ways of doing things are simply means—particular ways of realizing values.

Let's practice some deep discernment on just one piece of this puzzle. Everyone agrees that standing water is a problem because it breeds disease, keeps farmers from tilling the fields, and rots seed before it can germinate. What values are implicit in those statements?

People need to eat. And people need to be protected from disease.

Notice that this statement of values doesn't include a word about ditches. The ditches that carry the water away are not a value. They are simply one of many ways to secure fundamental values. Without the ditches we would be in big trouble: true. So we've got to maintain the ditches: false. Without the ditches we would be in big trouble *as we're currently organized*. But this particular form of organization isn't inevitable. It's just "how we do things around here." Humans created this system, so humans *could* reorganize.

How? You can't change the amount of rainfall the region receives. The farmers need fields dry enough for planting. I just don't see any alternative to digging ditches.

You're expressing the point of view of everyone invested in ditches: the farmers who have spent big bucks installing drainage tile, the manufacturers who make the tile, the hydrological engineers who understand how to construct ditches, and the construction companies that own the equipment for digging them. But let's set all that aside for a moment and think about the real problem.

Well, that seems pretty obvious. There's too much water!

"Too much" depends entirely on how people want to use the land. The water that covers a floodplain in the spring doesn't seem like too much, until people start building homes beside the river. The water that accumulates in low sections of a field doesn't seem like too much, until the farmer sets out to plant annual crops. Discernment helps us see that the apparent problem — too much water — is a problem only because people have organized themselves in certain ways. And reorganization is possible.

How? I'm not a specialist in agriculture, but I am a gardener, and I don't see how farmers can grow crops in soggy fields.

Practicing deep discernment helps us clarify our goals so we can rethink our means. If the goal is food production we might consider raising rice, which thrives in flooded paddies. Or maybe we could sidestep the problem of rotting seed by planting perennials, which don't need to be replanted from seed every year and have larger roots than annual plants. Those large roots absorb excess water so there's less runoff during rainy seasons, and they reach deep to find water when it's dry. Perennials can tolerate more variation in their environment, so "too much" or "too little" water becomes less of an issue.

Thinking carefully about values might lead us to other conclusions. Perhaps our goal is simply to pay the mortgage by growing a salable crop that thrives in waterlogged soil. In this case we might try switchgrass, a perennial that grows from Virginia to Missouri. Switchgrass can be converted into ethanol, and as a bonus it absorbs lots of phosphorus. Farmers who want to control flooding and keep excess fertilizer out of waterways can plant a hedgerow of switchgrass between a river and their field. Fields that are too soggy for some crops become an ideal environment for others. We can't see these possibilities unless we clarify our goals and rethink our means.

Asking Why

The practice of deep discernment reminds me of the persistent four-year-old who asks "Why?" over and over. Why are there ditches? To get rid of water. Why do we want to get rid of the water? Because there's too much. Why is too much water a problem? Because it rots the seeds. Why are we planting seeds? Because we need food. Is there some way to raise food without planting seeds that rot? Yes! Perennials and switchgrass. Hydroponics and shrimp.

Once you recognize the underlying issues, it often becomes clear that stubborn problems result directly from how we've organized ourselves. And there are always multiple ways of reorganizing. Here's another example. In colder climates people tend to pay high prices for produce because it has to be trucked long distances. At first glance it looks as though families have no choice but to tighten their budgets if they want to eat fresh vegetables during the winter.

But what if you could eliminate the costs of transportation? Farmers from Minnesota to upstate New York have borrowed greenhouse technology employed for generations in northern France and Belgium. Instead of fossil fuel these greenhouses use solar thermal arrays as their primary energy source. Even during the scarce daylight hours and weak sunshine of winter there's enough energy to heat tubes filled with water or glycol. The heat is stored in a reservoir of rocks buried beneath the greenhouse floor, then released during the long, cold nights, keeping the greenhouse temperature at the level needed for growing plants.

Deep discernment makes it clear that fresh produce and reasonably priced produce are both important values. The way things are usually organized, it's hard to have both because the produce is grown so far away. Figuring out how to heat local greenhouses inexpensively during the winter makes it possible to satisfy both values.

This kind of imaginative solution isn't likely unless we stop defending the usual means—in this case the practice of trucking winter produce from warm climates to cold ones. Once we've let that go, we can work on clarifying what really matters. That's the beauty of deep discernment. By focusing on the underlying values—productive farms, reliable food supplies, livable towns—we can see conflicts about ditches or trucked vegetables for what they truly are: disputes about means instead of ends.

The Trap of Tradition

Deep discernment comes more easily if you assume that traditional means are often ill suited to evolving circumstances. Sometimes the people who put a practice into place knew perfectly well that they were off the mark. Have you heard the story about the cook who always cut two inches off the tail of the Thanksgiving turkey before roasting it? When a friend asked why, the cook said it's traditional—her mother always did it that way. But now she's curious, so she asks her mother why she cuts two inches off the turkey. The answer: because *her* mother always did it that way. So the cook goes to her grandmother and asks where the tradition originated. Her grandmother pulls out a battered old roasting pan and says, "I had to make the turkey fit in the pan!"

The grandmother had a perfectly good reason for what she did, but when her granddaughter bought a larger roasting pan, that reason was no longer pertinent. Of course, by then the practice was tradition.

Even if the person who starts a practice knows it's a makeshift solution, it may become standard procedure. The farmers who first planted annual crops in Wood County were opportunists who took advantage of the dry land that became available when people dug ditches to extract oil. Once annual crops became established the ditches became "necessary," even though the original decision to grow annuals was as circumstantial as the act of cutting off the tail of the turkey. Grandma had to contend with the size of her pan. Farmers in Northwest Ohio had to contend with established markets in the surrounding regions. Habits form, one set of standard operating procedures becomes interlocked with others, and change becomes more disruptive.

Here's another example. When typewriters were invented, the hammers that created an imprint of the letters would hit each other and get stuck if secretaries typed too fast. The keyboard we know today was invented to solve that problem. The letters were deliberately arranged to make people type more slowly to accommodate the existing technology. Today, of course, "keyboarding" has nothing to do with typewriters. Computers are much faster than human fingers, but millions of people have been trained to use QWERTY—so we continue to sacrifice efficiency because of the way things have been organized.

I can see how people become attached to practices even after an original goal becomes obsolete. I can't imagine learning another keyboard configuration, even if it did make me a little faster. And the woman who cut the tail off the turkey may have used it as the basis for an especially delicious giblet gravy.

Sometimes tradition is harmless. I happen to like giblet gravy. However, we're really talking about cases in which standard operating procedure causes unanticipated harms. Maybe Uncle Bob has been diagnosed with heart disease, and all that extra fat in the gravy puts his arteries at risk. Then it's time to find a different way of making gravy. Maybe using the QWERTY keyboard is adding extra hours of labor or creating unnecessary strain in the hands of clerical workers. Then we need to invest in ergonomic keyboards or teach youngsters to use keyboards with a more efficient layout.

It's human nature to become attached to the way things are and to want a solution that leaves the environment as it's always been. But if an environment created by people is the source of harm, we need to change our ways. Sticking to the standard keyboard depresses productivity. Dredging all those ditches drains the public treasury. Trucking produce thousands of miles burns polluting fossil fuel. With discernment, we detach from familiar practices and think about more fundamental values.

This kind of discernment turns ordinary ideas of virtue upside-down. So often when we face stubborn problems, it seems virtuous to try harder.

When Working Harder Won't Work

Working harder at outmoded means isn't virtuous at all. Once we realize that our standard approach creates vulnerability, it's better to put effort into discerning what we're really trying to accomplish. Let's use a historical example: in the early twentieth century automobiles were built start to finish in the same factory. Once a business owner had invested in buildings and equipment, he assumed that the way to increase profits was to make more cars by encouraging workers to work harder. Henry Ford foresaw the unhappy, albeit unintended, results of this strategy: worker mistakes, resentment, and accidents.

His genius was in discerning his true purpose—building cars efficiently—and realizing it could be accomplished more readily if everything wasn't under the same roof.

Once he understood the factory as a means and not an end, Ford coordinated an early version of what today we call a supply chain. He figured out which parts could be manufactured and preassembled elsewhere. Then he delegated that work to suppliers, who found new efficiencies by becoming specialists in making starter engines or windshield wipers. Using a cooperative network of sub–assembly lines to make a complex product seems obvious today, but it wasn't when Ford did it. He practiced proactive compassion by anticipating harms to workers and consumers that might be caused by standard operating procedures. Then he practiced deep discernment by identifying his true goals: making cars more efficiently and profitably.

This seems like a very valuable distinction. Essential values like efficiency, security, and opportunity are pretty universal, but there's huge variation in how people pursue them.

When we loosen our attachment to means (easier said than done), conflict often falls away. Often people agree about the values that should be preserved. They may still disagree, sometimes vehemently, about how to realize those values, but those disagreements can actually spark intentional imagination—the subject of our next chapter.

If we separate means from ends we'll argue less about things that are really preferences rather than principles.

Up to a point, but "principles" can sound as though our values are fixed. That's not always true. Distinguishing ends from means can also help us understand how our values may change in response to changes in the environment. Let's think about ethanol, an energy source that became popular early in the twenty-first century. People were actively looking for alternatives because dependence on oil was causing negative externalities. In farming communities where corn was abundant, making ethanol seemed like a great way to use excess corn to produce the energy farmers needed for their tractors. As production expanded, however, other negative externalities emerged, in part because people didn't analyze ends and means.

As I recall, the price of corn shot up. And sometimes we couldn't buy sweet corn at the local farm stand because the farmer had planted field corn for ethanol. On a global level, serious food shortages led to violence in Africa and the Middle East.

We can understand these issues better if we look more carefully at the ends people were seeking. During the ten thousand years or so that humans have practiced agriculture, many practices have evolved—some of which now obscure the essential values that underlie farming. This makes agriculture ripe for discernment, so let's start with the four year-old's question: Why do we farm?

That's easy. People can't survive unless they eat.

Right. Before people started cultivating land, they had to wander around looking for things to eat, so finding food monopolized much of their time. Cultivating land was one way to secure a reliable source of edible calories. This goal explains why farmers have traditionally focused on annual crops that need reseeding every year. Annuals survive by producing lots of seeds, which are concentrated bundles of digestible energy. This makes them an ideal form of nourishment for both people and livestock.

For thousands of years agriculture has been organized around this premise: grow plants that produce edible, nourishing seeds. The premise has dictated mainline agricultural practices, so it's helpful to break it down. Because seeds must be planted each year, the soil must be prepared for each planting. Competitive plants become "weeds" to be cleared away. When crops are harvested, seeds must be separated—the biblical wheat from chaff. Most important, the seeds that are harvested should be used to nourish people, directly or indirectly.

When you put it that way, it seems like using corn to power vehicles creates a bad match between means and ends.

Growing corn is a reasonable means of getting to the end specified by traditional agriculture. Corn is tasty and easily digested, and provides concentrated energy for animals and people. We can argue, of course, about whether we should subsidize corn or turn it into syrup or use it for the relatively inefficient process of creating protein by feeding livestock. What we can agree on is that eating corn efficiently provides energy to people.

Now, however, we've introduced another goal: producing energy through combustion. If we're trying to power vehicles, the crop doesn't need to be tasty or digestible. Instead we need plants with lots of biomass that can be converted into fuel. Suddenly corn, with its compact, energy-dense kernels and large energy-deficient stalks, is no longer an obvious choice. We'll achieve our energy goals more readily with a crop like switchgrass, which distributes energy throughout the plant and is so productive that in many climates it can be cut once in midsummer and a second time after a killing frost.

The goal has changed, so we need to rethink the means. But we can't really do that unless we are as clear as possible about what we're trying to accomplish.

Achieving clarity about bedrock values requires real effort, especially when the environment is in flux. When change arises from multiple, uncontrolled sources, it's difficult to predict what will matter down the line, so deep discernment can't be done once and for all. We must continuously assess our goals to be sure they still make sense in a dynamic environment. And as we become aware of new technology and improved practice, we need to revise our means. Abundant food and efficient transportation are important and enduring values, but the ways we go about achieving them must be responsive and flexible.

I see how making the distinction between ends and means helps us discern what really matters, and whether our actions support or subvert those values. What's the second practice of deep discernment?

2. Be vigilant about accumulating harms

This practice grows from understanding that what people do can significantly change their environments. Technologies, practices, and procedures that support values when used on a small scale may create serious harm when we increase scale. Often we don't recognize this process because it happens in tiny increments. An innovation creates big benefits and little harms. People take notice and adopt the new practice. After a while the balance tips: the benefits may still be there, but those small harms have accumulated into something serious.

One preschooler jumping on the bed is having fun. The same preschooler jumping on the bed with four playmates is chaotic and even dangerous.

To an inexperienced parent this situation seems vaguely scary, and the response may well be: No more jumping on the bed. The discerning parent grasps that the scale of the activity has changed the environment, making it look as though the child's value (I want to have fun with my friends) conflicts with the parent's value (I want you to be safe). Clarifying those two values enables the discerning adult to redirect the child to another activity—perhaps a pillow fight.

In small social units like a family we can readily see how scale changes the acceptability of behavior. When it comes to larger, highly specialized social structures, it's more challenging to understand how harms that are all but invisible on a small scale can accumulate and undermine values. One local project funded by Congress may have genuine value and minimal impact on the federal budget, but funding 435 windfalls—just one for each Congressional district—adds up to real money and creates expectations of future subsidies.

The success of large-scale cooperation can lull us into the idea that more is always better and larger is always more efficient. Sometimes that's true, but not always. Deep discernment helps us recognize tipping points. What begins as an insignificant annoyance, easily tolerated given the benefits being created, can morph into a problem that overwhelms those benefits.

In the book that popularized the idea of tipping points, Malcolm Gladwell argued that ideas and even behaviors spread like viruses. Ordinarily viruses quietly coexist with other organisms. But under the right circumstances they literally "go viral" and create epidemics.

Detecting Unintended Consequences

When new ideas and behaviors are adopted on a large scale, the impacts are unpredictable. Here's an example: American homeowners are very attached to their lawns. But let's ask the four-year-old's question. Why do we have lawns? In the sixteenth and seventeenth centuries wealthy landowners often had large expanses of grass near their homes, usually for pasturing horses and other animals. Even after the rotary lawnmower was invented in 1832, keeping grass neatly trimmed was very labor intensive, an option for only the wealthy. Lawns for recreation didn't capture the imagination until after the Civil War, when Frederick Law Olmsted championed them as a way for urban Americans to sustain a connection to nature, originally in public parks.

I understand how important open space can be for city residents. When I lived in Manhattan, I was grateful to Olmsted for including the Great Lawn in Central Park.

Olmsted went on to design downtown Rochester, Belle Isle in Detroit, and many other public spaces treasured by urban residents. Those models were seductive, and the desire for what lawns represented trickled down to home-owners of modest means. When the first planned housing developments were built in the late nineteenth century, the homes featured small lawns that could easily be kept tidy with a push lawnmower.

Fast-forward to the early fifties. After World War II power mowers became affordable and lawns got much bigger. As any farmer knows, growing one crop over a large area makes it more vulnerable to pests and diseases. Sure enough, many homeowners learned that the only way to have a picture-perfect lawn was to use herbicides and pesticides. Suddenly we're looking at some serious unintended consequences, brought to our attention by Rachel Carson and others.

This is a conflict in my own backyard. My husband, a longtime apartment dweller, is very attached to having grass. I felt guilty about applying chemicals to our lawn in Ohio and even guiltier about watering grass when we moved to drought-stricken California!

On a small scale, what you do in your own backyard shouldn't be a problem. But when rainfall is scarce, keeping lawns green saps local water reserves. When pesticides and herbicides are used to kill bugs and weeds, those unwanted organisms build up immunities that make them peskier. When lawns are heavily fertilized, runoff stimulates algae growth that clogs and degrades waterways. Because the small engines in lawnmowers are inefficient, they produce considerably more air pollution per mile than the typical car.

Notice the contradiction. Lawns appeal because they make us feel more connected to the natural world, yet the way we care for lawns is creating serious harms for nature. Of course, most people resist the idea that they are doing damage by mowing their quarter acre. "Give me a break," they say. "How can what I do in my own backyard possibly be a problem?" It takes deep discernment to understand how scale morphs individually innocuous actions into practices so prevalent that they become pernicious.

I see how harms can accumulate when an idea really takes hold and persists. Scale matters!

But the impacts may not be obvious right away. It took years for experts to make the connection between people with respiratory disease and the air pollutants that power mowers emit. And it takes even longer to persuade the public that seemingly insignificant behaviors should be curtailed because cumulatively they are causing harms. Here's another case: I served on a committee that is supposed to decide when to declare "Ozone Action Days" in Northwest Ohio. At first it looks like a straightforward decision. If certain pollutants go above a certain level, we put out an alert.

The practice became contentious because specialists argued that different values deserved priority. People concerned about regional growth didn't want too many ozone days in a season because they feared it would discourage manufacturers from locating in the region. Others valued the economic benefits of tourism and thought the alerts might make the area less attractive to vacationers. Farmers and grocers worried that Ozone Action Days might discourage people from grilling as many steaks. In their own ways all these people were practicing proactive compassion, identifying prospective harms on behalf of different constituencies, themselves included. They resisted the costs of controlling air pollution because they discerned some, but not all, of the relevant values.

Poor air quality imposes costs. Those costs were obvious to healthcare specialists, especially people in local ERs who treated kids that showed up on days when air pollution became high. Health professionals don't sit on the Ozone Action committee, so one important value—kids being able to breathe without difficulty—doesn't even enter the discussion. The concerns that motivate resistance to air pollution standards certainly aren't trivial, but they aren't the whole story. Deep discernment says that breathable air is every bit as important a value as a vibrant economy.

Wow! I don't think the average lawn owner makes a connection between mowing the grass and asthmatic children in the emergency room. Lawns are supposed to be a wholesome, natural place where kids can play. Instead we're creating an absurd loop. Kids who should be running around on the grass can't do so in part because of the pollution from cutting the grass!

In a free society the presumption is that you can do what you please *if* it's not harming others. The challenge is to make the connection between the small things individuals do and the harm that occurs when many people do the same small thing. The aggregate effects of a once-benign behavior can threaten fundamental values. But if we keep values clearly in mind—in this case finding a bond with nature—we can start thinking of ways to achieve this without polluting the air or consuming scarce resources.

Connecting the Dots

Let's see if we can use deep discernment to understand the values underlying conflict in a more complicated arena: our car culture. In the early years of the twentieth century only the wealthy owned cars. Most people lived and worked on farms, so they didn't drive on a daily basis. The United States could easily produce all the gasoline our citizens needed, so energy for transportation wasn't a national priority. People liked driving, so they bought more cars and paved more roads. As time went on it became difficult to shop, much less get to work or school, without driving. As U.S. oil wells became less productive, we started looking to other countries to satisfy what the second President Bush called our "addiction" to oil. Before long we were taking an interest in the stability of oil-producing countries and sending troops to support—or topple—dictators. Even after fracking reinvigorated the domestic energy economy, we continued to be entangled in the politics of the Middle East.

Our collective enthusiasm for driving has changed the social environment. The freedom to go where we want when we want seems incompatible with our commitment to democracy and national security.

Deep discernment requires that we look carefully at all the relevant values in this situation. Being able to drive gives people more choices about what kind of work they'll do, where they shop, and what entertainment they seek out. But we also have to consider how we may compromise other values if everyone exercises this particular form of freedom.

Failure to connect the dots between behaviors and harms leads to a negative chain reaction. At some point traffic gets so snarled that it obliterates the benefits you hoped to secure by driving. The commute gets so long that it threatens the stability of vital relationships. We really have to pay attention, or we won't notice when standard operating practices begin to subvert other values.

I think most people would argue that, as individuals, we can't know when our actions are creating these cumulative harms.

No question. It's difficult for nonspecialists to spot externalities when they are being created by scale and changing environments, before they become serious. Within our specialized roles we must be alert for the thresholds at which standard procedures become problematic. And we must also recognize how our specializations shape, and in some cases limit, our understanding of the values at stake.

Here's an example of how roles can affect our perception of values. Like every other mammal on the planet I am constantly inhaling oxygen and exhaling carbon dioxide. Most of the time my breathing doesn't interfere with anyone else's health. There's plenty of oxygen, and plants convert carbon dioxide back to oxygen, so there's enough for all of us mammals.

Now change the environment to a large, enclosed building. When I'm alone in the building, my breathing still has negligible effects. But suppose I share a college classroom building with colleagues and several hundred students. As the proportion of carbon dioxide in the air increases, students get sleepy, professors become less incisive, and the building's function as a place of learning is compromised.

Let's see if I can discern the values that are at stake. I assume it's more efficient—and less expensive—to heat and cool enclosed systems. But clearly it's also important for students and professors to be mentally alert.

And different specialists have been assigned to each of those values. Professors understand that students learn best when their physical condition promotes mental alertness. Health researchers know that respiration releases carbon dioxide and excessive carbon dioxide slows brain function. Mechanical engineers are knowledgeable about air circulation systems and sensors that regulate CO_2 concentration. In each case the specialists have a rather narrow focus, so they may not notice what happens when more students crowd into a lecture hall.

The most serious problems of scale often emerge in the spaces between specializations. Within your area of expertise you may be following best practice and honoring the values that are obvious to you and your fellow specialists. You may find it difficult to understand how certain practices are causing harm because your specialized perspective makes it hard to see what matters to others. This brings us to the third practice for discernment:

3. Honor multiple points of view

What matters to me often seems like a given — any right-thinking person would care about that! And yet right-minded people are always coming to different conclusions about what's important. Let's think again about landscape design. When Frederick Law Olmsted began work on what would become Central Park, he looked for the most arresting scenery. Then he laid out paths and roads so people would have multiple opportunities to look at the best sites. He understood that a curved road multiplies the perspectives for viewing a landmark. Rounding a curve also modifies the view continuously, making subtle differences apparent and interesting. So, to maximize visitors' enjoyment of views from multiple vantage points, Olmsted created leisurely curves around the most scenic vistas.

I've visited national parks that feature those winding roads. It can be frustrating if you're trying to get somewhere, but I can see that the roads are designed to draw attention to scenic features in the landscape.

After the success of Central Park, other landscape architects borrowed Olmsted's ideas and applied them to other parks. In Glacier National Park, Going-to-the-Sun Road insists that you slow down and consider the scenery from different points of view.

Now let's think about two tourists, each stopping to take a picture of the same valley from a different scenic lookout. The photos will be different, of course, but it would be absurd to say that one tourist captured the right view and the other got it wrong. Each viewpoint reveals something that may not be visible from other vantage points.

Like those tourists, each of us sees things a little differently. Even if our experiences seem similar, our vantage may lead us to different conclusions about what is truly important. This is why we must make a deliberate effort to discern what other people value. In a complex, specialized world we operate in different environments that inevitably shape our point of view. A given environment could be defined by natural conditions: we live in a swampy region, or we're struggling with the same medical problem. It could be defined by social conditions: the farmers in a region have installed tile to drain their fields, or our parents were part of a particular religious tradition. Naturally we pay attention to the pertinent facts about the environments in which we find ourselves, and we connect most easily with people who share our understanding—perhaps because they've spent time in the same environment.

It's very easy to ignore people with points of view different from your own. Years ago I was at a meeting where school administrators boasted about using the Internet to improve communication with parents. When I asked how many parents in the school system were online, they said about half. The administrators in the room were internet users, so they were keenly aware of its benefits. They had identified a problem: poor communication with parents. But their solution made communication worse for parents who weren't comfortable online or didn't have easy internet access.

Expanding the Boundaries of Community

Deep discernment expands the boundaries of community to honor multiple viewpoints. Specialists, like those school administrators, may be legitimately focused on solving a problem in a way that's consistent with their experience and values, but that's not enough. A true solution must also incorporate the viewpoints of all affected by the proposed solution, as well as those who may be harmed when scale changes the nature of the problem.

Let's work through an example. All urban centers have sanitation engineers, who build sewers and sewage-processing plants to prevent human illness caused by proximity to waste. From the engineers' point of view, the goal is to prevent diseases like cholera. They feel successful when they create efficient sewer systems and effective sewage treatment facilities that bring them closer to those goals.

As it happens, treated sewage contains lots of nutrients, notably nitrogen and phosphorous. In small quantities that's not a problem, but when enough of those extra nutrients are discharged into a water body, rapid algae growth occurs. Again, that's not necessarily a problem unless the amount of algae reaches a threshold where its natural death and decay consume so much oxygen that fish suffocate. Then fishermen in the Chesapeake Bay and shrimpers in the Gulf of Mexico suffer reduced catches, enmeshing them in the decisions of upstream sanitation engineers. What's good from the viewpoint of sanitation engineers—reliable, safe, efficient sewage disposal—is bad from the viewpoint of fishermen because it destroys their opportunities to catch fish. The harm created by increasing the scale of sewage treatment, and the consequent algae growth, is most obvious and salient from the perspective of downstream fishermen and others who value the coastal environment.

Suddenly this looks like one of those impossible problems. The larger society needs both sewage treatment and abundant supplies of fish. Each of the groups has a legitimate point of view, and their goals seem incompatible.

When specialists work on a problem they must make a concerted effort to discern what matters to everyone involved. The sanitation engineers inevitably think about sewage problems faced by taxpayers in the city that hired them. The result matters to the taxpayers, but they don't need to think much about how it's accomplished. This is the power of specialization—you don't have to think about everything! The fishermen aren't part of the sewage treatment plan, but at a certain scale it has direct impacts on them. Instead of well-treated sewage they see dead fish.

The sewage treatment plan works very well from the viewpoint of those who value removing pathogens that would otherwise cause disease. It works terribly from the viewpoint of those who value an oxygen-rich estuary in which fish can thrive. These are *facts*, not *matters of opinion*. What the specialist does—even if it meets the original goal—may create unforeseen impacts, impeding goals that are obvious from other points of view.

In this situation the sanitation engineers must work extra hard to see things from the fishermen's point of view, and vice versa. We simply can't make progress on stubborn problems until we account for the fundamental values our apparent adversaries defend. People do things for reasons. The reasons are rooted in values, and the values grow out of experiences shaped by specific environments. If we want others to be reliable cooperative partners, we need to take their point of view as seriously as we take our own.

Excavating Values

Openness to other viewpoints is tough, even in small social units. After my first child was born, I had lots of deeply held ideas about how he should be raised. To my surprise, my husband had different, equally fervent assumptions. I was dumbfounded:

how could anyone think what he thought? It took us a while to figure out how to blend our values into coherent parenting.

You probably started by discerning and articulating your own point of view. Our assumptions about what really matters are often so deep that we can't readily explain them to other people. Getting at those values can be an almost therapeutic process that requires rigorous self-examination. To discern bedrock values you have to peel away familiar practices as well as unspoken assumptions rooted in the environments where those practices developed—in this case your own family of origin.

Besides clarifying your own values, you also need to understand the values that motivate the other parties in the conflict. Before you and your husband could become a parenting team, each of you had to understand and take seriously what was important to the other.

And that was frustrating. He also found it hard to believe that I was oblivious to things that seemed very important to him.

Conflict arises when we're unable or unwilling to appreciate the commitment to values generated by another person's experience. Getting beyond that impasse requires trust. Your husband had to believe that he was more than a means to your ends. To secure his cooperation you needed to convince him that you genuinely cared about what mattered to him—if only because it mattered to him. In all likelihood you were motivated to do that by recognizing you saw the clear benefits of raising a child with a cooperative partner.

In every successful cooperative relationship all the participants have to appreciate each other as people of goodwill who are trying to integrate various values, abilities, opportunities, and communities into a coherent, well-functioning whole. Take the town where I live. Bowling Green, Ohio, is a small community located on a major transportation corridor. It's an environment that could be conducive to crime because the youth population is high and the police force is small.

Thanks to collaboration among a wide range of community organizations, though, the crime rate is low. Civic leaders, including the police force, have been deliberate about seeking input from educators, mental health advocates, and volunteer groups such as the League of Women Voters. The people in these groups have specialized points of view and differing priorities, but they agree on an underlying value: everyone will benefit if the town is safe. By soliciting and affirming the validity of multiple points of view, local officials created a strong, cooperative consensus around a shared goal. The effort to locate shared values is essential in any cooperative venture: a family, a book club, or a musical group, as well as an international corporation, an NGO, or a government agency.

When conflicts arise in more intimate settings, I can work through them if I respect the other people. Then, even if they disagree with me, I trust that they have reasons for what they hold dear, and I try to understand.

The Power of Respect

Respect is always at the heart of deep discernment. When we make a sincere attempt to understand what's at stake for everyone involved in an apparent conflict, we demonstrate respect, setting the stage for cooperation that will produce genuine benefits. As we inquire about what matters to others, we make it clear that we don't regard them simply as a means to our ends. Instead we appreciate them as people who, like us, are trying to mold lives that seem good from their point of view.

I learned an important lesson about this kind of respect when I was only three. My mother, my six-month-old baby sister, and I were going out. This being the pre-stroller era, my mother put my sister in the baby buggy. When we got to the porch, she asked her "big boy" to wait with the baby while she ran inside to get something she'd forgotten.

My desire to be a cooperator was already very strong, and I wanted to help my mother. From my three year-old viewpoint, the obvious thing to do was to wheel the buggy down to the sidewalk. I rolled it to the edge of the stairs and braced myself as I'd seen adults do. Of course, buggy and baby weighed about fifty pounds—far more than my three year-old muscles could handle. I lost my grip and the buggy tumbled down the stairs, landing on top of the baby.

You must have been frightened—both because your sister could be hurt and because your mom would be upset.

Young as I was, I knew I had to tell my mother about this terrible accident. I ran into the house and, before I told her what had happened, made her promise she wouldn't get mad. She ran to rescue her crying baby, who was frightened but had escaped serious harm. Mom was understandably distressed, a feeling that could easily have translated into anger. But she'd promised not to be angry with me, and she'd heard me say I was trying to help. Taking those cues, she actually thanked me for telling her what had happened and for trying to be helpful. She assured me that my sister would be all right and pointed out that children have parents, whose wider experience helps them know what abilities a particular job requires. She told me I still had a lot to learn about how I could really help her.

What I learned from my mother's response was that, however much I had frightened her, she respected my intent. Decades later she recalled having decided that she had to honor her promise not to get angry. She understood that even though the harm was very real it was also unintended.

It's clear that by respecting your point of view your mother helped nurture your intent to create benefits through cooperation—even though things hadn't worked out well that morning, and she might easily have blamed or punished you.

My mother's response was a great lesson to me in how discerning and honoring what another person values, even when it seems wrongheaded from your perspective, can create a strong foundation for future cooperation. A sincere intention to solve problems or create benefits through cooperation deserves respect even when it creates unforeseen harms.

In many ways I see this as the heart of my work. I respect people for their positive intent even when their actions contribute to accumulating harms—like crowded roads or polluted lakes—that they couldn't foresee and didn't intend. Discerning the intention and the values behind the action lays the groundwork for future cooperation.

We often think of respect as a gesture we owe to leaders and experts because of their superior expertise or capabilities. But practicing deep discernment helps us see that, in a complex, global world, everyone deserves respect, because each of us has a distinct constellation of values shaped by our specialized experience in specific environments. In this new paradigm, respect means attentiveness to what matters to whoever is or wants to be a cooperative partner. Sometimes what we value grows out of training or experience; in other cases culture or individual predispositions play a more pivotal role. Regardless of how they emerge, our values define us. We cannot build sound cooperative arrangements unless we discern and respect what really matters to everyone those arrangements affect, and to everyone whose cooperation can improve the quality of community.

What you're describing sounds altruistic—until I realize it's the best way to ensure that I get the benefits of established cooperative arrangements. Unless those arrangements are coerced, the benefits will need to be mutual. Otherwise you won't want to cooperate, and I'll be left to deal with your indifference or fend off your hostility.

When Values Collide

Human life is social. Like bees in a hive, each of us has a role to play, and our communities will thrive only if each person does his or her part. But unlike bees, our roles are not predetermined. We can organize and reorganize ourselves to create benefits as mutual and as varied as human desire. To do so we must coordinate our efforts, and we must take the initiative to understand and support potential cooperative partners. As we alter the environments in which we interact, ongoing communication is needed to ensure that our efforts aren't damaging what others value.

Naturally we're most comfortable with our own ways. And given the benefits of specialization, we can ordinarily focus on only a small sliver of what matters. Still, when we detect harms or when conflict looms, we must try to detach from our own narrow goals and open up to other points of view. The practices of deep discernment enable us to devise forms of cooperation that are more durable because they honor more of what matters.

Most important, we have to assume goodwill even when things go wrong. When breakdowns occur, we have to resist feeling that the other party is "impossible" and conflict is "inevitable." It may look as though the other guy doesn't value what we value, but that's probably false. He just doesn't see how he can endorse what we want, given his perspective and commitments.

So when we find ourselves facing problems that seem rooted in the stubbornness of others, we have to expand our idea of community to figure out what they value.

Deep discernment is complex—because protocols, technologies, scales of organization, and the perspectives of multiple players are all in flux—but it is not nebulous or vague. At bottom it's the process of focusing on what matters fundamentally to people, so that our cooperative systems support mutually beneficial interactions. If we don't do this, conflicts become intractable. People dig in and refuse to budge, because what's at stake for them is some value for which no substitute is available.

Sometimes the values at the heart of a conflict are obscured by practices and techniques that have grown up to protect them. Then we have to strip away means to gain clarity about our ends. Sometimes values are threatened by practices that become harmful when adopted on a large scale. Then we must reappraise practices so they don't overwhelm key values. Sometimes values seem to be in conflict because they're rooted in points of view that arise from specialized circumstances. Then we must expand our own point of view to affirm insights revealed by other viewpoints.

I see how deep discernment helps us identify what's at stake for apparent adversaries, but how does that necessarily solve anything? All we've done is clarify that two or more parties see things differently. If everyone insists on what's valuable from her point of view, compromise and cooperation remain impossible.

I can see why you're frustrated, but we've made more progress than you think. Discerning the values in apparent conflict sets the stage for the next virtue: intentional imagination.

CHAPTER 4

Intentional Imagination
Expanding What's Possible

*A man will be imprisoned in a room with a door
that's unlocked and opens inwards, as long as it does not
occur to him to pull rather than push.*
Ludwig Wittgenstein

*If I had asked people what they wanted,
they would have said faster horses.*
Henry Ford

*We've been looking at problems that seem impossible to solve because we think some-
one will get hurt no matter what we do. Proactive compassion motivates us to solve
these problems: we don't want people hurt. Deep discernment clarifies the apparently
conflicting values that stand in the path of cooperation for mutual benefit.*

Sometimes deep discernment by itself extricates us from conflict. Once we
recognize the essential values—as opposed to standard practices or means—
we may be able to make cooperation work for everyone by adjusting technologies or procedures.

*But sometimes deep discernment can do nothing more than clarify why we are
in conflict. Then we experience gut-twisting anxiety because it looks like one
person or group can get what matters to them only by disregarding what matters
to others. Practicing compassion is motivating; practicing discernment is clarifying. But sometimes we're still stuck!*

And that's when we need to become very deliberate about practicing what I call
intentional imagination. When it seems that conflict is inevitable, we have to
look more carefully at our assumptions, make better use of known resources,
and tap into resources that have gone unrecognized or underutilized.

To reiterate, human survival hinges on cooperation that creates mutual benefits. The viability of the human community is put at risk whenever one party benefits, even unintentionally, at the expense of others. Deep discernment clarifies what's at stake for everyone involved, yet, as you've pointed out, sometimes those values seem hopelessly incompatible. When it looks as though working together simply won't produce mutual benefits, the stage is set for deception, coercion, and even violence. That's when we need to consider the possibility that the clash of values arises from how we've organized things. If we can imagine a different form of organization, conflict may fall away.

It's wonderful to imagine an alternative world in which conflicts dissolve, but I think most people consider imagination a gift, not a virtue. You either have it or you don't. When John Lennon sang his famous song, people really did dismiss him as a dreamer.

Learning to Imagine

Certainly it's common to regard imagination as an innate capability, but I think about intentional imagination as a learned virtue, a habit anyone can develop, a disposition we all can exercise. Just as people learn to drive a car or play a musical instrument, they can learn to exercise imagination to broaden the circumstances in which people share the benefits of cooperation. For people who intentionally cultivate the practices I'm about to describe, imagining becomes as natural as breathing.

To some extent intentional imagination resembles what we did spontaneously as children. When toddlers first learn to talk, they label the important features of their environment: dog, cookie, and so on. Then they learn to express what they want or value: "Up!" or "Me do it." From there they move quickly into imaginative play: "Let's pretend I'm a princess and the dog is a dragon." Their understanding of the physical world isn't yet fixed, so they move fluidly between what is and what could be. The pretend friend needs a seat at the dinner table, just like the playmate from next door.

Of course, children put a lot of imaginative effort into things that simply aren't going to happen. No matter how hard you pretend, the front porch won't be a rocket ship. A stick won't become a magic wand.

True. To be more than whimsy, adult imagination must distinguish between unchallengeable boundaries and boundaries that seem fixed but aren't.

Intentional imagination starts from the premise that the way people have organized activities, events, and spaces—even the way they think—contributes to or intensifies many harms. Current patterns of cooperation may have emerged in response to technology now obsolete or environments no longer existent. In other cases cooperative agreements ignored specialized concerns or discounted the values of people who are now affected. We practice intentional imagination when we challenge boundaries that are arbitrary or circumstantial. We can stimulate novel approaches to whatever folks are calling our current impasse by deliberately tapping into diverse viewpoints and specialized insights.

As you rightly point out, the world we inhabit includes some genuine boundaries: the laws of physics, existing markets, existing resources, and more. Flights of imagination that disregard such parameters may be entertaining—the genre of fantasy comes to mind—but aren't very productive. For imagination to function as a virtue, it must take into account the resources that are or may become available. How can technologies and time, people and protocols, be deployed differently so all cooperative partners enjoy substantial benefits? Intentional imagination boldly reconceives cooperative norms to address the harms revealed by compassion and accommodate the values revealed by discernment.

As you describe it, intentional imagination sounds like a way to rethink our circumstances so that apparently incompatible values can coexist, and suffering will be reduced. It's a very appealing prospect, and I'm curious about the practices that promote this virtue.

I've identified three approaches that unlock intentional imagination. Each helps us break down artificial barriers so we can reconfigure environments in a way that allows cooperation to thrive.

1. Examine assumptions.
2. Extend known resources.
3. Excavate concealed resources.

Anyone can cultivate these habits. And as they become engrained, their power over apparently insoluble problems is startling. Instead of the ache of anxiety because someone is going to lose, people feel the exhilaration of win-win possibilities.

1. *Examine assumptions*

One of the best ways to trigger intentional imagination is to question a premise accepted for so long that it seems like immutable fact. The other Monday at a choral practice I mentioned to the director that the choir had sounded better on the previous Wednesday. "That's how it always is," he replied. "Monday is Monday." What he meant, of course, was that Monday was the first rehearsal day after the weekend, so the chorus was rusty and less focused.

Still, the way he said it made me think. The formula "Monday is Monday" is the same as "business is business" or "war is war." Common maxims like these can mislead people, implying that there's an immutable logic to the situation.

"It is what it is!" There's simply nothing to be done.

When you examine these statements more closely, they don't really represent how things are. Instead they are statements about how things (like our weekday/weekend cycle) are organized. And that's not inevitable at all. We create cooperative structures to serve certain values. When new values come to our attention, there's no reason we can't reconceive our cooperation to accommodate more values. Statements like "Monday is Monday" promote a misplaced sense of resignation that is precisely the opposite of imagination. Indeed, that sense of resignation—there's nothing we can do because A is A—is often a call to intentional imagination.

When the choral director said, "Monday is Monday," he was assuming the chorus won't perform well after a lengthy break between rehearsals. Once you articulate the premise, it doesn't seem nearly so immutable. There probably are *ways to get the chorus to sing better on Mondays.*

For one thing, you might ask the singers to sit in a circle. That would help them listen more closely to each other and become more attentive to what they were doing. Alternatively the director might extend the warm-up, to be sure that voices and brains are limbered up and ready to focus on the music. All of a sudden Monday wouldn't be Monday in that negative sense. If we ask why we assume that Monday must be an off day, we challenge ourselves to find techniques that help choir members be as sharp as they were last Wednesday.

The problem of the lackluster choral practice got me thinking about other situations in which people don't perform well because their skills are rusty. Think about the first snowstorm each winter. Typically accidents spike at these times because people forget to adjust their driving habits to the changed environment. But highway safety managers don't just shrug and say, "Oh, well. Get the emergency rooms ready." The snowfall is fixed fact, but the accidents are the consequence of driving—something that's very much a product of human organization.

Lots of assumptions that make sense when conditions are dry must be examined when snow starts falling. And a good highway department does exactly that: analyzing what goes wrong and imagining new ways to organize things to prevent accidents. Highway crews get snowplows ready for service. They note where accidents have occurred in the past, and put extra salt on the curves and in low areas where snow and ice accumulate. They broadcast warnings about reduced visibility and slippery streets. They post signs alerting people that bridges and overpasses may freeze first. Anyone who lives in snow country knows the drill. The snow itself is inevitable, but many accidents are preventable when we reimagine the environment.

People created the entire infrastructure around driving. So people can reimagine it to minimize vulnerability.

Here's another example, quite literally a response to the "Monday is Monday" problem. In the 1970s American car manufacturers discovered that more defective cars were made on Monday than on other days of the week. After some analysis they discovered that workers were coming to work incapacitated from weekends that included alcohol and recreational drugs. And because the harms created by defective cars were potentially serious, management couldn't simply tolerate a "Monday is Monday" explanation.

Automakers started to imagine ways to get fully functional workers into the plants after the weekend. They enlisted the help of unions and talked to shop stewards. They developed antidrug policies and inserted cause-for-termination clauses into contracts. Before long, cars made on Monday were as good as those made during the rest of the week.

Accepting the "Monday is Monday" premise meant resigning themselves to the harms defective cars were creating for buyers and for their bottom lines. Once they questioned the inevitability of harm, this triggered a cluster of imaginative ideas for achieving consistent quality.

Questioning assumptions is at the root of every civil rights movement, too. People with disabilities, for example, started to challenge assumptions about what they couldn't do. The Americans with Disabilities Act was introduced in Congress by Senator Tom Harkin of Iowa, who saw that his deaf brother and others with disabilities were more likely to thrive if social environments were reorganized. Sure enough, something as simple as putting captions on televised programs opened up information and entertainment to people with hearing impairments.

When we see that a particular system causes harm and we ascribe inevitability to that way of doing things, we resign ourselves to the harm. But people rethink "inevitabilities" all the time. In the past it was a given that people had to stop working when it got dark, or that some children would get polio. Someone had to examine the underlying premises and consider the possibility that what seemed inevitable was actually variable. Once you do that, the floodgates open and alternatives start pouring out.

Practicing deep discernment started with the "Why?" of a persistent four-year-old. Maybe practicing intentional imagination starts with the classic question of a curious six-year-old: "What if . . . ?"

Let Go of the Way Things Are

Philosophers like to talk about possible worlds, a kind of thought experiment in which you alter specific things that seem fixed in the world as we know it. These experiments often yield a deeper understanding of a problem that seems irresolvable, and may even provide glimpses of a solution that couldn't be seen while we were constrained by our assumptions. The same technique is at work when employers encourage employees to "think outside the box" or when a facilitator tells a brainstorming group that all ideas, no matter how implausible, are welcome.

I was once involved with a nonprofit that had always raised money through a fundraiser whose centerpiece was a silent auction. It was assumed that this was the best way to raise money, even though finding donations for the auction sapped the energy and goodwill of board members and volunteers. Finally someone said in a meeting, "What if we didn't do the silent auction?" There was a moment of silence, and then the ideas started to come. What if we did a raffle? What if we put the auction online? What if we tried games of chance? Something that had felt like a chore began to seem like fun again.

This is intentional imagination in action. We want to cultivate the habit of asking whether the usual practice is absolutely necessary to the ends we seek. Could we get where we want to go in a different way? Notice how intentional imagination intersects with deep discernment. Practicing deep discernment leads to the liberating conclusion that ends are hugely divorceable from means. For the nonprofit, figuring out what they truly valued—raising money for a good cause and keeping the goodwill of volunteers—allowed them to let go of means that weren't working anymore. When we're firmly grounded in what truly matters, we can let go of assumptions about how things "should" be organized and start thinking about how things *could* be organized to achieve the ends we prioritize.

Of course, we'll want to consider the impact of scale on our actions. We must consider how many people the fundraiser will attract. Practicing discernment again, we must account for the viewpoints of all concerned parties, including people excluded from or even harmed by existing forms of cooperation. Perhaps the fundraiser is being held in a country club that discourages attendance by the less affluent. When we do these things, ideas start to flow. What if we adjust this variable? What if we tweak this technique? What if . . . ?

When people are really stuck, they may need a nudge to start examining assumptions. A few years ago, my husband and I were having the same arguments over and over. I wanted to do couples counseling and he didn't. We seemed to be at an impasse, so I finally decided to go to counseling on my own. When I explained the problem to the therapist, she said, "What if you simply stop arguing? If you have a disagreement, state your point of view and then drop it." As incredible as it sounds, this was a novel idea to me. My unexamined premise was that we had to resolve our disagreements because we were married. As soon as I let go of that assumption, everything shifted.

In fact, you challenged two assumptions. One was that counseling would be helpful only if you went together. By deciding to go on your own you gained the opportunity to acquire specialized knowledge and practices that might be relevant in improving your marriage. The therapist addressed the other assumption: that every argument must be resolved. As we've seen, when disputes involve values, a solution in which value A trumps value B is really just a way for people who hold value A to get what they want at the expense of those who care more about value B. With help you were able to imagine an alternative that didn't threaten either your or your husband's values.

Space for New Possibilities

Questioning both of these assumptions changed the environment in our home and opened new possibilities for my marriage.

In many ways this is the essence of sustainability. Like every other creature on the planet, we adapt to changes in our environment—especially the social environment that depends on cooperation. We cultivate trust, coordinate efforts, and assign responsibilities. We do all this because it reduces harms and increases benefits for everyone in the community—be it a family, a classroom, a church, a corporation, or a nation. Then, as the situation changes, we reassess trust, cooperate in different ways, and rearrange responsibilities.

So when I backed off and stopped insisting that my husband see things my way, I created an environment that was more respectful. That in turn opened up new and more creative ways of resolving conflicts. As I think about it, I can see that readjustments like this often happen spontaneously—especially in the early years of marriage, when people make subtle changes that improve their cooperation. She may learn that he is more open to negotiation after the first cup of coffee in the morning. He may discover that she's more willing to stick to a budget if it includes an allowance for a modest Saturday night out. They may discover how much they both enjoy a particular restaurant.

At every level of social organization, people make such adjustments without thinking much about it. As with the other virtues, however, we must practice intentional imagination more deliberately when we face conflicts that seem to have only win-lose solutions. In such cases we've invariably assumed that things must be organized the way they are because that's the way they're organized. Once we challenge this premise, we open the door to imagination.

Remember the farmers in Wood County, trying to cope with the runoff of water from farm fields that have been drained with ditches and underground drainage tile? What if we rethink the assumption that there's too much water? Maybe we could collect the water into places where it would do less harm or even create benefits. Maybe water preserves could be located in parks and available for recreation. Or, because northwest Ohio is an agricultural region, perhaps the collected water could be used to raise hydroponic produce or fish. Not far from where we live, a fellow has started a successful shrimp farm because he figured out an innovative way to make use of "excess" water.

Admittedly such solutions call for reorganizing agricultural resources. Local farmers know how to grow things on drained land, but they have to learn how to grow things in water. And they need markets for what they grow. Still, you can imagine that a farmer who is raising crops in water might even pay his neighbors for their runoff or at least accept it without charge. And local restaurants that like to feature local products might be enthusiastic about offering something that hasn't been available before. All sorts of interesting possibilities present themselves when you challenge the premise that raising food requires planting seeds.

This is exciting. Most people don't like being told, "Monday is Monday." They don't want to put up with things as they are but they feel as though they have no choice. You're saying there's always a choice when what stands in our way is something people have created. Then you can change what's "inevitable" by changing what people do.

Rethinking Lawns

Often we're motivated to practice intentional imagination once we've connected the dots between a specific behavior and the harm it causes. Take the problem of lawn care. As mentioned, running lawnmowers contributes to pollution because small gasoline engines are inefficient. Before we shrug and say, "Nothing I can do about that. Lawns are lawns," let's examine the premises.

One premise is that lawns can be cut only with gasoline engines. At Bowling Green State University and other colleges around the country, groundskeepers have reengineered lawnmowers to use french-fry oil—very plentiful on college campuses, as you can imagine. In the past the university paid to have used cooking oil hauled away. Now that it's burned in lawnmowers, the expense of disposal vanishes. And the university still has those lawns that look so wonderful on recruitment brochures—without the pollution created by standard mowing procedures.

Another premise is that lawns are a good idea in the first place. My wife and I challenged that premise when we built our retirement home and decided to leave the lawn out of our plans.

You have no lawn?

We were keenly aware of multiple harms created by lawns. Besides pollution from standard mowers, there's fertilizer runoff, which promotes algae growth in local waterways; diseases and pests that are encouraged by monoculture; the pesticides and herbicides used to control them; even the amount of time lawn care consumes. When we practiced deep discernment for ourselves, we recognized that what we really wanted was a satisfying natural environment around our home, including a small space for yard games with the grandchildren. A lawn was just one of many ways to achieve that goal.

Having challenged the underlying premise and made space for imagination, we uncovered many appealing alternatives. After some investigation we decided to install several rain gardens—specially designed perennial beds that absorb our torrential spring and summer rains. By using a layer of rock beneath the garden, we created a reservoir that absorbs and filters rainwater; therefore we have less erosion, less contaminated water, and fewer stagnant pools to breed mosquitoes. The rest of the yard consists mainly of native plants in mulched beds surrounded by wood-chip paths. For the grandchildren we planted a patch of short-growing native grasses I easily tend with an electric mower.

In California many people have abandoned their lawns because it's too expensive to water them. I've been impressed by the creative ways homeowners use succulents and drought-tolerant groundcovers. Still, I suspect that intentional imagination comes most easily to people who have been trained as philosophers, because philosophy encourages us to be skeptical about premises.

Philosophy and especially ethics can be useful specializations, but practicing intentional imagination isn't arcane or complicated. The first step is to acknowledge that there are *always* multiple ways to achieve our goals. In everyday life people understand this perfectly well. If you hear on the radio that there's a traffic jam on the highway, you don't give up on getting home. You take side roads. If you learn that a client can't be at a meeting, you don't write off the business; you reschedule or arrange a conference call or e-mail a proposal. Most people exercise such flexibility all day long, and those who don't are criticized for being rigid.

We must make it a habit to apply this same flexible approach to larger conflicts and apparently intransigent problems. What are the assumptions that underlie algae blooms in Chesapeake Bay or the ancient rivalries between Sunnis and Shiites? What do we accept as givens when we think about problems like high rates of high school dropouts, obesity, or mortgage foreclosures? I can't do the analysis for each of these problems, but specialists in these fields regularly need to challenge the inevitability of the given and ask *what if?* questions.

I can see how challenging assumptions opens the door for intentional imagination. What's the second practice?

2. Extend known resources

Many conflicts are rooted in a sense that resources are scarce. In the arid American West, for example, some constituencies are vigorously defending water rights originally distributed when water was more abundant than it is now (in part because there were with fewer people to claim it). We see conflict over budgets for the same reason. Disagreements can become vehement when people feel that there are competing claims to the limited amount of money available to a family, a school district, a corporate department, or a state government. Choosing to spend money on one thing means that it's not available for something else, so budget battles often become fierce as people try to protect what they regard as the most important priorities.

The perception that there's not enough to go around often rests on the assumption that things—especially resources—need to be organized as they've been in the past, but we've seen quite the contrary. Further, by using intentional imagination, we can reexamine known resources and find ways to extend them. Remember the family that couldn't afford department store coats? They generated new ideas about how to keep kids warm by thinking outside the budget. Yes, the pool of money was finite, but the pool of possibilities was significantly expandable.

When we were talking about that story, my first thought was about hand-me-downs. You don't need to spend money at all if you make what you have go further.

Confronting the apparent limits of known resources is always an opportunity for intentional imagination. Most people understand the idea of conserving what is valuable. Parents regularly nag kids to turn off lights when they leave the room, finish the food on their plates, or write on both sides of the paper. That's because they realize that the cheapest energy, food, paper, or any other commodity is what you don't use.

Conservation is invariably the least expensive way to go. Not only do we avoid immediate costs by conserving resources, but we also preserve the possibility of future benefits because resources will continue to be available. The history of incandescent, then fluorescent, then LED lighting is a case in point. Each new type of bulb used less electricity to provide the same illumination.

These habits emerge naturally during hard times. When the economy went south, many people found they could live perfectly well without buying nearly as much stuff.

During good times we sometimes treat conservation as what philosophers call a "supererogatory virtue"—something that's nice but not morally required. We figure we can afford the few pennies it costs to let the water run while we brush our teeth, forgetting that the insignificant actions of one person can create distressing externalities when performed by millions. If all Americans got in the habit of shutting off the water, we'd save four times the amount of water that flows down the Mississippi each year. What one household saves may be negligible, but what the community saves is significant.

By using resources efficiently now, we preserve options for the future.

That's important because, as we've seen, every configuration will create externalities sooner or later. We want to maximize benefits and minimize costs, but when costs increase or we discover costs we didn't anticipate, we'll be in a better position if we've been thinking all along about how to do more with less. In many ways this is the central question posed by intentional imagination: How can we satisfy ourselves without incurring unnecessary costs for ourselves or others?

Conserving Resources at Home

My wife and I were very deliberate about exercising intentional imagination when we built our retirement home. Like other retirees, we knew we'd have a finite supply of money and personal energy. We were also keenly aware of the negative externalities created by excessive energy use. Yet we're both enthusiastic computer users, and we wanted a house that would be comfortable for grandchildren. So in practicing intentional imagination we asked: How could we configure the available resources so we would have heat, computers, a fully functioning kitchen, and the many other amenities we enjoy, without using energy in the standard ways?

You give tours of your house to people who want to build green, so you must have come up with some good ideas.

We didn't have to do our imagining alone. Many specialists already had shared ideas about how to conserve energy. For example, simply designing the house so most windows face south significantly reduced heating and lighting costs. By adding appropriate overhangs on the south, we lowered cooling costs too. We knew about Energy Star windows but found that we could triple their insulating power by installing translucent honeycomb blinds. We raise the blinds when we want to warm the house on winter days and lower them to maintain the indoor temperature.

We also installed a geothermal heating system because the ground beneath the house remains at a relatively stable temperature all year long. By taking advantage of this we can cool the house in summer and warm it in winter without consuming fuel beyond what the system's compressor uses. The compressor itself generates some extra heat, and we use it to preheat water instead of letting it dissipate. We also installed a chronometer that sends hot water to our faucets at times when we're likely to want it. Water saved! And the bathroom fans have timers that turn them off when their job is done.

Most Americans pay for fuel to heat their homes and congratulate themselves if their furnace is 95 percent efficient (a ratio that compares the energy used to operate the furnace to the energy it produces). Our geothermal system taps into an underutilized resource under our house and has an efficiency rating of over 130 percent, because the heat it produces is much greater than the equivalent heat energy needed to operate the furnace. This technology, which quickly recoups its capital investment, cools our home at about 15 percent of the cost of traditional air conditioning.

In some cases you're conserving energy by making technological improvements—

the equipment is more efficient or makes better use of what nature gives you. In other cases you're changing your habits so you use less energy.

Experts have running debates about which approach is best: Should you install motion sensors or teach people to turn out lights when they leave a room? Depending on what they value, people come to different conclusions about the ideal ratio between technology and personal effort. A friend has decided that clothes dryers are superfluous, so he doesn't own one. As a result he organizes his time so that when the weather is dry he does laundry, and other obligations have to be juggled. My wife and I feel strongly about keeping social commitments regardless of the weather, so to minimize drying time we purchased an Energy Star washer that spins out most of the water, and we shop for clothes made from fabrics that dry easily.

The point is that when we start thinking about how to extend resources—especially scarce and/or costly resources—we can often extricate ourselves from problems that seem to have no solution. Water, for example, has become such a scarce resource in some parts of the country that people talk about "water wars." The standard way of thinking is zero-sum: if some people get as much as they need, others won't have enough. Intentionally imagining *what if?* generates thinking about how to use less, so everyone's needs are met.

Since we moved to California I've become very aware of ways to conserve water. What if we install drip irrigation so water goes only to the roots of plants? What if chronometers make the water drip at night to further minimize evaporation? What if we grow plants that make do with less water? What if we collect rainwater in cisterns? Many of these ideas aren't new. Native Americans in the Southwest were raising drought-resistant crops centuries ago.

We typically think that imagination is about coming up with a totally new idea. That rarely happens. Even the most creative people draw on ideas, tools, and techniques developed by others. What's imaginative is the way they rearrange the components. In the realm of conservation, intentional imagination isn't at all flashy, and its practitioners often don't get much credit for their insights. Take Gifford Pinchot, a scientist who became the first head of the U.S. Forest Service in the early twentieth century. Among other things he advocated protecting mountainside forests because they in turn preserve the snowpack. Pinchot understood that if the snow was shaded it melted more slowly, stretching the water supply throughout the summer.

Thinking about snow as a water storage system seems like a highly imaginative way to practice conservation.

Reconfiguring Resources

Daylight Saving Time is another example of imaginative conservation. During the summer, when the days are longer, it makes sense to have extra natural light in the evening when people are still active, rather than in the morning when many are still asleep. Obviously you can't "save" daylight — the amount of sunlight can't be controlled. But by shifting the clock you can conserve energy that would otherwise be used for lighting. There's some debate about how the energy calculation actually works out, but this reorganization yields other positive externalities. Having daylight last longer into summer evenings gives people more time for leisure activities, including exercise. Some communities have found that Daylight Saving Time can reduce traffic accidents and even crime.

Changing the way we use resources can create benefits without incurring huge costs. When I was a child, long-distance phone calls were expensive; you got one only if someone died. Long-distance lines were used primarily for business, during workdays. At night and on weekends the lines were mostly idle. But once the phone company spotted that underutilized resource, it started to offer discounted calls during off hours. For Ma Bell it was "found money" — the lines were already in place — and for families it became a popular way to stay in touch.

So when you talk about resources, you aren't just talking about natural commodities like energy and water.

Environmental ethics is my specialization, but I think of environments in very broad terms. Yes, we want to use intentional imagination to rethink the way we use natural resources, but we can also use it to make better use of human resources and the resources available in cooperative institutions — governments, corporations, universities, nonprofits, social clubs, and families.

Here's an example: when J. W. Marriott started his first hotel, he saw to it that his employees had good working conditions, and he even counseled them on personal problems, believing that happy employees would provide better service to guests. As the Marriott chain grew, its founder could no longer provide that kind of attention, but a culture of mentorship developed. New employees underwent a three-week training period, during which a senior hotel employee mentored them.

This practice created several positive externalities. Managers at Marriott became more attuned to the problems—and capabilities—of staff and could identify entry-level employees with the talent and drive to do more. Marriott has a reputation in the hospitality industry for grooming bell-hops, bartenders, and room attendants so they can be promoted to more responsible positions. Managers also were able to address workplace grievances before they became serious. Every company has senior employees who could take on the mentor role, and mentoring is now recognized as a fundamentally sound business tool.

Instead of paying a headhunter to recruit managers, Marriott is doing more with the people already on staff. I can see how it would be helpful to ask about extending resources in relation to almost everything we consume. Energy. Time. Healthcare. In every case it seems obvious that using less creates benefits.

Wasteful practices often evolve because the costs seem negligible. For example, middle-aged men and women don't necessarily think of muscle mass as a resource, so they squander it by making small decisions that seem insignificant at the time. They may decide they're too busy for exercise, or they may take on jobs that are more sedentary. But it's also well known that doing some simple exercises will conserve and strengthen muscles. This may not seem like an example of intentional imagination, but preserving muscle prevents harms and opens up opportunities, especially for older people. A fit person is less likely to fall. She can also take on more challenging activities and engage in more recreational pursuits than someone who has failed to conserve this resource.

The Flaw in Standard Operating Procedure

Unfortunately, practices that squander resources often get embedded in standard operating procedures, and then it's difficult to get people to conserve—even when they see the benefits. We can see this clearly in the construction industry. In the 1970s I hosted a European visitor who was shocked by the wastefulness on American construction sites. He couldn't believe how cavalier contractors were about tossing out extra materials. Today some contractors practice intentional imagination, making better use of materials because they see the benefits of more efficient practices. Others still operate under old assumptions about how construction should be done, in part because they don't want to assume the costs—and the risks—associated with implementing new practices.

The costs seem genuine. A contractor who wants to minimize waste must research better ways of doing things and retrain workers, among other things.

There is always risk associated with doing something differently, and we'll address that in our chapter on creative courage. However, we're motivated to practice intentional imagination because standard ways of doing things are causing harms and creating conflict, often because there are perceived shortages. In Dayton, Ohio, a faculty member at Sinclair Community College developed a course on construction techniques that were likely to save contractors money because they generated less waste. Any local university could offer such a class if administrators thought enough students would sign up, but Sinclair created demand for its course by mandating waste reduction in the contracts it put out for bid. Note that this change in policy didn't create excessive costs. The community college was happy to provide the course, and contractors were very willing to incur the associated expense if the course made them eligible to bid on lucrative contracts.

This is a great example of using imagination to reconfigure social resources. Once conservation became the new regional norm, there were plenty of positive externalities: Municipal landfill operations were spared unnecessary waste. Contractors saved money by reducing material costs and avoiding disposal costs. Competitive bidding passed those savings along to customers, including students. Everyone benefits.

It seems like consolidation is one of the best ways to practice intentional imagination. When we can increase the scale of what we're doing, we can usually eliminate duplication and waste. Resources become less scarce, so there's less conflict.

Not so fast. We always have to pay close attention to the impact of scale. Whenever small units do similar things, consolidation is a promising prospect as long as the environment is stable. For example, the size of the average farm in the United States has grown dramatically as farmers have realized that more acreage allows them to make better use of expensive specialized equipment.

Minimizing the time that a tractor or combine sits idle is definitely an imaginative way to conserve resources.

However, enterprises that become very large may find it difficult to practice intentional imagination changing environments. Changes in rainfall or fluctuations in average temperature, which affect the growing season, may require adaptations in the crops farmers grow—but corporate farms that have invested heavily in specialized equipment and practices may be slow to adapt.

Governments may even feel obliged to subsidize their inefficiency because they're "too big to fail."

You see the same pattern in relation to banks and car manufacturers. At first consolidation may create efficiencies. After all, techniques and procedures become standard operating procedure because they work well most of the time for most people under most circumstances. Now look at all the assumptions in that statement: What's an acceptable level of functioning? Which people have been considered? What circumstances are we talking about?

When the environment changes—because people want hybrid cars, perhaps, or because the government encourages home ownership—large institutions are often at a disadvantage because they are enmeshed in standard procedures whose premises may now be suspect. At such times smaller institutions may be in a better position to practice intentional imagination. Community banks, for example, can sometimes do more with less because they are attuned to changes in local opportunities and equipped to assess the plans and prospects of local enterprises.

For both large and small cooperative efforts it's easier to accommodate multiple values when people have a sense of abundance. If there seems to be enough for everyone, we can relax and be more creative about what we're doing. Because my wife and I spend less on energy we feel less anxious about buying presents for grandkids. Once we as a society started conserving daylight, people felt that they had more hours available to accomplish daytime goals. Contractors who waste less material find it easier to bring in projects under budget. This is the ultimate payoff of using intentional imagination to extend our known resources.

I see how we can practice intentional imagination by seeking out ways to use less of resources that are in demand. What's the third way to apply intentional imagination?

3. Excavate concealed resources

In addition to making better use of known resources, we can practice intentional imagination by looking around for resources that are undiscovered, underutilized, or even regarded as "waste." For years I've helped students understand this idea by using a standard puzzle that asks people to think quite literally "outside the box." The puzzle consists of a grid of nine dots. We are instructed to connect the dots without lifting the pencil, and using only four straight lines.

Typically people work within the confines of the grid, and, try as they may, all their solutions leave one dot untouched. The breakthrough comes when they realize that all of the white space beyond the grid is a resource to be used. If you extend the lines beyond the grid, the puzzle is readily solved. (To see the solution visually, visit cooperativewisdom.org.)

Another resource that may be unrecognized or undervalued is the specialized point of view. This became vivid for me when I presented the puzzle to a class that included a Japanese student. His point of view encompassed origami, so he asked if it would be okay to fold the paper. This had never occurred to me—or to any of my other students—but the instructions didn't preclude it. So I replied, "Yes, the goal of imagination is to uncover *anything* that is not absolutely impossible." The student promptly folded the top three dots over the center three, then did the same with the bottom three dots. Voila! With one line, he connected all the dots.

His point of view revealed imaginative possibilities that were invisible to others.

Hidden in Plain Sight

Often problems look insoluble because we cannot extricate ourselves from our own point of view. If we recruit others to imagine with us, we're more likely to spot resources we simply couldn't see alone. A school superintendent once came to me with a predicament I knew well: he was trying to finish a dissertation and couldn't find uninterrupted time to do the writing. Dave really wanted to finish the degree, but his job and family made significant and legitimate demands on his time. He couldn't see a way forward.

To stimulate imagination I started asking about resources he might have overlooked. I knew he was a morning person; his job demanded that he get up early to make decisions about whether the district school buses could safely make their morning run. Most days the decision was uncomplicated, so I suggested he could work on the dissertation during those two "found" hours when students were being transported to school. "Nope," he said. "When I'm at home, I see all the household chores that need to be done. I start on those, and before I know it I need to leave for work."

Now the missing resource became not time but a space where he could concentrate without distraction. I remembered that Dave was a committed church member: perhaps the church had space that went unused on weekday mornings? Sure enough, the pastor was glad to give him access to a desk, and Dave bought a small mobile locker where he could keep his supplies. Even better, the pastor became a support system, regularly asking Dave how his work was progressing.

The resources to solve this problem were hiding in plain sight. You practiced intentional imagination by asking what was needed and then looking for unconventional ways to meet those needs.

Discovering unappreciated resources through intentional imagination is exciting because it opens up the possibility that everyone can get what they want—even when known resources are scarce. My favorite example is wind energy. The Dutch have known and exploited this resource for centuries. Until recently most Americans have shrugged: the wind is blowing, big deal. But if we start asking *what if* questions, we can discover numerous ways to replace more expensive forms of energy with wind.

My wife and I discovered, for example, that we could produce 40 percent of the electricity we need to run our virtually all-electric home by installing a small wind turbine. (If we didn't live so close to our county airport, we could have built an even taller tower that would generate more energy.) The turbine creates no carbon footprint, and the local utility pays us for the power we contribute to the grid; combined with the savings on our bill, this enabled us to pay off the initial modest investment in seven years. Suddenly wind is a lot more than a pleasant sensation on a summer day. Using this underutilized resource lowers our bills, makes the local power grid more efficient, and decreases our contribution to climate instability. Win-win-win!

The habit of looking for previously unrecognized resources creates hopefulness. I regularly see this online. Social media started as a way for friends to share details about their lives, but it's also opened up opportunities for people to find community with strangers who share specific, and sometimes, difficult experiences. When a family member was diagnosed with an unusual type of cancer, I felt isolated because I didn't know anyone in the same boat. One night I was idly searching for information online and came across a support group devoted to this rare illness. Here was our lifeboat! And it was filled with survivors who found it comforting to share their own experiences.

Whenever it seems there isn't enough of something (in this case, empathy), it's time to start looking for alternative resources. You can see this clearly in the history of oil production in the United States. Around the turn of the millennium some experts believed we were at the peak of oil production, and that as consumption continued to rise, energy would inevitably become more expensive. That assumption proved to be false, and subsequent fluctuations in oil supplies and prices have significantly affected the world's economies. Rapid changes in the energy environment also obscured some of the bedrock values at stake.

By practicing deep discernment some people began to understand that the real value was available energy—not necessarily plenty of oil. That provided an opening for intentional imagination. What resources had been overlooked? Some turned their attention to wind, and now we have vast wind farms across the Great Plains. Others started thinking about solar, tidal, and geothermal energy. Still others started looking at technologies for extracting gas and oil that had been trapped in rock. Obviously we must be mindful about the externalities such technologies may create—especially if they are adopted on a large scale. Still, we open the door to new possibilities as soon as we start looking at resources that have been underappreciated in the past.

The emotional difference between those two points of views is huge. If you think about how to distribute diminishing resources, the future looks small, constrained, and dark. If you practice intentional imagination, prospects feel plentiful and hopeful.

Both viewpoints are deeply embedded in American history, in part because settlers who came to this country brought two versions of Christianity. Everyone knows about the Puritans, though we may not understand that their harsh rules grew out of an economy of scarcity. They were practicing a conservative form of imagination in which virtue is defined entirely by how you handle limited resources.

Limitless Frontiers

But Christianity also includes a more expansive way of thinking that is rooted in the idea of a benevolent Providence. From this point of view everything is provided to those who have faith. You can see how this idea permeates American thinking about the frontier. When John Locke said, "In the beginning, all the world was America," he was imagining an Eden-like environment filled with unclaimed resources, available for the taking.

The feeling that opportunity is limitless is part of what has always made this country so appealing to immigrants.

The first American frontier was physical and so were its resources. Settlers found land, timber, gold, and oil that weren't yet part of any codified system of property. To make use of them, all you had to do was claim them. Those early settlers were hugely vulnerable—there's always risk in doing what hasn't been done before—but they accepted the risk because they believed the quality of opportunity on the frontier was providential. Often they were correct. Think of John Jacob Astor. He made a huge fortune by connecting a resource that was plentiful in the American West—beaver pelts—to a European enthusiasm for beaver hats so intense that it had depleted the native population of these large rodents.

The rhetoric of the frontier has been applied to any realm where there are unclaimed resources, available to those who practice intentional imagination. America's physical frontier closed around 1890, but Americans quickly applied the frontier idea to technology—another arena in which one can discover resources simply by recognizing possibilities that haven't been appreciated in the past. Ford, Edison, Bell, and other tinkerers believed that anyone clever and persistent enough could invent machines that would solve problems and create new benefits. Instead of the hard physical work of appropriating land and its resources, this new frontier required the ingenuity to imagine how new technology could generate new opportunities.

I think people feel some of the same excitement about the Internet. Even now, anyone can come up with a clever domain name and stake a claim.

Today, as you point out, advances in technology have created an information frontier. In this era the initial success stories were about people who spotted new ways to configure or deliver data. Today data itself is a resource: because we can collect and analyze so much information, we can make predictions that allow us to avert harms and create new benefits. Companies can advertise directly to people whose search patterns suggest they might be interested in a new product. Health officials can aggregate search data to spot outbreaks of contagious diseases so medical teams can respond more effectively. Traffic apps can route drivers around jams by aggregating data from the cell phones of other drivers using surrounding streets.

Someone who does social media for the Red Cross said that the organization now monitors social networks to help identify where resources are needed during an emergency. Twitter and Facebook are resources that simply didn't exist in the past; now they're being used to pinpoint where people need food, shelter, and medical care.

Every era brings opportunities to imagine how previously unrecognized resources can promote cooperation in the society. In the 1930s, for example, changes in mortgage practices unleashed the community-building energies of Americans by making more working folks eligible to finance a home purchase. After World War II the G.I. Bill engaged the underutilized brainpower of millions of servicemen and women by giving them access to higher education. And in 1972, Title IX legislation unlocked the competitive spirit of an entire generation of young women. Instead of accepting the limited range of opportunities embedded in existing social structures, we can revise our structures to capture resources that haven't yet been recognized, much less developed.

All these enterprises share an optimistic spirit, a sense that anything is possible if we get in the habit of using intentional imagination.

Let's see how reimagining resources can operate in a place we've already explored in Chapter 3: the rivers of northwest Ohio. As you'll recall, they flood a lot. The most ecological form of flood control is allowing the rivers to meander and create wetlands that sop up extra water. When farmers near the rivers fertilize their fields, water that's sopped up contains extra nutrients from runoff. And when those extra nutrients reach Lake Erie, they can trigger explosive algae growth, which in turn depletes oxygen, kills fish, and—during one memorable summer—contaminated drinking water for five hundred thousand people.

So the needs of farmers, who depend upon the higher yields made possible by fertilizer, were pitted against those of people who want to harvest fish and drink water from the lake. This apparently insoluble problem was addressed in the 1970s by creating buffer strips—uncultivated land between the fertilized fields and the rivers—that trapped excess phosphorus so it didn't wind up in the river. By the turn of this century, however, the buffers were saturated and algae started to bloom again in the estuaries. Enlarging the buffers would cut into productive acreage, so intentional imagination was again required.

Where are the unrecognized resources? Phosphorus itself represents possibilities. Perennial grasses, like miscanthus and switchgrass, take up phosphorus and store it in their stems. These plants make ideal animal feed and can be harvested at the end of the growing season, when equipment might otherwise be idle. By planting these crops in the buffer strips, farmers can redirect the phosphorus away from waterways—and gain a cash crop. Indeed, miscanthus and switchgrass have been planted and profitably harvested even on land deemed too poor to cultivate for more conventional crops. Seeing the value in an unappreciated resource creates opportunity where there might otherwise be conflict.

Reconsidering Waste

Isn't trash often an underutilized resource? A long time ago I wrote a book about how to reuse things people might otherwise throw away. By the time I finished my research, I was amazed by all the highly imaginative ways people have found value in what otherwise would have been discarded.

When you think about it, "waste" is a description not of the material itself but of the way we think about it and handle it. Whenever we encounter cost in getting rid of something, we need to reframe our thinking. To stimulate intentional imagination we should start calling trash an "unappropriated by-product of human activity awaiting constructive use." Then it becomes a resource to be deployed rather than a problem to be eliminated.

Here's another place where scale can make a big difference. One soda can has no market value, but millions of them can be smelted to produce new aluminum products. That's why some people think about landfills as a legitimate way to store resources. In impoverished countries thousands make a living picking through garbage to find things that can be resold; it's the basis of an elaborate economy in the huge slums of India. In developed countries we may not have markets for these materials yet, but every landfill is an opportunity for intentional imagination. Often we can deflect conflict and create opportunities for cooperation by making better use of resources that have been dismissed simply because we weren't organized to make use of them.

So many American success stories involve someone who was able to see value that others had overlooked. I remember reading about how Henry Ford hated waste of any kind. The original Model T used a lot of wood in its frame, dashboard, and running board, so Ford bought his own timberland and built a sawmill. It really irked him to see that branches and sawdust were going to waste. But then he heard about a chemist at the University of Oregon who had figured out how to create lumps of fuel by mixing mill waste with tar and cornstarch. Ford built a plant for making "briquettes" next to the sawmill and hired E. G. Kingsford to run it. Before long, Ford dealerships were selling picnic kits that included miniature grills and, of course, Kingsford Briquets.

American history is replete with people who made fortunes by applying intentional imagination to the problem of waste disposal. In the late 1800s Gustavus Franklin Swift was able to sell butchered beef to New Yorkers for less than the cost of cattle on the hoof. How did he do that? First, the railroad boom made Chicago a hub for meat processing. Rail was an inexpensive way to bring cattle there from western ranches and then carry dressed beef to cities in the east. Second, the sheer number of animals prompted Swift to standardize and streamline techniques for slaughtering and dressing cattle. Chicago's "disassembly line" for beef was famous long before Ford's assembly line for cars.

Yet even these important innovations weren't enough to account for the savings Swift passed on to his customers. His genius was in recognizing the value of things that had been regarded as waste, like hooves and hides. A local butcher might not be able to make any use of those materials, but Swift understood the dynamics of scale. He had so many hooves and hides that he could develop profitable side markets in glue and leather goods. The profits from selling what had been waste allowed him to discount dressed beef, so that even factoring in transportation, the meat he sold cost less than beef from East Coast butchers.

Earlier we talked about how scale can create negative externalities, but in the case of waste more may create opportunities. This seems to be a Goldilocks predicament. Too much can be a problem but so can too little.

Thinking about the scale that's "just right" is part of intentional imagination—and the right scale may change depending on available technology. Here's another example. Ohio has lots of dairy farms, and the cows produce manure. On small traditional dairy farms, manure can be distributed in the fields without causing problems. But with the advent of Confined Animal Feeding Operations, aka CAFOs, odor becomes an issue, as does water pollution because the waste runs off into rivers and alters their ecology.

In many Ohio counties this seems like an intractable conflict. Large dairy and hog farmers claim they need more animals to function economically, but, as you can imagine, the manure from two thousand cows can produce serious problems. Nearby property owners are understandably worried about odor and water pollution. State regulations try to minimize runoff pollution by requiring farmers to have a certain number of acres on which they can spread each ton of manure. Even when farmers follow the rules, however, manure contaminates rivers and threatens groundwater whenever there's a hard rain. And there's the ongoing odor problem, which some communities have tried to address through nuisance regulations and even lawsuits.

This sounds like a major tangle of insoluble problems.

Which means it's a prime opportunity for intentional imagination! Joe Hirzel is a local farmer who also runs a vegetable cannery. The cannery dates back to Prohibition, when Hirzel's great-grandfather had to get out of the distillery business. The great-grandfather practiced intentional imagination, recognizing that the equipment and skills he had used to brew alcohol were very similar to those required by the emerging food processing industry. He founded the cannery that Hirzel runs today.

Like Henry Ford, Hirzel is concerned about disposing of waste products, especially from tomatoes. He'd like to avoid the costs—financial and environmental—associated with dumping waste generated by the cannery, so he has investigated biodigesters, a technology that captures the methane produced when organic material decomposes. Biodigesters run most efficiently when vegetable wastes are combined with animal wastes at a one-to-three ratio. Hirzel exercises intentional imagination by looking for sources of animal waste. Suddenly the large quantity of waste generated by CAFOS looks like a resource instead of a problem.

It's important to notice the impact of scale, both in creating problems and solving them. When people farmed as they did in the 1930s, manure wasn't an issue because nobody could care for that many cows. When the industry was mechanized, farmers could milk more cows, so manure became a liability. With another spin of the wheel, manure again becomes a non-issue—if you have enough to feed a digester that turns this unwanted byproduct into a valuable resource.

Imagination in Action

In my tai chi class we do an exercise called the Heavenly Jolt. You rise up on your toes and then let yourself drop. It's a funny little move but it jars things free. Imagining intentionally seems like that. Suddenly your world fills with resources where there didn't appear to be any.

Once they get the hang of it, most people really enjoy using intentional imagination. To see how practices work together, let's apply imagination—and the other virtues we've discussed—to a hypothetical situation. A local library loses a certain number of children's books each year, but there's no money in the budget to replace them. Compassion kicks in. Being deprived of books creates vulnerability, especially for children whose families can't afford to buy books. Practicing deep discernment reveals the key values: early access to books facilitates learning to read, and the library must stay within budget.

What are the assumptions that could lead to conflict? The only way to get books is to use the existing budget to buy them. At this point intentional imagination kicks in: What are the alternatives to buying books? Ask families to donate books their kids have outgrown. Find out if publishers donate books. Supplement the existing budget somehow. Seek grants for replacing books. Hold a fundraiser for the children's collection. Charge a fee for library cards.

We can also think about conserving known resources. How could we stretch the budget further? Find vendors that give deeper discounts. Join together with school or regional libraries to get discounts. How could we conserve the books themselves? Teach kids to be careful with them. Impose larger fines that get more books returned. Restrict some books to library-only use. Offer amnesty or even some kind of reward to people who return long-overdue books.

Where are the unrecognized resources? We might recruit volunteers to repair books that would otherwise be discarded. Salvage illustrations from damaged books, then frame and sell them. Study usage patterns in the library and staff only the hours when there are plenty of patrons, thus saving money to spend on books. Supplement the collection with e-books that children can view on tablets and home computers.

As you can see, using all three practices of intentional imagination opens creative options that avert conflict by preventing harms and increasing benefits. This is a fairly small-scale case, but questions about assumptions and resources can generate new possibilities even at the highest levels of public policy. Consider the end of World War II, when American policy makers anticipated the return of thousands of soldiers. High unemployment before the war had created social instability, so the goals were to bring soldiers home and keep unemployment low. These values seemed incompatible, creating opportunities for conflict—but also an opening for intentional imagination.

What were the assumptions?

Jobs had to come from the private sector. Soldiers would return home all at once. When policy makers let go of those "givens," new approaches became possible. What known resources could be conserved or redeployed? Existing jobs were clearly a known resource. To get the most mileage from them, policy makers decided to divert some people away from the workforce for a while. Keep soldiers stationed in Japan or Germany to stabilize those countries. Develop a professional officers corps. Persuade women to leave the workforce and raise families.

What resources were concealed or untapped? One: the country had a growing fleet of automobiles that were underutilized because roads were inadequate. Building and repairing highways created jobs—not only for people who could design or build roads but also for those who, given better roads, could more easily take their skills wherever jobs were available. Two: many soldiers were underemployed for lack of marketable skills. Using government help to pay for education deferred their entry into the workforce and gave them the skills to perform more sophisticated jobs, as well as to create new products and services. Professors were in demand and graduate education boomed. Implementing all of these ideas contributed to American prosperity for most of the rest of the century.

This seems like a case where imagination-driven progress in some areas contributed to problems in other places. Many of the women who were encouraged to become homemakers became frustrated when they couldn't use their skills and education.

Practicing intentional imagination is liberating. Whenever we identify new resources, we open up new cooperative possibilities. But the displacement of Rosie the Riveter illustrates the ongoing question of whether those possibilities can be realized in ways that integrate multiple values and create mutual benefits. Imagination alone can't answer that question.

CHAPTER 5

Inclusive Integrity

Reworking Cooperating So Everyone Can Thrive

As I would not be a slave, so I would not be a master.
Abraham Lincoln

*Good teams become great teams when the members trust
each other enough to surrender the "me" for the "we."*
Phil Jackson

*Let me try to summarize our progress so far. Proactive compassion motivates us
to respond when others are harmed, even if the harms are unintended. Deep
discernment grows from the realization that we endanger cooperation when we
confuse ends with means, ignore accumulating harms, or fail to embrace multiple
points of view. Intentional imagination opens up new possibilities by questioning
the status quo and systematically investigating resources that have been squan-
dered or unrecognized. Practicing intentional imagination exhilarates me, but
it also seems chaotic. If I'm planning a retreat for the sales department, asking,
"What if?" may allow me to imagine my colleagues in Brooklyn or the Caribbean
or even atop Mount Everest. But eventually I have to come to terms with goals
and budgets and schedules.*

The only way to translate what imagination promises into durable cooperative partnerships is to practice our fourth virtue: inclusive integrity. When
you first start thinking about any cooperative venture—like that sales retreat—
it's good to have a big pile of *what if's*, so imagination can be as open-ended as
science fiction. Intentional imagination is all about expanding possibilities, so
it should be oblivious to risk and real-world limitations, especially if standard
operating procedure straightjackets innovation or creates harms for bystanders.

Perhaps past retreats started on a weekend, making it difficult for parents to participate. Or maybe the event featured a golf tournament that gave golfers special privileges. Practicing intentional imagination enables us to burst such barriers.

But, yes, sooner or later you have to get real and figure out how to integrate the products of imagination into a working structure. Divorced from action, imagination is simply daydreaming. Endless *what if's* leave the world unchanged. Ungrounded ideas are like individual atoms: interesting, even beautiful, but not linked into functional molecules. Eventually we must commit to a specific cooperative structure that integrates what matters to everyone involved. Practicing inclusive integrity can help us find a coherent course of action toward a new cooperative system that honors the well-being of all affected parties. It's the habit of working with others to structure imaginative possibilities that will affirm and support the community of willing cooperators.

So someone organizing that sales retreat will need a plan that meets the goals of management, acknowledges the needs of a diverse sales force, and even considers the working conditions of support staff. This is really different from the traditional idea of integrity. I think most people regard integrity as an individual matter—how do I make my life consistent with my values?

As commonly used, integrity ends with such self-examination. And this kind of self-understanding is definitely an important part of the process. A person who practices inclusive integrity will certainly ask: Can I participate in a particular activity and maintain personal integrity? Will this form of cooperation violate what I believe in, stand for, or regard as fundamentally right, even if it advances some attractive goal? But limiting integrity to the self reminds me of adolescence, when the key developmental task is coming to terms with personal identity and figuring out what's important to *me*.

Integrity Is Fundamentally Social

As we mature, we become more settled with who we are and what we value. With personal integrity established, most people spend less time thinking about themselves and put more effort into creating strong social units—a committed marriage, a loving family, a functional workplace, an equitable government, and so on. In these cooperative settings a commitment to our own well-being isn't enough. Integrity has to be inclusive. For cooperation to work we must take the values of our cooperative partners as seriously as we take our own.

This reminds me of work done by John Gottman, a psychologist who has won media attention because he can reliably predict whether a couple is likely to get divorced. He's spent a lifetime studying happy marriages, and he concludes that the essential element is trust. As he puts it, happy couples essentially say to each other: "Baby, when you hurt, the world stops, and I listen and try to understand and empathize. I'm not going to leave you in pain. I'm there for you."

Exactly! Adults define themselves by the relationships they form and the projects in which they participate. Whether we're building connections with spouses, friends, colleagues, neighbors, or fellow citizens, cooperation is most likely to take root when we invest in what others care about, and they make a similar investment in what matters to us. In our complex, interconnected world people who are committed to cooperating for mutual benefit need an expanded sense of integrity that incorporates the values of their cooperative partners.

You're connecting self-respect with respect for others. In any cooperative relationship we have to ask, can I regard myself as a person of good character if my actions don't respect my partners' efforts and values?

We cannot possibly be persons of integrity if we acquiesce in social arrangements that undermine what matters to other people. A family won't work unless both partners truly care about what matters to their spouses and children. A company's success will be short-lived if its customers, employees, or suppliers come to feel like mere means to a corporate end. We practice inclusive integrity by conscientiously working toward new ways of organizing cooperative activities that take account of what matters to us and to our cooperative partners. *And* to those affected by our agreements.

You make it sound as if integrity isn't even possible in isolation.

Hence my term *inclusive integrity*. As social creatures our integrity depends on being part of a cooperative system in which each of us respects the efforts of every other person our actions affect. I want to make this very clear. The only way to respect people is to honor what is valuable *from their point of view.* No one is going to voluntarily cooperate with those who are callous toward or contemptuous of one's perspective. When it seems that someone's actions undermine what matters to them, people quickly become skeptical about cooperating. If they're free to do so, they may simply walk away; if constrained to participate, they may look for opportunities to disengage or even sabotage the project. In either case the potential of full-hearted investment in a mutual effort is lost.

The cooperative system is weakened if people feel that what they value isn't being taken seriously The integrity of the system depends upon mutual respect for values that may seem to be in conflict.

We originally conceived the cooperative bargain quite simply: I do this. You do that. We each benefit. But our ideas about vulnerability and harm, thriving and well-being are sure to be different depending upon our vantage points. If I'm the human resources manager of a company, I may be most concerned about the quality of the workplace and health or retirement benefits for employees. If you're the CFO, you may be focused on profitability and accountability to stockholders. Employees may be concerned about a diverse set of benefits, ranging from creative autonomy and congenial colleagues to paternity leave and profit-sharing.

As cooperators we affirm everyone's values. Our prospects for success are vastly improved if our alliance respects and affirms what matters to each of us and to those our alliance affects—say, everyone who lives in the community where this company is located, or the customers who buy the company's products. The goal of practicing inclusive integrity is to devise workable cooperative systems that allow diverse partners to flourish.

A New Response to Unintended Harm

I think most people would agree in principle that inclusivity is a good goal. In practice I keep bumping up against situations in which I'm being asked to give up something I care about because it causes inadvertent harms to others—even though I was just going about my own business, trying to practice personal integrity. This feels very discouraging. Creating any kind of cooperative enterprise is hard, and it's frustrating to discover that it's not working because of something you didn't or couldn't anticipate.

I don't see it that way. The idea that careful attention enables you to improve even your best ideas seems like a wonderfully optimistic view of the human enterprise. When harms to others become apparent, we can't be resentful just because they spoiled a plan that seemed to be working for us.

The transformative thought is that such complications are not a defeat. They aren't even a reason for discouragement. They're just the facts of the matter. People get attached to a particular way of doing things because it produces benefits for them, avoids known harms, and minimizes costs. That's all good stuff. But if we discover that our practices are endangering what matters to others, we must detach and work toward a new integration—a reimagined set of technologies, practices, and procedures that minimize harms and maximize benefits for all parties.

So when it becomes clear that something important to others is in jeopardy, we need to practice inclusive integrity, revising what we're doing so their goals as well as ours can be achieved. It seems like a daunting prospect. Can you describe practices that lead us to inclusive integrity?

Unlike intentional imagination, which can be utterly open-ended, inclusive integrity acknowledges real-world parameters that we must take into account as we try to renovate cooperative structures that have been found wanting. Three practices will help us in this effort:

1. Enlist flexible specialists.
2. Anticipate predictable weaknesses.
3. Treat every plan as a hypothesis.

These practices enable us to evaluate information accurately, stay on top of change, and adapt quickly when that's necessary.

1. Enlist flexible specialists

In pursuit of inclusive integrity we must take into account specialized information about particular environments, technologies, and practices. We'll need to consult with specialists who know things we don't know. The challenge is finding experts who are highly knowledgeable in their own field but also open to the possibilities created by imagination. We'll want to partner with specialists grounded in a set of established practices but ready to ask how those practices can be imaginatively applied and improved.

In my experience specialization often gets in the way of intentional imagination. If you're trying to generate new ideas, people with expertise often inhibit the process by explaining all the ways that new ideas are wrong.

Experts aren't always comfortable with the kind of intentional imagination that is a precursor to inclusive integrity. They've become experts by learning practices and technologies known to be effective in specific environments. We've all developed areas of expertise based on how we're situated in the world, our inborn abilities inevitably shaped by our environments. We've had access to certain educational opportunities. Particular teachers and mentors explained established practice and taught us its advantages. Life experiences have led us to specific conclusions.

By taking advantage of early opportunities to develop specialized knowledge and skills, we can become contributing partners in cooperative enterprises. Think about engineers. Their specialization provides known tools for dealing with particular environments. So situated, they can identify clear goals related to efficiency, effectiveness, reliability, and safety. Measurable standards determine whether a project meets those goals. Most engineers are very comfortable within such well-defined contexts.

And many feel quite uncomfortable if asked to move outside those boundaries. On the other hand, those who do often are responsible for breakthroughs. Think about the engineers who started to imagine cars without drivers.

Once we become bona fide specialists, our orientation has to shift a little. Because every specialist handles limited pieces of a complex project, we need to figure out how to coordinate what we do with what others are able to do. We won't be able to collaborate effectively, much less practice intentional imagination together, if we wear the blinders imposed by specialization. This is challenging, especially when things are in flux. It's natural to cling to what we think we know. It's scary to expose ignorance by talking, much less working, with people who know completely different things.

A congressional aide once told me he had no patience with environmentalists because their demands were extravagant and they were never satisfied, no matter how many concessions they won. I pointed out that health issues were often related to environmental problems, and that by anticipating and minimizing various kinds of pollution we could potentially realize huge savings in healthcare costs. The aide dismissed any prospect of following up on this connection; as he put it, "That's simply not how Congress operates."

Unfortunately, he's right. Different committees handle environmental issues and healthcare. Each has its own agenda and its own experts, so Congress rarely considers the intersection between these issues. Problems that could be nipped in the bud are allowed to become serious because two groups of specialists don't talk to each other!

When specialists are cut off from each other, opportunities for new, more inclusive integrations are missed. Let's push our example a little further. In healthcare there's general agreement that Medicare costs must be contained. On the environmental front, for two decades Congress blocked increased energy-efficiency standards for vehicles because they would cut into the revenues of American manufacturers. It might seem as though these issues are unconnected, but let's practice some deep discernment.

Why do the car companies need more revenue? In part so they can pay the runaway healthcare costs of their workers. And why are healthcare costs out of control? Well, at least some of those costs—for treating asthma, heart disease, and lung disease—are higher because poor air quality aggravates those diseases. And why is the air quality poor in some places? Because of stagnated pollutants from internal combustion engines. It's all interwoven.

Specialists who are fixated on their own area of expertise won't necessarily see how what they do creates externalities in other areas.

Becoming Virtuosos

Sometimes specialized training promotes a kind of hubris: Don't bother me, because I know this and you don't. Of course, that's a misunderstanding of the cooperative bargain. The reason I can specialize is because other people are taking care of many tasks crucial to my well-being. Conversely some specialists, as they go deeper into their field, become aware of how little, not how much, they know. Humbled by this awareness, they are good candidates to practice inclusive integrity. They realize how deeply they depend upon other specialists, and they're curious to know what new values and imagined possibilities other perspectives can deliver.

If we hope to practice inclusive integrity, each of us must be discerning enough to understand that the specialized knowledge and practices we have mastered are not ends. They are means that must constantly evolve in response to changing environments, technologies, and partners. Here's a simple example: a retired history professor was asked to do a guest lecture. He wanted to use a map as a visual aid, so he went to the department secretary and asked where the maps were stored. She looked at him blankly and said, "We don't have a map room anymore; all the maps are online."

Instantly the professor saw that this new configuration incorporated new values—ease of transport, no more outdated maps, availability of the map room for other uses. Still, it was a change from what had been standard practice, so it required flexibility of him. The professor made it his project to learn how to access and project the virtual maps. If he were giving the same lecture today, he would want to use time-lapse photography from satellites to demonstrate the growth of a transportation hub or the devastation of a tsunami.

Environments are constantly changing. We're better able to practice inclusive integrity if we acknowledge that what was important when we gained our expertise may not continue to be important. The values—in this case helping students understand how the world fits together—may persist, but the means are likely to change in response to developments in other areas of specialization, such as satellites and Google maps.

I've seen this in my own field, where the Internet has utterly changed the relationship between writers and readers. I spent years mastering the art of writing magazine articles that depended on lengthy interviews with experts. In online environments readers are more likely to skim and scan. There are fewer outlets for long-form journalism, so writers who hope to have an audience must retool so they can blog and tweet.

In any field of expertise, being secure in what we know liberates us from feeling defensive about what we don't know. A writer who is confident in her ability to communicate ideas with words will be more willing to experiment with new forms. In music there's a name for this kind of specialist: a virtuoso, someone who is extremely skilled. Although this musician's capabilities may be grounded in talent, virtuosity always requires dedication and sheer hard work. A virtuoso must continually practice, both to sustain a high level of skill and to make improvements so small only the most discerning will notice.

Such practice may seem like an end in itself, but it's not. Music is social. What matters is the imaginative integration that occurs among musicians and in the presence of an audience. In any memorable musical group—instrumental or vocal, classical or hip-hop—individuals cultivate their own expertise and then integrate their efforts to produce a unified and interesting interpretation of a piece of music.

My younger son plays jazz guitar, so I've often witnessed this kind of collaboration. In an ensemble each musician is a specialist, but the music comes alive when they listen to and play off each other. The drummer picks up the bass player's accents, the guitarist borrows a rhythm from the drummer, and the vocalist extends a line the guitar player improvised. Because they pay attention to each other, each is able to build on the expertise of the others.

Some exceptionally stirring music comes from people who deliberately seek out and incorporate musical ideas from different traditions. Think of Tony Bennett choosing to collaborate with Lady Gaga. Think of Yo-Yo Ma's Silk Road Project. He intentionally experimented with integrating instruments, sounds, and styles of playing from eastern and western musical traditions. Because he had so thoroughly mastered his own instrument, he could be open to new and sometimes challenging ideas.

Becoming a virtuoso in this way is an option for any expert. We practice inclusive integrity by cultivating a high level of expertise, then using that expertise strategically to construct a cooperative structure with broad benefits. We seek to become specialists so confident in our own skill and understanding that we can afford to be curious about how to integrate them with what other people do. We also want to seek out such specialists as partners. A virtuous specialist—a virtuoso, if you will—is always thinking about how her special expertise intersects with that of others.

Identifying specialists who have gained mastery in one area but are open to other points of view becomes the foundation for stronger forms of cooperation.

Finding Integrity on the Home Front

Here's a very personal example of how inclusive integrity rests on the efforts of flexible specialists. When my wife and I built our retirement home, we had lots of ideas about the conveniences and comforts we wanted. We also understood that we wouldn't be happy if we knew our home was contributing to problems for other people. This included our immediate neighbors, but we also hoped to avoid environmental harms resulting from standard construction procedures and conventional uses of energy.

Because many of those harms are cumulative, our grandchildren might feel the impact even if we escaped it. We didn't want our choices, especially in relation to burning fossil fuels and adding toxins to the environment, to diminish the quality of their lives. We also saw the possibility that, if we were creative about what we did, others might also be motivated to rethink their practices.

You're saying that your choices had to account for the impact they might have on others, now and in the future.

Building a home is a long-term, high-stakes investment for anyone. And we had an opportunity to make very visible choices in an area where we had some expertise. Our decisions weren't simply about what we wanted for ourselves. We wanted to set an example and build a reputation for being serious about sustainable cooperation.

Discerning and clearly stating our values and goals opened up space for the fun of imagination. When we asked "What if?" some experts explained in detail why we couldn't possibly do what we wanted. We learned to listen very carefully to those explanations because they were invariably about values that needed to be incorporated into our plan. But we didn't defer to those experts.

Practicing intentional imagination generated a long list of possibilities, but eventually we had to come to terms with certain facts. We had purchased a particular piece of land and saved a specific amount of money. We had access to specialists who knew how to do some things and not others. Some technologies would work best when bundled with other technologies.

And that's when you needed to enlist flexible specialists.

Again and again we found partners who brought specialized training or experience that we didn't have. For example, we chose our general contractor in part because he had earned an Energy Star rating, indicating that he worked regularly with insulators, plumbers, and electricians who used reliable, energy-conserving technologies. Another litmus test for cooperative partners was that they listened carefully to us, discerning our values and taking them seriously. This was important because what we wanted often forced them to go beyond standard practices in their specialization.

Our heating system is a case in point. We live in a place where the average temperature is 71 degrees F in summer and 26 degrees F in winter. Most people cope with the cold winter temperatures by burning some sort of fossil fuel, but, as we saw in the last chapter, practicing intentional imagination revealed other possibilities. Geothermal energy is an under-recognized, often ignored resource—not because it's expensive or controversial but because it's outside the mainstream. Because our contractor was open to working with other specialists, we were able to tap this resource, installing two-inch pipes just below the frost line. Glycol flowing through the pipes is heated in winter and cooled in summer. A compressor separates cooler molecules from warmer ones, using those appropriate to the season to heat or cool the house and returning the others to storage until they become seasonally appropriate.

As we sought out experts who were willing to share knowledge and coordinate their practices, we discovered ways to integrate many values dear to us—including some declared impossible by less-flexible specialists. Our electrician, for example, bluntly admitted that he'd never heard of some of the things we were proposing. He was, however, willing to talk to an expert in wind technology. In this way he learned about and employed energy-storage practices that were standard in another field.

Integrating Across Specialties

New ways of doing things often emerge at the edges of established disciplines, it seems. Online, the term mashup does a good job of describing such creative opportunities. Infographics, for example, emerged from the intersection of big data and graphic design.

You see people exploiting these opportunities in medicine, too. In the late twentieth century, specialization created huge benefits in healthcare. After all, one general practitioner can know only so much; once a person has been diagnosed with a specific problem such as heart disease or diabetes, it's to the patient's advantage to work with someone specially trained to treat that condition.

But there's a growing understanding that a person is more than the sum of his or her conditions. To achieve health outcomes that reflect their patients' values, specialists need to share information and coordinate their efforts. If they don't practice inclusive integrity, they may miss diagnostic cues and cause harm. A doctor should be interested in what a patient's dentist knows, for example. Gum disease and high blood pressure are both red flags for stroke, but these facts are often locked in separate filing cabinets, to the detriment of many patients.

To their credit, many doctors now practice integrative medicine, an approach that embodies inclusive integrity. Along with the values embedded in traditional medicine, such physicians are receptive to insights from experts in nutrition, exercise, and alternative treatments such as acupuncture. Breaking down walls between medical specialties has led to improved outcomes for many patients. It is also redefining the general practitioner's office as the integrator of specialists' knowledge.

Clearly it will be easier to find new and improved ways of cooperating if we can enlist experts who are open to creative collaboration. Still, those new collaborations will be vulnerable to changing circumstances. How can we make new social configurations durable?

That question leads directly to our second practice.

2. Anticipate predictable weaknesses

When we are renovating and reintegrating a cooperative structure, all partners invest time, effort, and resources—so we want our new structure to be as robust as possible. The best way to do this is to anticipate places where breakdowns may occur. I've found a helpful metaphor in thinking about a river. To the unobservant, rivers may look the same day after day. But anyone who lives near a river knows it is always changing—along the banks and downstream, but also in the speed and depth of the current.

Using this analogy, we improve the integrity of our cooperative efforts by considering what will happen at the margins, what kinds of problems are likely to accumulate, and how we can adapt to fluctuating currents of change without undermining what we've done. These questions direct our attention to zones where vulnerabilities are likely to emerge.

Let's start with the banks of the river. It seems that most cooperative plans are organized to operate well in the mainstream.

Vulnerability at the Margins

Every cooperative system is designed with particular circumstances in mind. It's easiest to see this in construction and other engineering fields, where people regularly talk about the "tolerances" of certain materials or practices. Safe construction practices must stay within the tolerances of the materials they employ. Engineers practice proactive compassion by making sure that the demands on a material don't exceed its tolerance.

Like the banks of a river, tolerances clarify the parameters within which we must operate as we pull together our plan. When we say that something is "safe" or "acceptable," we really mean that, under ordinary circumstances and normal management practices, risks can be managed so as to avoid serious harm. Having clear tolerances also allows partners to hold each other accountable. Being precise about these boundaries makes it more likely that specialists will coordinate their efforts successfully to achieve a mutual goal.

I can sue you if the joist you installed doesn't hold up my roof. You can rebut my claims if I used roofing tiles that were too heavy.

The concept of tolerances is employed explicitly in fields using materials whose properties are easily quantified. But it's also useful in thinking about social interactions. A teacher knows from experience that ten homework problems help clarify what's been taught in class, but twenty will induce boredom and perhaps noncompliance. A supervisor sees that mistakes increase if workers go too long without a break. Sustained cooperation depends upon boundaries that make interactions predictable and productive for both parties.

A large part of what parents do is to help children understand social tolerance. It starts with simple rules—be punctual, a good handshake is firm but not too tight, and so on. Staying within these boundaries demonstrates a willingness and ability to cooperate. As young people are entrusted with responsibilities, they often test the edges of social tolerance. Will Mom and Dad still trust me with the car if I come home ten minutes after curfew?

What will my employer do if I have a visible tattoo? Most quickly learn that things flow along most smoothly when they stay in the mainstream, with its clearly defined norms.

Of course, not everyone fits into the mainstream. When my deaf daughter went to our local school, she struggled. She's every bit as bright as her brothers, but school was much harder for her because it's set up with the assumption that students can hear.

This is a good example of how our cooperative systems are always vulnerable at the edges. We can strengthen them by asking questions about people, practices, and circumstances at the margins. What can be done about vulnerabilities that will affect some people some of the time? And how do changes in the environment create problems—or opportunities—at the edges of our cooperative structures? In the case of students with special needs, new technologies may open up new possibilities. Perhaps deaf students should be able to use cell phones to text with the teacher.

Sometimes integrations inadvertently exclude people because their needs fall outside the focus of our specialized viewpoint. In a restaurant, for example, the thermostat is set to keep most customers comfortable most of the time. But what about an infant or an elderly person or someone just getting over a cold? They may be vulnerable at a temperature that's perfectly acceptable to other people. And what about the table near the kitchen or the entryway? Those microenvironments may suit some customers but not others.

The same thing is true in a classroom, where the experience is designed for "typical" students. The lessons may be boring for bright students and baffling to students with less ability.

In situations like these we have two choices. We can make the vulnerable individual responsible for the success of the cooperative effort, or we can revise the cooperative structure so that more people benefit. The restaurant owner might assume that people will take the initiative and bring sweaters for babies or elderly relatives. Or he might decide that it's good business to make the environment comfortable for a wider range of patrons: by installing insulation to reduce drafts or building a double door entry to minimize the cold air that blows in.

The school district makes a similar analysis. Administrators could expect parents to compensate for individual variations in the abilities of children by getting a tutor for a child who is struggling or providing enrichment for one who's bored. Or they might decide that the school would be improved by providing those services on location. They might create instructional options for students who need extra time to master new concepts as well as for students who grasp new material easily.

It looks as though it's easier and less expensive to ask individuals to compensate for their own vulnerability.

That's what we tend to assume, but cooperative systems often become more durable if protections are built right into the system. Drunk driving is an example. The number of people who drink too much to make responsible decisions about driving is marginal, but the harm they do affects not only themselves but many others. We may want individuals to take responsibility for their alcohol consumption, but that isn't a very effective way to reduce accidents caused by drunk driving. As a society we've achieved much better results by addressing this problem from the viewpoint of people who might be injured by drunk drivers. How can we build safeguards into the system?

First, accidents involving drunk drivers are most likely to occur between two and three o'clock in the morning—typically the hour after bars close. If police patrol the streets around bars during those hours, accidents from drunk driving decrease. If liability laws assign some responsibility to businesses that serve alcohol, bartenders have an incentive to find alternate transportation for inebriated drivers. If judges have access to new technologies, they can mandate the use of a device that immobilizes a vehicle until the driver proves he's sober by taking a breath test. All these changes strengthen the system by protecting innocent people as well as those drunk drivers on the margins.

We could think about the vulnerabilities created by drunk drivers in an even broader way. Could you design a vehicle that cannot leave the road or one that will stop before it hits another vehicle? If so, you limit vulnerability regardless of how the driver behaves. Interestingly enough you also create benefits for people who would never think of getting behind the wheel after they've had a drink. A vehicle that slows in anticipation of an impending collision would be valuable to sleepy or elderly drivers or even those who suffer a stroke while driving.

This reminds me of something that happened when my daughter was in high school. We pushed hard to get captioning for her classes so she could better understand what teachers were saying. It wasn't easy, and sometimes I felt guilty because her needs seemed so different from those of her typical classmates. Still, once we got the problems worked out teachers found that hearing kids read the captions too. And many of them did better by seeing as well as hearing what was said in class.

Expanding the benefit zone on behalf of a minority at the margins regularly creates opportunities for the majority. When the Americans with Disabilities Act forced hotels to build accessible floors, some protested because the modifications seemed aimed at the relatively small number of people confined to wheelchairs. Then it turned out that other people liked those floors too. Suddenly travel was more feasible for older folks, people with injuries, and people suffering fatigue because of an illness. Even though the benefits weren't intended for them, the new arrangements encouraged these people to consider trips they might not have taken, thus expanding the pool of potential cooperators—namely, paying customers for the hotel!

It's easy to dismiss the problems of small, specialized populations outside the mainstream, but all of us are disadvantaged at one time or another by specialized environments. Whenever specialists work together to create new forms of cooperation, they do well to consider what risks, and opportunities, are created for people at the margins.

The Internet is a clear example of what you're describing. It was devised by academics and the military so experts could share very specific kinds of information. Today, of course, nonspecialists use it for commerce and social networking without beginning to understand its complexities. As a result they are left vulnerable to viruses and malware and international e-mail scams. Success stories from the Web are often about entrepreneurs who saw a vulnerability and tried to minimize it for the rest of us. Amazon made it safe for people to use a credit card to buy things; Facebook reduced the risks of talking to people online.

Service providers often see reducing vulnerability at the margins as an unnecessary expense, but that's incredibly shortsighted. Expanding the safety zone multiplies the number of people for whom cooperation will create benefits that are assuredly mutual. We can practice inclusive integrity by paying attention to what's happening at the edges and building concern for those people into our cooperative plans.

Planning for Downstream Impacts

Our cooperative plans are always stronger and more durable when we make an effort to anticipate externalities. So we'll also want to look ahead to see how our plans might impact people distant from us in time or space. Some plans may seem feasible and inexpensive because any problems they create will affect only people we can't see, in a future we can't quite imagine. But the future will arrive, and those harmed will understandably object. To use our river analogy, cooperative systems are always stronger when we foresee rather than ignore problems that may emerge downstream.

The downstream metaphor comes from pioneer days, when people believed that flowing water purified itself every six miles. As long as homesteads were six miles apart, folks thought, they didn't have to worry that something entering the water on their property would have a harmful impact on their neighbors. That assumption is one root of the fiercely held idea that you should be able to do whatever you want on your own land. Similar thinking led to my mother's assurance that the smoke I worried about as a boy would go away because the sky is so big.

Whatever else it may have accomplished, the environmental movement made it clear that what people do to land, water, or air often has tremendous implications for others.

If we hope to practice inclusive integrity, we have to consider the long-term implications of our actions. Ellen Swallow Richards, who in 1894 became the first woman trustee at Vassar College, had this kind of vision. At that time the college needed to improve its sewage treatment. Until then sewage had been dumped into the local stream, but as the college grew, farmers downstream started complaining that their cows were getting sick. The trustees figured that they simply needed a bigger waterway, so they proposed digging a canal to carry sewage directly into the Hudson River.

This sounds like a problem of scale. When there were only a few students, the pollution was negligible. With more sewage, they needed a bigger river to carry it away.

The notion that problems disappear if we can't see them is naïve at best. Even in 1894 Richards understood this. The first woman to graduate from MIT, she spent her career advocating for what is now known as public health. She understood that the waste problem would be more difficult to solve once sewage was dispersed into the river, and that harms would accumulate for New York City residents, who depended on the Hudson for drinking water.

Despite resistance she persuaded the trustees to contain the sewage in leach fields. Her imaginative plan actually saved the college money because it eliminated the costs of digging the canal. It also created positive instead of negative externalities. The fields in what came to be known as Vassar Farms were enriched by nutrients in the sewage, and annual yields greatly increased. Instead of passing on the harms of serious pollution to those downstream, Richards imagined a new way to reorganize resources to capture real benefits.

This seems harder than identifying people at the margins. Downstream externalities often accumulate into serious harms without ever coming into focus. Nobody planned for them to happen, and even the people who are suffering may not make the connection between what's happening to them and actions upstream.

People at the margins are vulnerable right now. In contrast, downstream problems occur at a distance or in the future, so they require us to anticipate and respond to unseen and potential vulnerabilities. When we don't adequately foresee the future, we—or our successors—face the more difficult challenge of cleaning up our mistakes. So we'd do well to project as best we can how the environment might change, particularly in response to our actions.

The pork industry is a good example of how this can work. On contemporary farms hogs are raised in large barns. For many years it was standard practice to store pig wastes in open lagoons, which would overflow during heavy rains, contaminating local waterways. Hog farmers have strengthened their industry by looking quite literally downstream. Modern hog facilities allow excrement to fall through grids into basements, where waste can easily be collected and stored until it can be spread on the fields. Not only have farmers spared their neighbors the problems of contaminated water, but they've also increased their own profits because the wastes from the barns fertilize soybeans and corn that feed a new generation of pigs. They've closed the loop.

This reminds me of proactive compassion, but instead of anticipating harms from our own point of view we practice inclusive integrity by coordinating with others and anticipating harms from multiple points of view.

The idea of looking downstream may be most easily understood with examples that involve water, but the concept applies to any deferred liability. Think about parenting. When children are young, doing things for them is much more efficient. It takes time and patience to teach a child how to make a bed, prepare vegetables, or pack his own suitcase for a family trip. But look downstream. Most parents want adolescents who can take care of themselves and cooperate willingly in family tasks. You're more likely to get that result if you start teaching skills early, when children are eager to be Mommy's little helper.

A future in which children become teenagers is pretty easy to anticipate. The challenge of inclusive integrity is to foresee less obvious changes in the environment. In particular we have to consider how the environment might change *because* our plan is successful. As we've seen, when we expand the scale of our actions, downstream consequences may be magnified—especially for those who aren't directly involved in the original cooperative system.

As we devise plans that account for known problems, we and our cooperative partners need to think about trends to which we contribute—and how small, seemingly insignificant flaws in our plans can accumulate into serious problems.

Think about student debt. Everyone agrees that education is a good. Educated people tend to have better jobs, so the motivation to get a higher education is especially high among young people from families that can't afford to pay their tuition. Financial aid packages were originally designed to make education affordable, in part by deferring payment until a student armed with a degree could land a well-paying job.

Everyone was so focused on the prospective good of education that few thought clearly about the downstream harms that students' accumulated debt could cause. Bankers, financial aid officers, policy makers, and even parents failed to look beyond the moment and think through the possible consequences of so many young people borrowing so much money. A few young people struggling with student debt wasn't a huge problem, especially if they came out of school with professional skills. Today, however, 40 percent of people under age thirty-five graduate with significant debt—the average outstanding balance is around $30,000. The sheer numbers have changed the economic and social environment. At an age when they would ordinarily be buying cars and houses, these young people are struggling to pay off college loans rather than starting families.

I'm beginning to understand. We almost have to think like science fiction writers, projecting our actions into the future and trying to imagine negative as well as positive outcomes. Whenever we can anticipate future conditions and work them into our cooperative plan, changes in the environment are less likely to be devastating.

We want people to imagine cooperative agreements that produce mutual benefits. Downstream externalities may not be obvious when we first start thinking about a new way of doing things, yet we know they are inevitable. If we integrate this understanding into our projections, they still won't be infallible, but when vulnerabilities emerge we will be alert and ready to revise. If we don't do this, we condemn ourselves or our descendants to remediation after the fact. We practice inclusive integrity when we devise social configurations that from the outset take seriously the concerns of those downstream.

I see how we can sidestep some problems if we calibrate our planning to account for people who are downstream or at the edges of the mainstream. How else can we anticipate and correct flaws when revising our cooperative systems?

Adjusting to the Pace of Change

Our cooperative configurations will be more durable if we build in mechanisms that adjust to the pace of change. Sometimes the environment we're in is relatively stable: imagine a slow-moving river at the end of summer. Sometimes it's changing rapidly: imagine that same river during a spring thaw.

Change occurs in both environments, but the pace is different. Each situation presents its own challenges and opportunities. In a stable environment standardization and consolidation create efficiency. If something works well today, it will probably work well tomorrow; imagining lots of new possibilities and trying to integrate them into our plans may squander resources. Think about healthy adults. Most thirty-year-olds reasonably view their bodies as environments that will be easily sustained during the next decade. Physiological systems operate according to genetic programming: at this time of life cells die and are replenished without any special attention.

Because of this relative stability most young adults develop a set of healthy practices that support, or at least do not quickly undermine, these bodily integrations. They eat foods that agree with them. They commit to an exercise regimen of some sort. They establish a sleep schedule. They also make connections with social networks that promote sustainable health: visiting the dentist, getting a flu shot in the fall, enrolling in extra exercise classes after lapses during the holidays, and so on. A healthy adult may tweak this regimen now and then, but most don't need to give it a huge amount of thought.

If I decide a bowl of oatmeal is a good breakfast for me, I might as well stick with that. Perusing the endless cereal aisle will take time without producing better results.

That's true as long as the environment is stable. If, on the other hand, an environment is changing rapidly, attempting to maintain standard practices may not produce standard benefits. The most dramatic example is cancer, which interrupts the normal, healthy program of human development and aging. Now cells are growing faster than they die off. If metastasis occurs, cells that ordinarily grow in one part of the body—the kidney, perhaps—begin to grow in other organs. Suddenly the body that seemed stable becomes a fast-changing and potentially endangered environment.

By its very nature an unstable environment is harder to understand. What worked yesterday may not work today, so any plans we put in place must be flexible and easily revised. That's why oncologists see their patients so often. They know that their understanding of this environment is temporary because so many variables are in flux. The long-term goal is stable functioning, but in the short term, plans are highly provisional. The oncologist tries a combination of treatments, monitors the effects, and makes constant adjustments.

In 2009 my youngest sister was diagnosed with an especially virulent form of cancer. Her doctors conferred with various specialists and tried various treatments. And some of them worked. On some tumors. For a period of time. The treatment plan kept changing, which was both stressful and hopeful.

In any rapidly changing, poorly understood environment, the best strategy is to make lots of small-scale adjustments, knowing that some will work better than others. You see this process in the natural world, where organisms must respond as environments change. Otherwise they die out and something, perhaps offspring with a slight mutation, replaces them. Some observers have described this process as wasteful. It definitely takes extra energy to create new forms of integration. Still, our limited knowledge means that in a fast-changing, unstable environment the best bet is a hedged bet.

The recent history of American media illustrates the contrast between strategies that work in stable versus unstable environments. After the upheaval of World War II the nation settled into a period of relative stability, and so did the media. People were informed about current events through a monolithic news apparatus of three television networks and dominant city newspapers. Because of this consolidation most people received the same news, which reinforced relative consensus about national issues. Then along came the Internet, and the environment became unstable. New technology enabled minute-to-minute updates by anyone with a cell phone. The old model of gathering news, submitting it to the scrutiny of an editor, and then releasing it once a day was supplanted. News became available around the clock from many sources, and public opinion fragmented.

What happens online may not be authoritative journalism, but it is nimble. Individuals have a highly effective way to communicate what they see, think, and feel—often right in the middle of unfolding events. Of course, without the filters built into traditional media it's harder to know which tweet is credible.

An integration that works well when an environment is stable can become a liability in a disrupted environment, as many media companies have learned. In many cases large, established companies with entrenched ways of doing things are struggling, while smaller, more nimble start-ups are attracting an audience. The strongest forms of cooperation allow us to expand or contract depending on circumstances. We can scale up when environments are more stable, and get smaller and more local in response to disruption.

The federal system created by the Founding Fathers is precisely this kind of system. During periods of minimal change, large-scale government does a good job of collecting and disseminating information about best practices—in everything from food safety to banking. A centralized system can also ensure evenhandedness, which to a large extent is about setting ground rules and making them easy to follow. Having national norms can remove social barriers to large national markets and may even encourage innovation, because some risks have been extracted from the system. Our founders understood all this when they established a federal treasury and a national currency good "for all debts public and private."

When the environment is in flux, one-size-fits-all rules don't work nearly as well, so our federal system also promotes local responsiveness. A recession, for example, looks like a harm to the entire nation. Yet in every recession some regions and industries suffer more than others. If Congress decides that a stimulus program is in the national interest, it may leave the administrative details to be worked out by state officials, who can respond more flexibly to rapidly changing and sometimes highly local circumstances. After the economic downturn of 2008–09 some stimulus money was earmarked for transportation, but states had discretion in how to use it. Depending on local needs, some states spent the money on building and repairing roads; others spent it on public transportation. The federal system is brilliant and resilient, because it can wield national authority to create efficiencies when environments are stable and disperse authority to encourage imaginative responses when change is occurring rapidly.

Standard ways of doing things produce reliable benefits — until the environment changes. When things are in flux we'll get better results from smaller, more provisional projects because we don't yet know what will work in the new environment.

We practice inclusive integrity by building social configurations that function well in stable environments but don't fall apart during periods of rapid change. The company 3M, for example, has survived for a century because both capabilities are built into its corporate structure. It was originally a mining company, founded by five businessmen who invested in a mine meant to produce abrasive minerals for grinding wheels. The mine was a failure, but the company's founders were committed to research and innovation. In the 1920s, 3M developed waterproof sandpaper as well as masking tape.

Like other companies, 3M features products with proven commercial value: masking tape is still going strong. At the same time the company is built around small, nimble teams able to spot opportunities that would go unnoticed if it focused only on what had been successful in the past. Its leadership actively encourages innovation by holding an annual competition that fosters team building, collaboration, and management skills among employees. Researchers are encouraged to practice intentional imagination, and the teams with the best ideas are awarded development funding. Not every idea is a winner, of course, but the competition keeps 3M responsive to changes in the environment it might otherwise miss, and its array of successful products — sticky notes, pet hair removers, respirators, solar mirror film — showcase the resilience of this approach.

Reengineering the System

Let me summarize: We practice inclusive integrity by making sure that our cooperative systems are responsive to the concerns of as many people as possible. To get maximum return on our efforts, we should consider the needs of people at the margins, anticipate externalities for people and environments downstream, and build in flexibility that enables us to adjust to the pace of change.

Now let's work through a situation in which all these approaches to integration come into play. A colleague of mine has an interest in the huge dairy farms we were discussing earlier. They produce an obvious benefit: milk. They also produce manure in quantities that can be problematic. My colleague started with a big *what if* question: What if someone created a product that made constructive use of milk *and* manure?

That's practicing intentional imagination.

He fooled around with a lot of ideas. Finally he focused in on yogurt, a product that uses milk as its raw ingredient. So far, so good, but what about the manure? He started talking to experts about waste digesters: contraptions that process manure and produce the low-level heat needed to make yogurt. Now the situation starts to look like an opportunity for inclusive integration. Multiple values are in play: make a healthy dairy product, reduce the impact of animal waste, and, of course, generate income.

As it happens, the digesters also produce methane, which can be burned to produce electricity. My friend did some calculations and figured he could make a profit if he sold the excess electricity for 8.6 cents per kilowatt hour. But in Ohio, unfortunately, the wholesale rate to buy electricity was then below 8.6 cents.

So the configuration he's considering wouldn't work in Ohio. But maybe there were opportunities at the margins.

Just so. In any market environment prices are a measure of value within a range of conditions. Accordingly, "wholesale electric price" has different meanings in different market environments. In Wisconsin, for example, the wholesale electric rate was higher, and my friend's proposed cooperative structure could potentially work quite well in that environment. Of course, he would need to consider the stability of the energy environment. What factors might cause energy costs to increase or decrease? Was the pace of change likely to be gradual or sudden?

My friend also had to think about the downstream implications of relocating to Wisconsin. His wife had compelling reasons to be in Ohio. What were the long-term implications for their relationship of spending significant amounts of time apart? What could they do to mitigate negative externalities? Alternatively, if he wanted to locate the plant in Ohio, more imagining was in order. Could production costs be trimmed? Could he justify a higher price for the yogurt? Could he find an untapped source of heat—perhaps waste heat someone needed to exhaust?

What you're describing sounds like the work of a good engineer: consider tolerances, anticipate future problems, evaluate the stability of the environment. The process is methodical and open-minded. If one approach doesn't work, try another.

And it's important to acknowledge that, no matter how hard we try, we can't anticipate every externality. We can strengthen our collaborations enormously by identifying weak points and incorporating diverse points of view. Still, we are fallible. Our plans will fail to foresee some eventualities and will overlook the concerns of some affected parties. Our third practice addresses these failings.

3. Treat every plan as a hypothesis

Whenever we try to integrate a range of values into a cooperative system, we must regard any proposal we develop as a hypothesis. Inclusive integrity starts with a set of goals and possible ways of reaching them. Those goals must be clear, even though we know they may change as we become aware of emerging facts and values. Things may not go as planned, often because we don't know enough about the environment or about our cooperative partners. Treating plans as provisional is more challenging than it may sound, however, because our instinct is to stick with the known. We'll need to continually use proactive compassion to detect emerging harms, deep discernment to perceive hidden values, and intentional imagination to reconfigure resources.

This makes me think about the years when my children were young. Just when I thought I'd discovered the secret to happy family life, things would change. We were committed to eating dinner together every night—until the kids started playing sports, and practice times made it impossible for everyone to be in the same place at the same time.

A family is a social environment, thriving when cooperation produces benefits for all. The benefits will differ depending on the child, and they'll change as the children grow. Parents can't know in advance what will catch on with any particular child, and wise parents offer a range of activities without becoming too attached to any particular configuration. What bores a child at one stage may become a passion. Or something that seems like a talent may turn out to be only a temporary fascination. A healthy family continually reevaluates benefits and harms so that multiple values are recognized and supported. We need to preserve the values embedded in established practices and affirm new values as we become aware of them.

When our kids started playing sports, I could clearly see the benefits even though I wasn't an athlete. In addition to physical skills they developed friendships and even a work ethic. So to maintain my commitment to shared meals, we made Sunday brunch a big deal for a while. It was a meal everyone enjoyed, and we could linger around the table talking about the week.

The same need for flexibility applies to other social units. Consider a typical faith community. Worship is always a priority, of course, but congregants may have different ideas about everything from the length of services to the kind of music that should be played. Some members may be chiefly concerned about doctrine, and others may give priority to ministry—ministering to members of the congregation in distress or to vulnerabilities they see in the whole community. A healthy congregation will evolve, responding to new circumstances while preserving the values on which its tradition rests.

In my own church, for example, members became aware that a growing number of local families were tending aging relatives who had cognitive impairments. Burnout was a real risk, especially for those trying to raise children and working outside the home. The congregation decided it could use church facilities to start an adult daycare program offering respite care. Putting this in place required considerable patience to coordinate the concerns of families, church elders, healthcare providers, geriatric specialists, and government agencies.

I certainly see how conflicts could arise. Members rely on the church for benefits that are well established. New circumstances—a rise in the number of seniors with cognitive issues—create vulnerabilities. Trying to address those needs without disrupting established goods will be a challenge.

Achieving flexibility is more likely when we assume that any form of cooperation is hypothetical and subject to change. If we discover that what we're doing causes unintended harms, or that the environment has changed, we have to recalibrate. We use intentional imagination to generate possibilities, then settle on a set of techniques and protocols that seems promising—at least for the present.

As we put our new plan into practice, we must ask lots of questions. Are we achieving the stated goals? If not, what can be changed? Did we encounter costs that seemed unnecessary? Did we get results we didn't anticipate? Did implementing our plan change the environment in unanticipated and undesirable ways? Or have we discovered other benefits we should incorporate into our goals? In the case of the adult daycare center a good combination of physical activity and mental stimulation might slow cognitive decline for some participants.

It sounds like we should be wary whenever it seems that things are settled. Stability is at best a temporary illusion.

Even the Best Plans Won't Work Forever

Cooperation may settle into workable structures for a while, but then we risk becoming complacent. Let's look at efforts to address a certain source of water pollution. As we discussed earlier, fertilizer contains phosphorus to make plants grow better, but when it rains, phosphorus washes off fields and into streams. In Northwest Ohio those streams run into Lake Erie, where the phosphorus stimulates algae growth in warm weather. Eventually the algae die and decay, a process that sucks up oxygen in the water. If there's excessive algae, the oxygen becomes so depleted that fish actually suffocate.

Nutrient pollution is a big problem in many of the world's estuaries: Chesapeake Bay suffers from the same pathology as the Gulf of Mexico. It's taken time, but specialists now understand how excessive nutrients produced by industries, farms, and sanitation facilities contribute to excessive algae growth, declining catches for fishermen, and, even farther downstream, increased air pollution.

In the 1970s phosphorus-fueled algae growth became a very serious problem in Lake Erie. Specialists applied imagination, asking: What if we took phosphorus out of laundry detergents? What if we created fertilizer-free buffer zones along the lake and at the edge of farm fields? New legislation forced manufacturers to reformulate detergents and incentivized farmers not to plant crops requiring fertilizer in the buffer zones. In other words, flexible specialists practiced inclusive integrity, reengineering social configurations to consider values that hadn't been well-understood in the past.

It sounds like a good plan, but I bet they didn't anticipate all the externalities.

For many years it looked as though the phosphorus problem had been solved. Plants that grew naturally in the buffer zones absorbed much of the phosphorus that seeped in. The algae blooms went away and the fish did better. Over time, however, issues of scale emerged. When the buffer strips were established their capacity seemed immense, but eventually they became saturated with pollutants. Early in the twenty-first century algae blooms began appearing again in Maumee Bay, a shallow area at the western end of the lake.

So the plan that looked like a permanent solution was actually a hypothesis. And issues of scale proved the hypothesis wrong.

In such situations it's tempting to blame the experts, who were supposed to come up with a plan that would solve the problem once and for all. But if we think of the Lake Erie plan as a hypothesis, we can see the need to consider new variables as the environment changes. Perhaps we could have anticipated that the buffers would fill up and stop functioning as planned, but when an old problem resurfaces—or a new problem emerges—we must exercise inclusive integrity to address it. Expanding the buffer zones might look like one obvious solution. Unfortunately, taking more farmland out of production significantly increases costs and diminishes benefits.

This sounds like an opportunity for intentional imagination.

When I got involved with this issue, I asked what if questions about the buffer zones. Phosphorus was showing up in the lake because the zones were filled to capacity. What if the buffer zones could be emptied and refilled over and over? I didn't know the answer, so I started talking to specialists. Eventually I found agronomists who knew about perennial grasses that absorb tremendous amounts of phosphorus. What if these phosphorus-hungry crops were grown in the buffer strips? For one thing, they would need to be harvested, or the phosphorus would go back into the soil when they decomposed.

Then what would you do with all that grass?

Well, the grass contains lots of calories, but it's not all that digestible. Still, calories represent energy. What if we used the energy in some other way? Many utilities in Ohio burn coal, which, as everyone knows, generates pollution that can be prevented only by installing costly scrubbing equipment. So some utilities have begun to ask if they could cut costs by retrofitting their facilities to use biomass—mostly wood chips and (aha!) grasses. So there could be a market for cellulosic grasses grown to absorb the phosphorus in the buffer strips. At the time farmers were being paid not to grow crops in the buffer strips. What if, instead, farmers planted perennial grasses in those strips and sold the harvested grass to the utilities? Suddenly we're avoiding old costs and creating new benefits.

Your plan is very imaginative, but it sounds too good to be true. There must be externalities.

Of course, and some are actually positive. First, perennials have long roots that sequester carbon by storing it in the ground. To the extent that carbon dioxide contributes to climate change, having perennials absorb CO_2 creates a genuine benefit. Second, as we've seen, perennial roots soak up water, so they can play a part in flood control. Third, since phosphorus is stored in the grass blade, not in the roots, harvesting removes this unwanted mineral from the vulnerable ecosystem.

It's easy to get carried away and again assume that we've found a permanent solution. But there may be other, less positive, externalities. Perennials become established in about three years, after which they produce a reliable crop year after year into the indefinite future. Profits for farmers will be higher if they plant only grasses with the highest yields. If they do this on a large scale, there will be acres and acres of the same plant. And we know from sad experience (including the Irish potato famine) that depending too heavily on any one crop invites vulnerability to disease and other environmental stresses. Our plan will be stronger if we encourage farmers to establish a mix of grasses so that some will thrive regardless of variable weather and other growing conditions. Yet, even with this kind of forward thinking, we must acknowledge that there are things we don't know, possibilities we haven't taken into account.

Plan, Respond, Revise, Repeat

The dynamics of intentional imagination and inclusive integrity remind me of the deep breathing I learned to do in tai chi. First we inhale and expand to take in all of life's possibilities—that feels like imagination. Then we contract and exhale as we strike or punch. That seems like integration. Imagine new possibilities; integrate those possibilities into practice. Evaluate. Repeat.

Applying the virtues is always a repetitive process. Every time we revise a cooperative structure, we are proposing a hypothesis about how to avoid harms and create benefits for multiple parties. And no matter how wonderful the plan is, it will produce externalities that eluded us because of our specific focus. The farmers are thinking about making a living, so they don't necessarily see how planting the same crop as their neighbors may contribute to blight.

Nor can the plan possibly anticipate every change in the physical, much less the social, environment. The physical world changes both independently of us and because of us. The human world changes because those cooperating on a particular project are not the only agents whose actions have consequences. The market for biofuels may fluctuate. Demand may decrease because increased fracking makes natural gas less expensive. No matter how brilliant the plan, how carefully we implement it, or how vigilant we are for externalities, new vulnerabilities will emerge, and we'll need to reactivate the virtues.

When harms emerge, often there's a gotcha moment when everyone wants to blame someone. That's what happened when an algae bloom in Lake Erie threatened the water supply in Toledo. But you're saying that breakdowns are inevitable because we aren't omniscient.

When harms become apparent it's easy to feel resentful because they spoiled what looked like a really great plan. Often the harms were unpredictable, based on what we knew when developing the integration. Think about the plastics revolution after World War II. DuPont's unironic slogan back then was "Better things for better living . . . through chemistry." Introducing plastics widely into the physical environment brought a host of externalities, some of which we're still discovering—such as the way PCBs concentrate in the tissues of marine mammals. But they were utterly unanticipated.

Of course, every plan for integrating a set of values entails costs of some kind. People are more likely to agree to costs if they believe the system will create problem-free benefits for the foreseeable future. I've often used that argument in favor of wind turbines. Yes, there's capital investment up front, but then the turbines produce power with minimal maintenance for many years after start-up costs have been recovered. The same reasoning applies to the costly research required to develop a new drug. Still, we need to make a distinction between reasonable, balanced costs and the serious harms that damage other people's ability to thrive, or the natural or social systems on which we depend.

Cost versus Harms: The Moral Contract

The distinction between costs and harms is interesting. Costs are something I accept in exchange for benefits. What you're calling harms are costs imposed on me. Either I didn't consent or I don't get benefits.

We don't practice the virtues in a utopia. The real world calls for constant analysis of costs and benefits. We do this all the time: I don't perceive the grocery bill as a harm because I got to choose ingredients for a dinner I will enjoy with my wife. If we aim for inclusive integrity in our cooperative arrangements, we must continually check in with each other to be sure costs and benefits are balanced and reasonably distributed. Do benefits you enjoy interfere with what matters to me, or do my benefits come at your expense? How can we integrate our values into a cooperative system in which partners willingly accept certain costs in exchange for benefits important to them, but none of those benefits imposes unacceptable costs on others?

To find some clues about how this works, let's take another example related to fisheries. Many are in collapse because overfishing has depleted breeding stocks and the fish population cannot sustain itself. In both East and West Coast fishing communities this erosion happened gradually. Fishing practices developed during a time when "all the fish in the sea" was an unimaginably large number. A century ago fishermen would have laughed at the idea that fish stocks could be depleted. Even in the 1990s it was hard to convince fishermen that standard practices were destroying their industry. Some explained away scientific forecasts by arguing that the fish had learned to evade their nets or moved to other locations.

In coal mining, too, change snuck up on communities. The environment changed slowly or in subtle ways that weren't detected as they were unfolding. Then one morning people discovered that their accustomed and meaningful way of life was under attack. When a livelihood is also a way of life, people are even more reluctant to change their ways.

Change is occurring even when things seem stable. The cooperative arrangement that seems like a win-win today may look quite different tomorrow—especially if we discover that it affects people who weren't involved in the original plan. Obviously individual fishermen never intended to undermine their own livelihoods or that of others, but the scale of fishing operations was having precisely this effect.

By the turn of the twenty-first century most fishermen could see that their catch was seriously diminished. The only hope for keeping some fisheries alive was to inventory available stocks and adjust catch sizes so the fish could replenish themselves. Regulations went into place and quotas were established. From the outset it was clear that limiting catches would result in fewer boats going out and less business for fishing supply shops. In several communities plans emerged that accounted for this consolidation by offering buyouts to some boat owners and suppliers.

That must have been wrenching for those individuals.

Some young folks saw the handwriting on the wall and opted to pursue education to equip themselves for careers they couldn't practice in their hometowns. Others imagined how to preserve what they valued about fishing as a way of life. What if we farmed fish? What if we harvested something else from the sea? What if we used our boats for whale watching or scuba diving? Clearly these fisherman would have been more comfortable hanging onto traditional assumptions and practices. But the environment had changed—in part because of those assumptions and practices.

To sustain what they most valued, people who continued to fish also had to imagine and integrate a new set of practices around which to reorganize a fishing economy. In one West Coast salmon fishing area, a mediator from a nonprofit conservation group helped community members hammer out a plan based on population data supplied by government scientists. The plan allocated a three-month quota to each fishing boat. Each captain decided when to go fishing, but once he hit his quota his boat couldn't go out until the next cycle.

The premise seems simple: each crew can make a living selling its quota of fish, and everyone has to stick to the quota to ensure an adequate catch next year and the year after. On paper it sounds like a perfect solution.

In settling on a specific plan the fishermen committed themselves to one of many alternatives, then created a set of practices that integrated multiple values. To stabilize the fish population we'll do X. To provide a viable living for fishermen we'll do Y. To minimize harm for those who won't be fishing we'll do Z.

It was a big improvement, but when this system went into practice, vulnerabilities became apparent. As each captain got close to the agreed quota, he had to make his (or her) best guess about what he was catching. Because he couldn't see underwater he had to make precise calculations based on imprecise information. If the net was down fifteen minutes too long, he might take too many fish. The new rules required that those fish be tossed back—although by the time those fish hit the water, they were dead. Since the goal of the project was to sustain the fishery by increasing the number of living fish, dead fish were a problem.

This sounds like another intractable problem. Limiting the catch is necessary to sustain the fishery. Fishing up to the quarterly quota is the only way fishermen can earn a living wage. Fishing isn't a precise science, so they wind up killing too many fish.

Feeling at an impasse comes directly from believing that the plan adopted was the only feasible plan. But if we treat it as a hypothesis, then the new information about dead fish gives us a chance to rework our thinking with another dose of intentional imagination. What if we change the way the quota is set? Eventually the plan was revised to make the quota annual. Now the fishermen must try to guess whether they have enough fish only once a year. That should reduce the number of dead fish thrown back by 75 percent — not bad. The cost of ignorance is reduced. The fishermen maximize income without depleting the fishery.

Mind you, the system still isn't perfect. Within a given year captains are free to fish whenever they want, but there's still a lot they don't know. How many fish will there be on a given day? How stormy is the weather at different times of year? What's the relative risk to the boat? What will the market price be in different seasons? If you get too far ahead of your quota, will you miss out on prime fishing days when the fish are running strong?

All these areas of ignorance are potential sources of error and vulnerability, so there's still plenty of room for improvement — and imagination.

In this example people practiced inclusive integrity by designing a solution that takes into account both the values of local people who support their families through fishing, and those of the federal scientists and regulators who collect data showing how that fishery fits into larger concerns about sustainable populations. Both sides must continue to cooperate if they hope to minimize vulnerabilities that may not be obvious in their initial plan.

Dynamic Integrity

Any hypothesis can be strengthened by integrating the knowledge and concerns of those who can step back to see the big picture and those who cope with day-to-day details. Earlier we saw how large-scale integrations can be more efficient and small-scale integrations can be more flexible. The federal government, with its research and policy capabilities, may be in a better position to set a large-scale policy with firm goals. But decisions about how to achieve those goals are often left to local governments and in some cases to private industry.

For example, federal regulators have established rules about high fuel efficiency and low emissions for the fleet of vehicles traveling U.S. highways. Individual car companies work within that framework to figure out how to meet these goals. Manufacturers can aim for different market segments. They can put resources into vehicles with varying performance characteristics and fuel requirements. They can develop lightweight alloys that do not sacrifice strength, or automated systems that improve typical driver performance. Each manufacturer must assess its historical strengths and market appeal to develop its own best response.

In short, inclusive integrity takes a set of what if's generated by imagination and works through the implications for a specific environment. If you get stuck, you ask "What if?" again and generate a new hypothesis about how to rework the social coordination to secure the most widespread benefits and minimize newly understood harms.

Inclusive integrity is a way to test the viability of what we imagine. We work to establish improved social configurations in response to vulnerabilities identified through proactive compassion, values clarified with deep discernment, and possibilities generated by intentional imagination. We make our renovated cooperative structures sounder and more durable by encouraging flexibility in specialists, paying extra attention to predictable areas of weakness, and treating every plan as a hypothesis.

Even with all this effort, we can never devise social arrangements that will work forever. Our cooperative efforts depend on the parameters of particular environments. We understand some of those parameters, but others will be obscure or will shift as the environment changes. Successful cooperation must be a dynamic process that evolves as we evaluate what we've attempted, diagnose problems, and imagine revisions that integrate values not obvious at the outset. Accepting the imperative to revise and reintegrate always feels risky. But for the social animals that we are, the potential benefits of cooperation make the risk worth taking.

CHAPTER 6

Creative Courage
Embracing the Risks of Engagement

History, despite its wrenching pain, cannot be unlived,
but if faced with courage, need not be lived again.
Maya Angelou

Success is not final, failure is not fatal;
it is the courage to continue that counts.
Winston Churchill

I see how practicing inclusive integrity can improve cooperative efforts. Yet it
also introduces new vulnerabilities. Previous forms of cooperation have proven
benefits. When you ask people to integrate new values into a revised structure,
there's a risk things won't work out. The new benefits seem speculative and easily
outweighed if established benefits are jeopardized and new harms introduced.

You're forgetting what motivates us to practice the virtues in the first place.
The status quo may create benefits for some, but sometimes it creates harms
for others and ignores the well-being of still more people. That imbalance
is inherently unstable. Yes, there's risk in changing integrations that have
worked in the past. But there is also risk in defending structures justified only
by such a selective focus.

In the face of conflict people often adopt a me-against-the-world stance:
"How can *I* still get what *I* want—or am I going to have to compromise
something that's important to *me?*" Practicing the social virtues changes
this orientation. If I'm a responsible cooperator, it's not enough that I get
benefits. Once I make a commitment to an environment that promotes
mutual flourishing, I stop thinking in terms of us and them. Now I want
to know: What are the conditions under which we all can thrive? Staying

focused on mutual well-being rather than individual interest is at the core of creative courage.

Practicing inclusive integrity can create a virtuous cycle. Once other people believe that I'm serious about integrating their concerns into a project, conflict falls away.

Yes! When I make it clear that I'm committed to our mutual well-being rather than individual interest, my cooperative partners take a renewed interest in the success of our enterprise. And when I see them strengthening a project that matters to me, I'm inspired to step up my own efforts. It doesn't matter whether our mutual project is the successful market launch of a new product or a fund drive by a worthy charity or a treaty between two countries on the verge of conflict. If we can engage the talents and goodwill of all participants, we generate energy that contributes to the vitality of the entire community.

No question. It's wonderful to be part of an effort in which everyone works together for benefits that are truly mutual. We hope mutual benefits will be self-reinforcing, so the community is improved by the synergies cooperation yields. But then there are also stubborn cases where, despite our best efforts, harms persist and conflict seems inevitable.

Whatever our hopes, cooperative efforts always carry uncertainty and risk. We start with the premise that cooperation will create mutual benefits, but there's never any guarantee that this will happen. Maybe partners who played crucial roles in the past become unable or unwilling to support proposed improvements. Maybe the prospect of revising an existing cooperative structure puts established benefits at risk and introduces new vulnerabilities. Under such circumstances disagreements become more vehement and people grow discouraged.

No matter how much we want the benefits of cooperation, there will always be difficult questions with uncertain answers. Within what parameters must we stay to ensure safety? What are the indicators of success? What are the costs of action, or inaction? Are our cooperative partners trustworthy and capable of handling their assigned responsibilities? Will our efforts create disproportionate benefits for some or inadvertent harms for others? Will environments, either natural or social, change in ways that undermine our efforts?

Given all the ways our plans may fall apart, we need courage to stay committed to the cooperative enterprise. No cooperative effort stands a chance unless the participants embrace the risks of engagement. When we become aware that our hopes for mutual benefits are foundering, we must summon the courage to take on whatever risks are involved in restoring and strengthening social configurations that create genuine benefits for all willing cooperators.

Traditionally courage is regarded as a big, brash virtue—someone charging into a real or metaphorical battle.

That kind of courage comes into play when cooperation has broken down so badly that the only alternative is to go for broke and risk everything—including possibly one's life. Mayhem and destruction often result. The virtue I'm describing is different because it keeps our goal—cooperation for mutual benefit—firmly in mind. It's creative because it pushes us to envision and work toward circumstances in which everyone can thrive even in the face of imminent conflict. When we fix our sights on that prize, we can better assess our response to risk: Which actions are cowardly, which would be reckless, and which are creatively courageous?

Three Positions in the Cooperative Structure

We must also be aware that our responses and opportunities will vary depending on where we find ourselves in the cooperative structure. When unexpected harms occur and cooperation threatens to unravel, people tend to identify with one of three groups: those who are satisfied with the status quo, those who find themselves burdened with costs, and those who are largely unaffected.

Sometimes these characterizations seem fluid. Online, for example, parents worry that adult predators will victimize their children, even though peers are likely to be the ones involved in harassment. And most kids adopt multiple roles at one time or another: aggressor in one setting, victim in another. More often they are bystanders, distressed because they don't know what to do when they see someone bullied.

We tend to wish these boundaries were fixed, if only because firm boundaries help us determine responsibility in the face of harm. After a natural catastrophe, for example, people often look for villains: someone should have seen it coming; someone else profits after the fact. Even in less dire circumstances it's easy to complain about lazy bureaucrats, companies that exploit workers, schools that don't function, even family members who don't do their fair share. But in situations of chronic conflict things aren't that simple. If you earn a paycheck from a business that pollutes the water your family drinks, are you a beneficiary or a victim? If you buy products from that factory, are you a bystander or a beneficiary?

Our perspectives also change as we move from one environment to another. I may be harmed if my neighbor uses an herbicide that leaches into my well water; I may also belong to the homeowners' association whose rules forbid unsightly weeds. I may benefit if the value of my stock increases because a company underpays its workers, yet I may feel unfairly used if my property taxes go up to subsidize school lunches for those workers' children.

So response-ability will vary depending on where we stand in complicated situations.

It will, but regardless of which position we occupy we can exercise creative courage by knowing as much as possible about what is at stake and what we're able to risk. What resources—time, materials, energy, training, technology, and goodwill—are available to initiate or rescue a cooperative project? Because resources are not unlimited, our choices cannot be naïve or reckless. As we renovate existing cooperative structures to address newly discovered harms, we don't want to imperil the benefits those structures were originally designed to deliver. As environments change, we must continually assess what's at stake. What benefits are still being created? Are our goals worthy? What harms have been brought to our attention? How can they be alleviated?

Three practices help us answer these questions, making it more likely that—regardless of our perspective on a given conflict—we will recognize and take legitimate risks on behalf of the community of responsible cooperators:

1. Address the failing hypothesis.
2. Confront imbalanced benefits without undue blame.
3. Hold tight to the cooperative vision.

This is where the rubber meets the road. Backing away from risk when the goal is worthy is cowardly. Taking on more risk than the goal warrants is reckless. If we hope to strengthen the cooperative systems on which we all depend, we must use creative courage to identify risks that are both justified and necessary.

1. Address the failing hypothesis

As we've discussed, every cooperative effort is a hypothesis. Motivated by compassion, we discern multiple values and imagine cooperative systems within which we can integrate those values into a coherent, cooperative routine. But no matter how conscientiously we practice the social virtues, some cooperative projects simply don't work out the way we hoped.

We've talked about many of the reasons a hypothesis might fail. Our partners disappoint us or disengage from the project. Technologies fail to deliver as promised. Procedures for coordination are too vague or ambiguous to implement. Or environments change in ways we didn't anticipate.

We may also find that a certain form of cooperation has outlived its usefulness. Think about classes that teach students skills that are now obsolete or government programs targeting problems that are no longer urgent. In other cases the reasons for cooperating may still be valid, but changes in the environment make the means questionable.

In the 1980s, for example, the Reagan administration responded to deep inadequacies and even abuses in institutionalized care for people with mental illnesses such as schizophrenia or bipolar disorder. New laws and regulations shifted resources toward smaller residential facilities. In that deinstitutionalized environment law enforcement officers were often the first to interact with people whose deviant behaviors attracted public attention. Encounters led to warnings and repeated warnings led to incarceration. Eventually persons with mental health issues became a significant portion of the prison population. In some communities social service specialists began to lobby for additional training for a specialized cadre of police officers who could handle such confrontations. Officers learned to deescalate conflict, prevent violence, and direct mentally ill people to agencies where they could get needed services.

The initial impulse was a compassionate effort to address harms created by institutionalization. But putting mentally ill people into the community changed the environment, especially for police officers. Standard law enforcement procedure sent some people with mental problems to prisons — institutions even less able to provide appropriate care.

In this case both social service and law enforcement agencies got better results by tweaking their procedures. Humans are inveterate tinkerers; when we're attached to an existing form of cooperation, our first inclination when new harms arise is to make little fixes. Such small adjustments sometimes address the harms while preserving the benefits of the original plan. We put sanitizer dispensers in lavatories when we realize that microbes are prevalent in that environment. We install air circulation systems in libraries when we discover that closely packed books are at risk of disintegration from mold or the acid in their paper. We make accounting procedures more transparent when it becomes clear that murky practices make it easy to misappropriate funds. Such creative tweaks—which are the product of intentional imagination — may get cooperative projects back on track.

It's extremely satisfying (and potentially lucrative) when an applied researcher, entrepreneur, or official can design a product, service, or practice that responds to newly understood vulnerabilities.

The Limits of Knowledge

But sometimes we can't tinker our way out of our problems. And then we have to admit that a cherished hypothesis has proved false. Think about a parent who's convinced that learning to play the piano will enrich her child's life. Her intentions may be excellent, but every child develops differently, and there's no way to know in advance what's going to be best for this particular kid. If she clings to her hypothesis, parent and child may soon find themselves locked into destructive battles over piano practice.

The further we get into a plan, the more we become attached to hopeful outcomes. As we invest in any form of cooperation, we may forget that it began as a hypothesis and begin to believe that the plan must create benefits simply because we have poured so much effort into it. We practice creative courage by regularly reminding ourselves that anticipated benefits might not materialize, and a trend towards unanticipated harms may prove overwhelming.

It's not easy to acknowledge a false start. The parent in your example may have invested in a piano as well as lessons. It takes courage to step back from the original hypothesis and find a wiser way to secure the benefits music lessons were supposed to provide.

In larger institutions, too, people are called upon to restructure in the face of a failing hypothesis. Take the case of JCPenney, a veteran retailer that faced a precipitous decline in market share early in the twenty-first century. Ron Johnson, brought on as CEO in 2011, had developed highly successful retail strategies for Apple and Target; the JCPenney board hypothesized that he was a flexible specialist who could imagine ways to develop new markets and turn their company around. For his part, Johnson hypothesized that installing multiple boutiques within each JCPenney store would appeal to current customers and attract new upscale shoppers.

As it turned out, his plan alienated existing customers and failed to attract new ones. Seventeen months and millions of dollars later, the JCPenney board concluded that their hypothesis had failed, and Johnson's contract was terminated. The board practiced creative courage by assessing the situation honestly and acknowledging that their promising plans weren't adequately addressing harms, much less creating benefits.

Such failures strike at the heart of the cooperative bargain. We did X. You did Y. Lots of other people put in time, labor, and other resources. Yet benefits aren't forthcoming.

People heavily invested in a given structure, specialists in particular, often defend it because they've poured their hearts into the work and followed best practice. In truth, "best practice" should always carry an asterisk because it's "best" as developed out of knowledge base B, in conditions C, for people aiming at goal G. Best practice needs constant review and revision as new information comes to light, new environments emerge, and new goals come into focus. We must constantly acknowledge the limits of what we knew when we developed our hypothesis.

Even the most knowledgeable specialists have areas of ignorance that may lead to a faulty and potentially harmful hypothesis. Firefighters are a dramatic example. Despite their rigorous training, they know that every fire is unpredictable. Even familiar natural environments can change because winds may shift and variations in terrain and vegetation may affect the rate at which a forest dries out. Social environments also change: buildings from different eras are constructed and wired differently. At different times, a company may store supplies that are more or less flammable. All these variables create unknowns and heighten risk.

Firefighters must use available information to formulate a hypothesis about an effective strategy for each fire. What are the features of the environment where the fire is burning? How far has the fire progressed? How hot is it? What combustible material is within the fire's reach? But no matter how skilled the firefighters are, this knowledge is limited, so they must be ready to adjust swiftly as new vulnerabilities appear. It would be cowardly to simply abandon the effort to put out the fire, but it would be reckless to persist in a strategy that has stopped working. Firefighters need creative courage as they assess when and how to make such adjustments.

Getting Past the Defensive Response

Aren't we most willing to address a failing hypothesis when we are the ones at risk? If a cooperative structure is still working for me, I'm likely to resist the idea that it should be reorganized.

Certainly when we're enjoying benefits from a cooperative system, it's much more challenging — yet necessary — to acknowledge that the same system is harming others. Most of us think of ourselves as decent people who care about the welfare of all. So if other people accuse us of benefiting from a cooperative plan at their expense, our first reaction is likely to be defensive: "This works for me. I'm sorry if it doesn't work for you, but that's really not my problem."

We may also be tempted to dismiss or minimize problems identified by others: "Why are you bringing that up now? In the context of what we're doing, that problem is insignificant. You're making a mountain out of a molehill." It may seem inconvenient or downright risky to acknowledge the perspective of those who claim to have been harmed by what we're doing.

However understandable these reactions may be, we violate the terms of the cooperative agreement if some people are harmed so we can enjoy benefits. We practice creative courage by setting aside our defensive, self-justifying responses and seriously considering how to rework the cooperative structure to alleviate harms and expand benefits.

If we push people to acquiesce to arrangements that create benefits for us but not for them, we're in danger of becoming predatory.

Yes, and there's this too: If we're in the fortunate position of enjoying benefits created by cooperation, we have access to resources that aren't available to others. That gives us response-ability, and we must exercise it to strengthen the cooperative system. When we discover that our hypothesis about mutual benefits is faulty, we must be prepared to risk time, energy, and other resources to correct it. If we're embedded in a cooperative system that works for us, response-ability calls us to stake our capital against whatever harms others endure, to restore the mutuality of benefits.

People in this position may face very real risks if they insist that attention be paid to harms, especially if others are reluctant to acknowledge those harms.

True — and this debate can occur internally when dual roles put us in an ambivalent position. A researcher who gets a paycheck from a drug company needs courage to draw attention to newly detected side effects caused by a popular and profitable drug. A salesman whose bonuses depend on writing more mortgages practices creative courage by calling out company guidelines that encourage loans to people who won't be able to repay them. A politician who takes campaign contributions from a factory owner exercises creative courage in voting for legislation that will regulate pollution from that factory.

It may be tempting to ignore a problem when you're a bystander in the situation, neither a victim of harm nor responsible for causing it. But that's a misreading of how complex and interconnected we are. Think about our justice system, which depends on every citizen being equal before the law. After several high-profile incidents in which unarmed black citizens were killed by police officers, white citizens began to question the evenhandedness of law enforcement. Even though their own experiences with the police may have been positive, it became harder for white people to have confidence in the system once they became aware of how often black citizens suffer harm when interacting with police.

Cooperation fails if benefits no longer appear mutual, so we all need to be looking out for each other. It's not enough for me to be safe and secure if the disengaged way I live contributes to undermining other people's potential.

Taking Risks to Restore Mutual Benefits

Whenever we become aware that cooperative structures benefiting us also cause harms, even inadvertently, we must risk our own assets to repair the social fabric. At the personal level this often happens spontaneously. A spouse who has said harsh things during an argument may attempt to heal the hurt by spending time on a special meal or money on an unexpected gift. Even in these situations creative courage is required. You know you need to remediate harm, but you can't be sure how your overture will be received.

The same principle applies to companies, countries, and other social institutions. They too must take courageous action if it becomes clear that well-intentioned practices and policies have caused harm. One leader who did so is the innovative businessman Ray Anderson, who in the 1970s built Interface, a very successful carpet company that produced modular carpet tiles for commercial buildings. The carpet was made from petrochemicals, which release fumes during manufacture and after installation. The tiles also created disposal problems, adding toxic bulk to landfills. Like other executives, Anderson accepted these environmental costs because he was focused on the company's bottom line and the benefits his company produced for customers, employees, and shareholders.

When the benefits are genuine, the focus seems legitimate.

But the harms were also genuine. Anderson made this connection in 1994 when he read Paul Hawken's *The Ecology of Commerce*. Suddenly he became aware that the company he had so carefully nurtured was implicated in a wide range of destructive practices. His recollection of that moment was dramatic: "I got it. I was a plunderer of Earth, and that is not the legacy one wants to leave behind."

At that point Anderson saw his current business model as a failed hypothesis, and compassion motivated him to take action. He discerned the crucial values: running a profitable company and minimizing the harms created by toxic chemicals. He applied intentional imagination to every aspect of the company and implemented new integrations that promised to create benefits while reducing harms. Products were redesigned to minimize toxins; processes were reconceived to promote recycling and reduce wastes. Most dramatically, Interface stopped *selling* carpet. Instead they leased their products, maintaining control so they could reuse the fibers once the carpet tiles wore out. The company remained profitable as Anderson courageously and creatively incorporated these newly understood values into the company's mission and operation.

It sounds as though Anderson had a sort of conversion experience. When he read Hawken, he realized how his company was implicated in harms. As CEO he had response-ability, and he exercised creative courage by reworking a failed hypothesis, turning Interface into a contemporary model of both profitability and environmental responsibility.

When we discover that the existing environment tilts the game in our favor, it takes creative courage to put our own assets on the line.

The Courage to Step Away

There are also situations in which an existing cooperative structure simply cannot be repaired or salvaged. We may be very attached to the benefits we hoped to achieve, but even our most imaginative efforts aren't working. A local charity collapses after the sudden death of its founder. A new technology dries up the market for a product crucial to another company's bottom line. A spouse abandons the family. A hypothesis about successful cooperation may be utterly refuted when goals are beyond reach, a changed environment makes goals irrelevant, or a crucial partner proves unreliable.

In situations like these we're tempted to give in to anger, bitterness, or even despair. All that effort for nothing! It's easy to see how people might lash out or give up.

Creative courage points us in a different direction. When any particular means of cooperation fails to produce mutual benefits, we need to become more deliberate about looking for other ways cooperation can fulfill its promise. What vulnerabilities remain? What values endure? What resources have been freed up?

Yes, we will feel discouraged because we had high hopes for our original plan. But now it's time to step back so we can discern what's really worth defending. This isn't a matter of abandoning our cooperating partners. We need to survey the damages created by our failed hypothesis so we can attend to pain and address immediate risks. At the same time we must also reassess our goals so we can identify new cooperative possibilities, enlist willing collaborators, and seek out enabling resources.

This is the difficult realization of couples that decide to divorce or nonprofits that disband or companies that decide to sell or close a division.

When things fall apart, even small efforts to create benefits through cooperation can make a big difference. Not only do you reaffirm your intention to be a responsible cooperator, but you also open up possibilities for others. Let's say that a divorced parent invites former in-laws to a birthday party. This invitation acknowledges the constructive role grandparents can continue to play with their grandchildren.

Or maybe the director of the failed nonprofit actively helps people from the defunct organization find new positions that will utilize their talents. Or she shares insights about harms to be avoided with organizations that have a similar mission. In this way she minimizes the scope of the "failure" in the hypothesis and continues her commitment to fruitful collaboration whenever it's possible.

A company that has to lay off workers can provide counseling or training that will help workers find new positions. And the workers themselves can open up to new ways of cooperating with colleagues, family members, and the community at large.

Such actions strengthen the larger cooperative community and may even change the environment in ways that make our original goals more feasible. Remember that children's game called pick-up sticks? After the sticks are scattered on the table, you try to remove one without jostling the others. Sometimes one stick seems totally stuck — until an adjacent stick is moved. In the same way, actively looking for new ways to promote mutual thriving changes the environment in ways that may even allow us eventually to revisit our original hypothesis.

I see how it's courageous to admit that a plan we care about has failed in some fundamental way. How should we handle situations in which some people insist on defending a plan that creates benefits for them even though it also creates harms for others?

Cooperation unravels when benefits are imbalanced. Understanding this leads us to regularly apply the social virtues. Regardless of whether we are beneficiaries, victims, or bystanders in an arrangement, we look for ways to be sure that all willing cooperators enjoy proportionate benefits and don't suffer undue harms. Unfortunately people do lose track of this fundamental premise of cooperation. The second practice that promotes creative courage insists that imbalances be addressed without assuming predatory intentions.

2. Confront imbalanced benefits without undue blame

Sometimes people become entirely focused on benefits that cooperation produces for them and become indifferent or oblivious to harms imposed on others. They may be predators, very aware that they are exploiting others. More often they are simply self-involved and unwilling to acknowledge their place in the social fabric. They may be driven by fear of losing what they have, or they may believe, for whatever reasons, that they're entitled to more consideration than others.

George Orwell aptly summed up this failing in his famous quote: "All animals are equal. But some animals are more equal than others."

Whatever the motivation, this situation contains enormous risk. People quickly lose interest in the cooperative bargain if it seems that, even if they do their part, they aren't going to get what's important to them. This feeling fuels the anger that's become so prominent in American politics. As the middle class shrinks, many Americans suspect that the cooperative bargain at the heart of the American dream may be corrupted by people who claim an excess share of benefits.

This sense of imbalance is often at the heart of stubborn conflicts. Both sides are intransigent because they are convinced that benefits for others come at their expense.

The Costs of Exclusion

In persistent conflicts, people who have more power may decide that the best way to protect their interests is to circle the wagons. In the Middle Ages people built walls around towns. Even in the twenty-first century, gated communities are built to keep out perceived predators. And human history is filled with stories of people who tried to limit vulnerability by shrinking the group eligible for cooperative benefits.

Discrimination in various forms is another way of restricting benefits to people we feel we can trust because they are like us. As recently as the middle of the last century women were discouraged from getting a college education because it would be "wasted" if they got married and raised children. In college towns today, local governments often resist participation by students because college kids "don't care" or "won't be around long enough" to make a positive difference. Such exclusionary strategies are invariably defended as the best way to protect benefits for a core group, such as men in the workforce or taxpayers in the college town.

But these arguments obscure the larger truth: benefits are more likely to multiply when the network of cooperators is expanded. Exclusion always carries costs. At minimum the community misses out on the very real contributions that educated women and engaged college students might make. In my town, for example, local officials have been receptive to initiatives by college students who wanted to collect and recycle carryout containers made of cardboard, glass, or plastic. By treating students as full-fledged partners the entire community can enjoy benefits, including reduced pressure on the local landfill and lower disposal costs for local businesses.

Exclusion also sacrifices the resilience that comes from examining problems from various perspectives. Again and again we've seen that the most imaginative solutions to conflict often come from people whose point of view enables them to spot resources invisible to others.

In addition to forgoing benefits, communities that exclude people who want to enjoy the benefits of cooperation expose themselves to significant harms. This truth was at the heart of uprisings in the Middle East during the Arab Spring of 2011. The systems that produced benefits for insiders in those countries created large and escalating harms for people outside the power structure. When people feel victimized they may try to evade those who seem to be taking advantage. If what they value seems to be under assault, they may feel they have no choice but to actively and strenuously defend what matters to them. Sure enough, citizens of many Middle Eastern countries took to the streets to express their unhappiness at being excluded from the benefits of cooperation.

Whenever they can, people resist social arrangements that exploit them so others can benefit. When situations become adversarial, attention shifts away from the benefits that cooperation might create and toward outmaneuvering perceived predators. Initially people on both sides may think, "If conflict arises, we'll just have to put up with it." Before long that changes to "There *will* be conflict, and we'll simply have to bear its costs because the alternative—giving up on what matters to us—is unacceptable." Instead of looking for ways to increase benefits, both sides may become resigned to harms.

I see how tempting it is to subvert a system that seems rigged against you. I remember how, during the mortgage crisis of 2008, some homeowners simply walked away from mortgages because they couldn't see any way to pay the bank and provide for their families.

In that unfortunate situation cooperation collapsed. Ordinarily the partnership between a bank and a prospective homeowner creates obvious benefits: the bank earns a return on the money it loans, and a family gets a stable place to live. When banks started making loans to subprime lenders and then packaging those loans to sell to investors, the environment changed in ways not entirely understood by banks or borrowers. Instead of imagining creative ways to maintain cooperative benefits in the changed environment, bankers and homeowners became adversaries, each determined to protect their benefits at the expense of the other party.

This kind of defensive response usually stimulates adversaries to become even more aggressive. Computer code that's supposed to prevent malicious viruses spurs hackers to create even more devious code. Antibiotics developed to snuff out microbes stimulate the evolution of superbugs. A stockpile of weapons meant to deter aggression creates anxieties that lead other countries to assemble an even bigger stockpile. In situations like these you wind up with an arms race that's likely to escalate until one side runs out of resources — or both sides are left in ruins.

Improve Prospects by Extracting Blame

Are you suggesting that people suck it up and ignore people who are benefiting at their expense?

Absolutely not. Using power to extract disproportionate benefits from other people is predatory, and those exploited are right to resist such arrangements. Obviously we shouldn't continue to cooperate with partners who consistently coopt disproportionate benefits for themselves. Better to disengage as soon as possible and, where appropriate, turn to the legal system for remedies. We all have an interest in punishing exploitive practices because they undermine the agreement at the heart of cooperation.

However, those who feel victimized must also consider the possibility that behavior that looks predatory may arise from ignorance and narrow focus. We practice creative courage when we give our adversaries the benefit of the doubt, staying engaged even when they seem indifferent or hostile to our concerns. We face the real risk that the other party is a genuine predator who intends to benefit at our expense. Yet in the absence of clear-cut evidence, we deliberately embrace that risk by holding in mind two seemingly contradictory principles:

we must protest imbalances in burdens and benefits and we must affirm the value of cooperation. It would be cowardly to acquiesce in social arrangements that run roughshod over the values of people who lack power. And it's reckless to disregard the benefits that can be created only through cooperation. If at all possible we want to assume that even those who look like exploiters want to be cooperators.

As I recall, John Stuart Mill talked about the idea of "innocent error." Sometimes harms occur even when people act in good faith. There's no point in assigning blame, because no one set out to cause the problem.

Mill is talking about situations in which unhappy consequences result from sincere efforts to do what's right or to pursue novel opportunities. If the outcome really was unforeseeable, given what the agent could know at the time, condemning the effort may be satisfying but doesn't resolve the problem. It's more helpful to point out the undesirable outcome and work toward improving results. By extracting blame from the process we can open up space for beneficiaries to acknowledge their regrets, then proceed with revising cooperative arrangements to prevent future harms.

Even when it seems clear that one party's action has caused or contributed to harm, victims and bystanders practice creative courage by assuming that apparent beneficiaries will be unhappy with the result once harms are brought to their attention. We want to appeal to the person's sense of response-ability: given the kind of person you are, you'll obviously want to take steps to correct what's happened and put a stop to the harm.

Hospitals take this approach with morbidity-and-mortality committees. When something bad happens to a patient, the committee investigates. The intention is not necessarily to assign blame, though blame may be appropriate if culpable ignorance, willful negligence, or malfeasance were involved. More often the goal is to learn from adverse experience. How did specialists coordinate or not? What can we do differently next time? Refusing to demonize the other parties in a dispute is a way of practicing creative courage.

This form of courage seems powerful because it enlists the goodwill of people who are in a position to make changes.

People accused of creating harms or taking undeserved benefits will naturally defend themselves. They resist apology because it implies liability. So, lacking evidence to the contrary, it's better to assume that harms are unintended. In many cases this is a reasonable assumption because people don't come with identical values, priorities, and judgments. Each of us has a specific set of life experiences, formed in certain environments. Our differences are built in, and even the most well-intentioned cooperative partners sometimes surprise, puzzle, or disappoint each other. Instead of pushing people who look like exploiters into a defensive posture, we may be able to draw them back into the cooperative process by assuming that they too want an outcome that produces benefits for everyone involved.

Of course, some beneficiaries seem blind to the possibility that their benefits come at the expense of others.

Speaking Truth to Power

Sometimes beneficiaries defend their privileges because they can't step outside their own point of view. Their biases may make them deeply resistant to the perspective of those who claim to be victims. In such cases bystanders can play an important role by confronting beneficiaries in a way that draws them back into genuine cooperation.

My favorite example of this kind of creative courage comes from the Bible. When David became king in Israel, the idea of political organization beyond the clan was just emerging. In societies of that place and time, kings were tyrants who made and enforced laws. With no separation of powers there was no way to challenge the king. He was above the law.

David fell in love with Bathsheba, a very beautiful woman who was the wife of Uriah, a soldier in David's army. While Uriah was deployed, David impregnated Bathsheba. When David learned of the pregnancy, he realized that his subjects wouldn't be happy with a king who slept with a loyal soldier's wife. He urged Uriah to go home to visit his wife so it would seem plausible the child was his. But Uriah was such a loyal soldier that he refused to take comfort from his family while his fellow soldiers fought. His tactic foiled, David encouraged his generals to send Uriah to the front line, where he was predictably killed.

This seems like a very obvious case in which all the benefits are on one side and all the harms on the other.

By sleeping with Uriah's wife and then manipulating his death, David disrupted the agreement at the heart of a cooperative society: benefits must be mutual. Even the king should not exploit citizens, especially by bringing about the death of a soldier-citizen. Nathan, a prophet in Israel, understood the Mosaic traditions of right and wrong that predated the kingship, and he recognized wickedness when he saw it.

Obviously Nathan would be taking a serious risk in confronting David. The person who had taken disproportionate benefits and engineered undeserved harm also had absolute power. Even if the king didn't impose his wrath, he could simply ignore Nathan. There was, after all, no court of appeal. Beyond Nathan's passion and willingness to speak out, the society provided no mechanism for holding David accountable.

Nathan faced the risk of speaking truth to power.

Knowing that a direct accusation was likely to make David defensive and possibly vengeful, Nathan told the king a story: Once upon a time there was a simple shepherd who lived next door to a rich man. The rich man had many flocks of sheep, but the shepherd had one lamb, and he loved it with all his heart. One day guests came to visit the rich man. Instead of butchering a sheep from his own flocks, the rich man served the guests his neighbor's lamb.

David was outraged. His compassion was awakened, and he responded viscerally to the shepherd's vulnerability. That sort of behavior should be punished, and as king he had the power to punish. He demanded that Nathan name the culprit. That's when Nathan looked him in the eye and said, "You are that man."

I love the way Nathan changed the dynamics of an impossible situation by telling a story. It's such an effective way of getting David to imagine another person's point of view.

Nathan's crucial insight was that David thought of himself as a moral man — a cooperator, who wouldn't exploit vulnerability. When he engaged David's sympathies with a story about the abuse of power, he also activated David's sense of integrity. The king's defenses were down because he thought he was a bystander listening to a story. When it turned out to be his story, he couldn't avoid judgment, because in his outrage he had already pronounced it.

Standing Up for the Good of the Community

Nathan's action also captures the power of those who practice creative courage on behalf of the larger community. Nathan could have ignored David's misdeeds, because he wasn't directly involved. Instead he was motivated by compassion because someone had been harmed. He discerned the apparently conflicting values: On the one hand, the king's power benefits the community in that he takes responsibility for maintaining social order. On the other hand, citizens must be protected from abuse of authority. Then Nathan used imagination to tell a story that brought the values into coherence.

And he certainly practiced creative courage when he announced, "You are that man."

These days harms are more often created by complex networks than by powerful individuals. Standing up to those networks requires enormous courage because these networks invariably create benefits — including jobs, services, products, and profits — as well as harms. Rachel Carson began to understand these networks during World War II. Trained as a naturalist, she had long shared a common assumption of her era: that the vastness of the natural world made it impervious to human action. She wrote hugely popular books about the natural world, particularly the marine world.

During the war Carson worked for the government, using her scientific background to synthesize and publicize the contributions of fellow scientists. At that point she began to see a pattern in their research. Chemicals that were benign in small quantities caused serious problems when they accumulated in natural environments. Pesticides used by farmers to protect crops from insects were changing the genetics of the pests they hoped to eradicate. Fertilizer applied to increase yields was running off into rivers and changing the environment of the sea itself. Antibiotics, created by medical researchers to cure common diseases, were encouraging more virulent pathogens.

In the process of creating genuine benefits, human actions were also creating enormous unintended hazards.

Carson's ongoing correspondence with scores of scientists in different disciplines allowed her to recognize clear and disturbing trends. Changes in social environments, including farms, factories, and laboratories, were eroding the vitality of natural ecosystems. It would take years of patient science to pinpoint the mechanisms of these changes. Some were physical: accumulations of minerals, diffusion of light, concentrations of anthropogenic chemicals. Some were biological: the introduction of exotics, vulnerabilities created by monoculture, resistance to pathogens.

But even without the benefit of these details Carson knew she had to sound the alarm. Although she was struggling with breast cancer, she synthesized the research from a vast network of scientists and exercised creative courage to describe a destructive trajectory. In the early pages of *Silent Spring* she follows Nathan's lead, telling a story so disturbing that an entire generation was forced to see the consequences of its actions.

Predictably, experts who were attached to the benefits derived from standard practices dismissed her findings. Carson would not be deterred, though. Even after her cancer had metastasized she testified before Congress, insisting that we needed to rework existing forms of cooperation in the face of potentially catastrophic environmental changes.

Nathan confronted a king. Carson testified before Congress. Most of us don't operate on such a grand scale.

But we practice creative courage whenever we speak up on behalf of those who are unfairly disadvantaged by the way a cooperative system is organized. Maybe we defend students who score poorly on standardized tests that fail to take cultural differences into account. Or we object to excluding committed gay couples from benefits enjoyed by heterosexual couples. Or we protest the tax code that allows professional football teams to enjoy the benefits of nonprofits.

Such protests require courage because the people who benefit from the arrangements are powerful and likely to push back. Our goal, however, is not simply to engage them as adversaries. If we are to restore the benefits of cooperation, we need to be creative about converting adversaries into allies who will use their advantages to restore a balance of benefits.

This seems like a lot to ask.

Practicing the social virtues requires an ongoing commitment to the good that can come only through cooperative effort. Think about what Nathan and Rachel Carson had in common. Even when things looked very dark, they didn't give up. Like Winston Churchill in World War II, they scoured their circumstances for every resource they could imagine or invent. They enlisted whatever allies they could recruit and searched for new social synergies. They simply refused to give up on the promise of cooperation even when things looked very dark — and this brings us to our third practice.

3. Hold tight to the cooperative vision

The third practice of creative courage is simple to describe and extremely difficult to carry out. As you'll recall, the cooperative premise has three parts: 1. I do my part. 2. You (and millions of others) do your parts. 3. We are all better off.

In complex interconnected systems, however, things can go wrong at every stage. So far we've discussed how creative courage can address the risk of breakdown when our hypothesis about mutual benefit is mistaken (part three) and when some of our partners enjoy benefits without doing their fair share or by imposing costs on others (part two).

Now we must go back to part one. Given all the ways cooperation can unravel, it's often tempting to give up — to decide that doing my part is just too tough. But regardless of what others do or what negative externalities emerge, we must persist in looking for ways to cooperate. We practice creative courage by staying committed to the role of the consistent, reliable cooperator, no matter what position we currently occupy in the benefits equation. We accept the risk of doing whatever we are able to do, exercising response-ability wherever we can, hoping but never certain that our efforts will contribute to an environment in which everyone can thrive.

People give up on cooperation for several reasons. They may feel they're doing more than their fair share. Or they are overwhelmed by change. Or their contribution feels small and insignificant.

Creative courage entails facing these complexities head on, staying committed to the larger vision of what cooperation makes possible even when it seems to unravel in specific circumstances. Let's address each of the three concerns you've just mentioned.

Accept the Risk of Imperfect Partners

Counting on other people is always risky, particularly in complex networks that require many specialized partners to coordinate. Hundreds of people were involved in building the car I drive, growing the food I eat, and making the medications I swallow each morning. I count on them even though I don't know them. Thousands of others have agreed to play a role in educating my grandchildren, identifying toxins in the environment, or working out trade agreements with other countries. I trust them to be conscientious about what they do, and they in turn trust me to do my specialized part.

Trust always carries the risk of betrayal. When we work together in families, schools, faith communities, businesses, and governments, we will sometimes feel that others have failed to live up to the terms of some cooperative agreement. And they may feel likewise about us. Human beings don't always execute their responsibilities flawlessly. And when we're focused on benefits that are obvious from our specialized point of view, we can lose track of what matters to other people. We practice creative courage by refusing to retreat to our respective corners. We start with the dual hypotheses that any betrayal is unintended, and that our partners want the benefits of cooperation just as much as we do.

Can't we minimize the risks of cooperation by working with known partners?

Certainly. On any given day my wife and I may disagree. Even after years of cooperation we occupy different vantage points formed by gender, family background, education, experience, friendship, and so on. Still, our long history of cooperation gives me confidence that we'll find a solution with genuinely mutual benefits. The same idea holds in other settings. Partners in a law firm may feel more confident about hiring graduates of schools they attended. On the international level, countries that have enjoyed the benefits of trade over time are more likely to work peacefully through other disputes. Choosing familiar partners extracts some of the risk from cooperative ventures.

But that strategy is limited. In today's complex environments we're often called on to interact with people we don't know directly or whose values don't seem to have any relationship to ours. In some cooperative efforts we become entangled with others unintentionally because our actions had an adverse impact on them. Corporate efforts to maintain quality by establishing standards may make it impossible for franchisees to succeed in local markets. Local governments may find it difficult to implement mandates enacted by well-intentioned state lawmakers. A developer may feel blindsided by the objections of environmentalists, while the environmentalists feel threatened by the developer's plans.

Respectful Engagement

Whenever we encounter people who seem antagonistic toward our values, it's tempting to retreat back into the safety of a community that reinforces our point of view. That's precisely when we need courage creative enough to imagine the world from other points of view. We expand benefits when we expand the pool of cooperators. Taking a compassionate and discerning interest in the viewpoints of others is the best way to encourage them to become responsible cooperative partners.

Persuading someone that you care about what matters to them is especially difficult if one person or group feels their values have been disregarded in the past.

Feeling exploited or betrayed in a cooperative relationship is a difficult reality to come to terms with. What happened in the past isn't what you wanted. Under some circumstances people may need to grieve for what they've lost. This painful process becomes a little easier if those who benefited from the dynamic acknowledge past harms and commit to practices that will prevent future harms.

This was the insight of Nelson Mandela. Despite South Africa's long record of racial animosity, he sensed that many in the white community were uncomfortable with the privileges they had enjoyed under apartheid at the expense of black people and would welcome an opportunity to make things right. It took truly creative courage to enlist former adversaries as allies, establishing the Truth and Reconciliation Commission so both blacks and whites could bear witness to the systematic harms caused by an unjust social structure. Taking harms seriously is often the first step toward repairing trust and restoring cooperation for mutual benefits. Without such acknowledgment, opportunities for cooperation may be foreclosed by unresolved anger and suspicion.

Reparations made to black South Africans transformed apologies from the white community into more than lip service. Sincere apology paves the way to forgiveness. Renewed cooperation is possible once people feel that, regardless of what's happened in the past, their values are now being taken seriously.

Don't Be Overwhelmed by Change

Even when cooperative partners can overcome distrust, people may be tempted to give up on cooperation in changing, unsettled environments. As we struggle to find integrations that create mutual benefits, we will adopt and abandon goals, discover or exhaust resources, discard or become adept at using tools. These variables always introduce uncertainty and risk into our interactions, but they are especially disruptive when environments are changing rapidly, giving rise to inadvertent and unpredicted harms. Commitments made in one set of circumstances may seem inappropriate or irrelevant in changed circumstances. We may even question the desirability of the benefits we were trying to secure. We practice creative courage by facing these complexities head on.

When I become aware of a new project that's likely to bring changes in my community, I try to attend the earliest planning meetings. These sessions are invariably tedious and complicated because experts are trying to figure out how to integrate known values into a changing landscape. The specialists may be well intentioned, but they have a finite list of values in mind and probably haven't thought through all the ways their plans could go awry, especially in our local setting. If I want what I value to be part of the integration, I must be willing to invest time and patience, knowing that there may not be much to show for it.

Risking those personal resources is a way of practicing creative courage.

When environments are in flux, social coordinations are undefined and nebulous. At that point it's especially important to stay involved, anticipating harms and speaking up from our point of view. When college students proposed ways of expanding recycling in downtown Bowling Green, I thought that encouraging young people to do something constructive in the community was obviously a good idea. This value wasn't as clear to others who lacked my perspective as a professor, so I made an effort to participate in early discussions. The values we hold most dear often seem so evident to us that we may not grasp the need to articulate them for others. When change is unfolding we have an obligation to strengthen cooperative structures by speaking up about vulnerabilities and benefits visible from our unique point of view.

Speaking out invariably requires courage, especially if you're confronting specialists who are attached to practices that have worked in the past or who have alliances with familiar partners. You have to do the hard work of clarifying what's important from your point of view. You may need to recruit allies, dig out research, or uncover case histories that bolster your argument. Most of all you need to maintain a cooperative stance that acknowledges existing values while insisting on values not yet integrated into the plan.

People are more likely to be disadvantaged by social arrangements when they don't participate in negotiations as early as possible. Once cooperators settle on a plan that creates benefits for some parties, it's harder to insist on revisions.

Unfortunately, this happens more often than it should. Sometimes people are left out because they're invisible to those devising the integrations or because no one understands their point of view. In other cases specialists may wrongly assume they don't need to consult a particular group because they are the ones who know "best practice." But when environments are changing, best practice has to change too.

I had the opportunity to think deeply about this problem several years ago when I served on a team evaluating the response to oil spills. Staff members at the National Oceanic and Atmospheric Administration understood that there was an ethical dimension to restoring the environment after a spill, so they asked for input from an ethicist. In oil spills—and in other fast-moving environmental events—the response generally has two phases. The short-term objective is to minimize harm. Experts in the spill containment network know what their jobs are, what equipment is needed, how to coordinate teams of specialists, and how to respond to environmental variations such as channeled currents and wave patterns. Input from the public is minimal because speed is essential and everyone agrees that containment is the goal.

In one oil spill off our local coast in California, officials actually asked concerned citizens not to show up on the beaches because they made it more difficult for experts to do their jobs.

The second phase is restoration, which unfolds more gradually after the precipitous change has occurred. At first it might seem that the goal for this phase is obvious: restore the environment to what it was before the spill. As our team examined cases, however, it became apparent that replication isn't always possible. After a major spill the physical environment is out of equi-librium for five to ten years, but more immediate needs confront the human community. People can't simply go into hibernation. Fishermen have to feed their families. Businesses that depend on tourism close their doors. The lon-ger a cleanup takes, the less likely it is that a community can be reassembled as it was before the disaster.

That's what happened to New Orleans after Katrina. Many people simply moved away and started new lives elsewhere.

Even if you could stop the clock in these situations, there are serious ques-tions experts simply cannot answer without significant input from the people directly involved. What if the quality of the community before the catastrophe wasn't great? Does it make sense to "restore" a dilapidated community? And if not, who pays for improvements? What if some peo-ple liked things as they were before and others didn't? Who decides what qualifies as improvement?

Staying engaged in these conversations isn't easy. A mutually beneficial plan for restoration must integrate concerns that become obvious only in the wake of the crisis. Insurance companies may pay for a rebuild only if it minimizes the risk of repeated catastrophe. Rather than try to reintegrate people into their former environment, governments may underwrite reloca-tions that match willing workers with job opportunities. Participants must practice creative courage, risking time and effort to sort out what was valu-able about the old environment while looking for ways to thrive in the new one. When outcomes are uncertain, staying connected to the cooperative process becomes even more crucial.

Collective Courage

I think people often disengage from cooperative efforts because they feel there's little they can do.

We often assume our individual efforts will be insignificant, especially if a problem doesn't directly affect us. The fallacy of this thinking is captured in an old story about a village that was planning a celebration. Town leaders asked villagers each to contribute a cup of milk to a vat to make a pudding everyone could share, but when the vat was sampled it contained nothing but water. The cooperative benefit of a delicious pudding became impossible because each villager decided his little bit of milk wouldn't make a difference.

It's natural to hang back when we can't be sure our efforts will make a difference. And certainly we need to be selective about how we expend scarce resources such as time, energy, money, and specialized knowledge, for which there will always be competing claims. Creative courage rises above these concerns. Instead of pleading insignificance we should always look for situations where we can exercise response-ability. What talents and resources can we risk to foster environments in which everyone can thrive? Where can we find allies who will expand our effectiveness?

This reminds me of the "stone soup" story, where two scamps come into a village and announce that they can make soup from stones. They succeed because impoverished villagers decide they each can spare an onion or a carrot to go into the common pot.

The collective power of creative courage can be immense. Even when resources seem scarce, we can create cooperative benefits by pooling our efforts. In a company facing bankruptcy, for example, managers may believe their only choice is to cut back on staff, further diminishing the potential for cooperation. In some cases, however, employees have courageously pooled their resources to buy the firms that employ them. When it works, employee ownership can harness the benefits of scale, creating new possibilities by aggregating small contributions from individuals. By redistributing benefits and burdens, employees may preserve an integration that secures ongoing employment and even adds to the benefits of shareholders, despite the costs and liabilities.

Civil resistance offers another example of the power of collective action. When citizens of the former Soviet Union faced repression, what resources did they have? Not much in the way of money, material, or power. They did, however, have time, energy, and the willingness to resist injustice. Around the same time, citizens of Czechoslovakia and Hungary called on collective memories of the role civil disobedience had played in their histories. As individuals they might be ineffective, but when they joined together they were able to resist an oppressive government.

You're saying we practice creative courage whenever we step out of our comfort zone to improve the likelihood that cooperation will produce genuine and mutual benefits. If I see people being harmed or threatened by change, I need to think, "That's my cue. What can I do differently to strengthen the cooperative community?"

Whenever it's within our power to promote human flourishing, we need to find our part and step up. The response might be very simple. If I realize my neighbors are suffering from flooding, I might install rain gardens or collect water in a cistern so I'm not contributing to future flooding and suffering. I might also decide to raise the bar a little and teach others these practices by offering tours of the gardens or a class in landscape practices that minimize runoff. I might develop more expertise by attending local or regional meetings on water management.

For our actions to make a lasting impact we must invariably depend on and coordinate with others who have specialized capabilities. When Rachel Carson died in 1964 it wasn't clear that society would heed her warnings. It took years of patient collaboration by scientists, activists, and policy makers to address the questions she had raised. What could be learned from the failures of early environmental laws? How could regulations be improved to increase compliance and make enforcement more effective? We may not remember the names of those who worked out the answers that led to the Clean Air and Water Acts of the 1970s, but collectively they took response-ability, sparing the rest of us from serious harms of pollution.

The Power of Bystanders

Many of those people were doing their jobs, of course. But when we aren't directly involved it's easy to think, "I'm not responsible for this."

Bystanders aren't beneficiaries and they aren't being harmed. They operate in a comfortable, relatively stable environment that allows them to pursue their goals without constant personal worry about harms. That environment tends to feature good salaries, health insurance, occasional vacations, and other social goods. Tenured professors fall into this category. So do healthcare workers, government employees, and retirees with trustworthy pensions.

We shouldn't overstate the safety of this zone. Life is unpredictable, and changes in the physical or social environment may turn a bystander into a victim or a beneficiary. A tornado or a fire might destroy one's house. A rare misfortune may strike: say, an outbreak of infectious disease or a jar of tainted peanut butter. Local authorities might confiscate property to build a road. Fracking that happens miles upstream may contaminate groundwater. A stock crash may jeopardize a pension system. Yet even acknowledging the possibility of disruption, many people lead comfortable lives in which benefits don't come at obvious expense to others and the probability of inflicted harms is small.

In relation to any problem large enough to command national attention, I guess most of us could be regarded as bystanders.

If my own situation seems sustainable, it's tempting to relax and enjoy my good fortune. My well-being, though, continues to depend on the health of the cooperative community, and I still need to take risks actively to strengthen the cooperative network. What harms have been overlooked? What values aren't being integrated into the cooperative structures around me? How can we anticipate and mitigate unintended harms? How can bystanders use imagination to expand and strengthen the cooperative network? No one can do everything, of course, but everyone can do something.

This kind of creative courage is being practiced by a new generation of retirees who have taken on second careers or significant volunteer projects such as VISTA. These people have raised their families and probably put away enough for a comfortable retirement. But rather than go fishing, they use their time, talent, and expertise to replenish cooperative systems that have benefited them.

The man who built my Energy Star home is an example of someone who voluntarily takes on risk for the good of the community. Bill Decker was well past an age when he could retire, and given the success of his construction company he didn't *need* to build anything. Yet he had become aware of harms caused by standard practices in the construction industry. Lumber is harvested unsustainably, eroding hillsides and disrupting ecosystems. Inferior insulation practices result in discomfort and wasteful energy consumption. Plumbing and landscaping practices make inefficient use of water. These practices remain well established and profitable because the harms can be ignored: costs are widely distributed or accrue over time.

Understanding all this, Decker is unwilling to ignore the harms and has committed himself to the relatively risky project of building with more sustainable methods. He's taken on the burdens of meeting a payroll and arguing with regulatory agencies because he believes construction practices need improvement. Although he isn't being directly harmed and can't be sure that his efforts will lead to reforms, he sees an opportunity to prevent harms and strengthen the community through his specialized knowledge. So he stays engaged. Every day he practices creative courage by working to implement new practices — often in the face of opposition from people who don't understand what he's trying to accomplish.

I guess I accepted a similar kind of risk when I became a board member for our local school foundation. The district had devoted resources to educating our three children, including our deaf daughter. It seemed only right that I invest my own resources to make sure such opportunities would be available to other students.

On a global scale we saw creative courage in action during the meetings about climate disruption that resulted in the Paris accords of 2015. Conference delegates from 180 countries faced all the risks we've described. They were understandably wary about committing their citizens to sacrifices that might not be shared evenly. They confronted the prospect of rapid and potentially catastrophic change. And they understood that piecemeal efforts were doomed to insignificance.

To complicate matters further, the United Nations lacks the executive strength to enforce compliance. The success or failure of the delegates' efforts would depend entirely on voluntary cooperation. With that in mind they came up with an ingenious plan. The overall goal was to keep the rise of global temperature to no more than 2 degrees Celsius, ideally 1.5 degrees. Using this goal, each country was asked to reduce greenhouse pollutants by a specific percentage. How to meet those targets was left to the countries: since each is organized differently, with varying powers of enforcement and access to resources, there would likely be wide variation in their choices.

It sounds like the participants clarified the common value — reducing the pollution that contributes to climate disruption — without specifying the means. That opens the door to imagination but creates significant risk. What happens if a country doesn't hit the target?

The countries that signed the accord agreed to collect, verify, and publish data showing how well they are doing on their various efforts to reduce emissions as measured by commonly understood metrics. Disputes may arise at first about the effectiveness of different plans. As time goes on, however, a growing body of public data will indicate how successful countries have been in achieving their goals. The countries also agreed to reconvene every five years to assess progress, individually and collectively.

The courage on display in Paris was creative in part because the cooperators didn't try to tell each other what to do. Instead they established a common goal and then asked each country to accept response-ability. Risk is minimized because a procedure for collecting data will confirm or falsify proposed hypotheses about how to reduce pollution. Each country has an ongoing incentive to do its part because its reputation as a reliable cooperator is on the line.

Success isn't guaranteed, but cooperation makes it more likely. No one has the power to force countries to make changes that will reduce pollution. But the benefits of working together are pretty dramatic, and the likelihood of success increases because clear standards have been set and data collection will be used to determine whether specific integrations are working.

This is the heart of responsible cooperation in action. Regardless of our circumstances, the third practice of creative courage is to hold fast to the cooperative vision, constantly looking for ways to strengthen the cooperative community. We accept response-ability whenever we can. We seek allies willing to step outside their own comfort zones to help the larger community flourish. If we encounter obstacles, we take another path. If one project falters or the environment changes, we make adjustments. We keep our eyes on the ultimate prize: cooperative systems that enable the entire community to thrive. We exercise creative courage by refusing to accept halfway measures flawed by partiality to any benefit or party, or disdain for any harm or victim.

What you're saying reminds me of a quotation I once saw in a classroom for hearing-impaired children: "Courage doesn't always roar. Sometimes courage is the quiet voice at the end of the day that says, 'I will try again tomorrow.'"

Each of us, again and again, must take risks to strengthen or remake the vast, interconnected social configurations on which we all depend. The nature of those risks will vary, and we may not see the results of our efforts. We'll surely encounter breakdowns and bottlenecks that produce imbalances in benefits, but we can't be deterred. Wherever we see openings for cooperation we must accept the risk of doing our part, taking whatever steps we can to strengthen and protect environments in which all responsible cooperators can flourish.

CHAPTER 7

Cooperative Wisdom

The Social Virtues in Action

All ethics so far evolved rest upon a single premise:
that the individual is a member of
a community of interdependent parts.

Aldo Leopold

If everyone helps to hold up the sky, then one person does not become tired.
Tshi proverb, collected by Askari Johnson Hodari

Practicing creative courage, with so many risks involved, seems very tough,
especially in an environment that's constantly changing.

Cultivating any of the social virtues is challenging. Many of the practices we've outlined will feel unfamiliar. Deploying new strategies is always difficult, especially in the face of change and conflict.

In my experience, however, the rewards more than justify the effort. Those who master the virtues don't get discouraged when problems emerge in their cooperative projects. They see opportunities where others see discord. They discover creative ways to improve relationships in every area of their lives. They cultivate, contribute to, and are supported by communities in which everyone participates, senses their own value, and feels encouraged.

All of this sounds a lot like what is traditionally called wisdom. It's an appealing goal. But when I was trying to master these new ways of responding to conflict, I remember feeling overwhelmed. Five virtues. Fifteen practices. It's a lot to absorb.

That feeling is understandable. Remember, what we've been calling virtues are habits of mind, reflexive ways of responding to challenging circumstances. And most people start out with a different set of reflexes, grounded in our traditional understanding of virtue. From the time children are quite young, parents encourage simple forms of cooperation because everyone is better off when we work together. We learn to do our part and demonstrate the kind of responsibility that leads to mutual benefits. Under ordinary circumstances we protect those benefits by continually making small adjustments that ease tension and defuse conflict.

Sometimes the standard reflexes serve us well, but they don't necessarily prepare us for the changing technologies and complex networks that increasingly dominate our lives. When harms occur even though everyone was trying to do the right thing, we typically resort to deflecting blame and denying responsibility. We end up damaging alliances and scrambling to make amends.

We'd all like to believe that if we work hard and practice the traditional virtues, everything will fall into place. We'll live happily ever after if we can just find the right mate, land the ideal job, get better organized, employ the killer technology, pass the needed law, win the decisive battle.

We grow up with fairy tales that promise we can achieve sustainable happiness by getting things right. Wisdom starts with the insight that stability is a mirage. Whenever we believe we've nailed it, we put ourselves at risk. We live in dynamic, open-ended environments — both natural and social — so even our best-laid plans are vulnerable to disruption. And even our most careful cooperative efforts need ongoing revision.

Trying to get things right once and for all makes us frustrated, angry, and cynical.

When we become aware of benefits available only through cooperation, it's natural to want to nail things down with commitments and contracts, institutions and regulations. But the environment is always in flux. When we engineer procedures or technologies that "feel right," the most charitable interpretation of this feeling is that we're hypothesizing mutually beneficial outcomes within a specific environment. But the environment will change, and then standard operating procedures can't continue to yield their customary benefits.

When what's right is no longer obvious, we feel overwhelmed, unable to act constructively.

In complex environments we regularly experience the inadvertent harms described in Chapter 2. No one can keep track of everything, so problems show up in places where everyone thought someone else was paying attention. Changes in scale can result in disruption: more is better until it isn't. And assumptions about norms prove invalid — especially when unusual cases arise or tolerances prove fragile, as we saw when discussing inclusive integrity. In all these ways changing environments expose the limits of our standard reflexes.

When breakdowns occur and harms become apparent, the "old" reflexes tend to kick in, but they don't serve us well. If things have gone wrong despite our willingness to cooperate, it's all too easy to abandon the co-operative project. Rather than seeking to exercise response-ability, we try to deflect blame. Rather than trying to discern what others value, we grow suspicious of each other: "I'd better get you before you get me." Rather than working to expand benefits, we begin to take advantage of cooperation: "Why shouldn't I cheat whenever I can get away with it?" Pretty soon the social environment becomes cutthroat rather than oriented toward the benefits of cooperation.

Cultivating new reflexes associated with the five social virtues short-circuits this unhappy sequence. We start with the compassionate observation that change takes us all by surprise, confounding our assumptions about the benefits cooperation is supposed to produce and creating vulnerability where we thought there would be mutual advantage. Deep discernment makes us aware that very few of our conflicts begin with malice. If we hope to continue to enjoy the benefits of cooperation, we must be attuned to changes in both natural and social environments, responsive to what others value, and committed to the ideal that benefits for some must not impose harms on others. The social virtues I espouse may not be reflexive for most people, but when we work deliberately to adopt and internalize them, they transform our approach to conflict.

How the Virtues Work Together

Practicing the virtues has had profound effects in my own life. My relationships are richer, and I have a vision of the future that is optimistic but not naïve. I also remember that it took a long time before the practices came naturally.

These renovated virtues are most powerful when they become embedded in character. Making a commitment to the practices is the only way this can happen. To help readers keep the big picture in focus, we've listed all the virtues and their corresponding practices at the end of the book, page 217.

On our website (cooperativewisdom.org), readers can download and print a PDF of the list if they want a hard-copy "cheat sheet" close at hand.

Look for opportunities to put the practices into action — at home, at work, in your community life. When you observe other people trying to strengthen cooperation, take notice and point it out. Over time your reflexes will evolve. Eventually, when you find yourself facing any of the usual disrupters of cooperation, you'll automatically look for ways to restore and expand mutual benefits.

The process is subtle and usually slow, but the rewards are very real.

Think about a child learning to play a musical instrument. The teacher encourages the child to practice simple exercises. At first every note is an effort, but with time and practice the notes start to flow together. The fingers come to know where they're supposed to be. Then the child can tackle pieces of greater complexity.

Similarly, the practices associated with each social virtue may at first seem difficult or even beside the point. But as they become more familiar you'll learn to recognize occasions to use them. Alternative responses occur to you spontaneously. Hidden vulnerabilities, previously invisible resources, and overlooked solutions come into focus. Sometimes you'll even discover opportunities to integrate once-reluctant allies into reenvisioned projects.

This reminds me of my experience as a student of tai chi. Initially I was over-whelmed by the intricacies of the movements. Fortunately my teacher was very patient, teaching the same motion over and over. In time the movements began to feel natural and then started to flow one into the next.

As you'll recall, the social virtues were distilled from the study of situations in which people had been able to restore mutual concern, respect, and coopera-tion even in disrupted and degraded environments. As a professor of applied ethics I spent years teaching these practices to students and saw dramatic changes in what they were able to accomplish. Often my graduate students took internships in settings where people had never worked with an ethicist. I taught them to analyze work environments and write proposals that helped organizations foresee the benefits of addressing neglected, harmful external-ities. Even when students had expertise in areas I didn't understand, I was able to help them apply the virtues so they could renegotiate cooperative arrangements, redeploy resources, and rethink standard operating procedure.

Over the years I marveled at the benefits that resulted from people practicing the five social virtues in a wide range of difficult circumstances. I can't imagine telling people how to live. All I can do is bear witness to the transformative possibilities that are activated when these virtues become reflexive. Changes that could have been disruptive became opportunities for growth instead of occasions of conflict.

As we've talked about cases I've noticed that, even though all the virtues are in play, one often proves to be pivotal.

The virtues and their practices work in synergy to address disruption and conflict. Compassion is often the trigger, but there's nothing magical about the sequence. Sometimes one of the virtues will seem obviously suited to unlocking the conflict at hand. If a particular practice calls to you in a specific situation, build it into your hypothesis about how you can promote cooperation.

It's also important to recognize that not everyone will be equally good at every virtue. Because of training or temperament, some of us are especially drawn to discernment, adept at finding integrated solutions, or ready to take risks. It's perfectly natural to turn to a partner who "knows how to handle stuff like this" — in all likelihood because that person is already proficient in a particular virtue. For instance, people often turn to me for imaginative analysis that produces a new way to approach a persistent problem. I in turn often reach out to colleagues who have technical, scientific, or historical perspectives that strengthen a proposed integration.

It helps to know that exercising the social virtues with a good team will yield benefits even if you aren't proficient in every practice.

Each of the social virtues shifts our orientation. Instead of thinking only about what's good from my point of view, I enlarge my scope to include anyone who wants to be a responsible cooperator. To see how the virtues work in tandem, let's look at five cases in which cooperation was at risk of breaking down because of unintended harms. In each case all the social virtues are relevant, but one plays a decisive part in producing solutions that strengthen communities of cooperators.

Proactive Compassion and the Challenges of Dementia

Proactive compassion was on display when members of my congregation decided to lend church facilities to a respite care program for elders in the early stages of Alzheimer's and other forms of dementia. As people live longer, more and more families face stressful questions about the care and safety of loved ones who are not cognitively competent. To avoid institutionalization many families try to absorb the elder into their household, but caregivers often feel uncomfortable and overburdened when they assume significant responsibilities for formerly autonomous parents or spouses.

Members of our congregation became aware that this issue was causing harm to families in our community. Caregivers were experiencing severe stress as they tried to cope with jobs and children along with the nonstop supervision of elders whose judgment could no longer be trusted. Specialists at the local council on aging were also tuned into the problem. They were able to mobilize staff members trained in gerontology and dementia-related issues, but they didn't have a facility. The congregation, however, had facilities that went unused during the workweek.

This sounds like a problem of scale and tolerance. Caregivers start with good intentions but are gradually overwhelmed as the disease progresses and the burdens of caregiving become more onerous. Members of your congregation along with experts at the council on aging anticipated the kinds of breakdown that might occur, and they exercised response-ability.

A plan emerged to provide eldercare for one day each month so caregivers could take a break. Experts from the council helped make the environment provided by the church safe and offered forms of stimulation that could slow cognitive decline. Caregivers appreciated the service, but gradually it became clear that one day a month wasn't enough to relieve the day-to-day stress of caring for someone with diminished cognitive capacities. And the gerontologists were frustrated because one day of programming did little to retard the progress of dementia.

At this point some deep discernment was called for. Caregivers needed regular breaks to maintain their own physical and mental health; those with full-time jobs needed support throughout every workday. Seniors with dementia needed a sense of dignity and opportunities for engagement. The council on aging, which had expertise but no infrastructure for delivering services, needed partners. The congregation needed to see the connection between the program and its ministry to the community.

In this case deep discernment wasn't so much about resolving conflict, because it sounds like everyone was on the same page. The challenge was to find resources to alleviate several acknowledged vulnerabilities without imposing excessive costs on any of the partners.

Understanding these basic values laid the groundwork for practicing intentional imagination. What if a program were available every day during the workweek? Could the church still house it? How could food preparation and hygiene issues be handled? How could costs be kept down so the program could serve the most vulnerable families, who didn't have much money to spare?

Once the questions had been asked, people started to come forward with resources. Some did research, finding a church in South Carolina that had developed a ministry specifically for aging community members — both Christian and Muslim — and their families. This church was eager to share the nondenominational materials it had developed.

The council on aging had access to grants that would minimize costs to families. The congregation faced the need to renovate church bathrooms to meet ADA requirements, but could arrange for food delivery instead of upgrading kitchen facilities to commercial standards. A for-profit company that manages residential facilities was willing to partner, administering and finding staff for the enlarged program. Ties to internship programs at the local university made it possible to reduce the cost of all-day adult day-care services while giving students an opportunity to cultivate skills they would need as certified professionals.

This kind of inclusive integration is rooted in proactive compassion. People were willing to do what they could because they clearly understood the vulnerabilities created by the situation and were determined to alleviate them.

Courage also played a part, because as circumstances changed some part-ners reevaluated the nature of their participation. In practice this is how the social virtues interact. One day you're trying to anticipate vulnerability. At another time you may be working on an integration that needs revising because someone has discerned a value that wasn't clear before. Or you may need creative courage to insist that vulnerabilities visible from your perspective are taken into account. And, of course, you're constantly imagining new ways to improve cooperation so more partners get more of what they need to thrive.

Deep Discernment and Protecting Habitat

In another case, one of my graduate students cracked open a conflict by practicing deep discernment. In 2004, Marybeth Bauer was an intern with the Environmental Defense Fund, working on the difficult challenge of protecting endangered species. The fund's efforts were impeded by conflict between the U.S. Fish and Wildlife Service, which is responsible for developing plans that protect habitat and mitigate harms for endangered and threatened species, and property owners who complained that mitigation often burdened them with unfair and costly requirements. In many places the FWS would propose regulations, and landowners would do everything they could to evade and sabotage those rules.

In their own ways both sides were practicing compassion. Their specialized points of view made them sensitive to different but very real vulnerabilities.

My student spent time with the owners of one property, the Hickory Pass Ranch, a three thousand–acre spread in the Texas hill country. The ranch was home to the golden-cheeked warbler, an endangered bird with a vivid golden head and a distinctive song. Protecting the warblers also meant protecting the Ashe juniper because the birds use its bark to make their nests. Even though the habitat was essential to the warbler's survival, federal agencies didn't have the money to acquire the land, and in any case the family that owned the ranch didn't want to sell.

Practicing deep discernment revealed that the ranch was important to this family because it was part of their legacy—the "setting for stories made and told across generations," as Marybeth wrote. To pass on the ranch to the next generation, the family needed to keep it profitable, and like other landowners they feared that regulations might strangle economic options. They weren't antagonistic toward those who wanted to protect the warbler's habitat. Like many Texans they had a sentimental attachment to the warbler; they just didn't want its needs to take precedence over theirs.

I can see how the insights produced by deep discernment set the stage for intentional imagination here. What if there were a land management strategy that preserved habitat for warblers and generated income for landowners?

Asking that *what if* question led to new ideas, including that of a conservation bank. Now operating in many states, conservation banks give landowners a way to earn money in exchange for preserving habitat. In the case of Hickory Pass Ranch the landowners set aside five hundred acres to be managed in perpetuity as habitat for the warblers. In return they received five hundred conservation credits that could be sold to developers who were impinging on the warbler's habitat elsewhere. The revenue from the credits pays the costs of managing the preserved land.

This integration created positive externalities. The cost of paying someone to supervise five hundred acres of warbler habitat was less than what the Fish and Wildlife Service had been paying a regulator who was trying to impose rules on resistant ranchers. The warblers were much more likely to survive and thrive if their habitat was managed with the landowners' cooperation. Both sides still faced uncertainty and risk, of course, but what had seemed like an impasse was transformed into an opportunity for everyone—including the warblers—to benefit through human cooperation.

The key moment seems to be when each side opened up to the viewpoint of those who seemed like adversaries. That openness became possible because a key person practiced deep discernment with both parties, untangling means from ends, paying attention to accumulating harms, and embracing the legitimacy of multiple viewpoints.

Intentional Imagination and the Sandwich Shop

Intentional imagination provided the key that unlocked a seemingly hopeless situation in Great Barrington, Massachusetts. In 1991 a popular sub shop in that town lost its lease. Besides selling delicious sandwiches, the shop had been a meeting place where residents exchanged views about politics and other local issues.

Around the same time a national franchise selling subs had opened in Great Barrington. In addition, competition from chain stores and malls was threatening the economic viability of many small downtowns. In that economic environment, when deli owner Frank Tortoriello tried to borrow money to move his business across the street, the bank decided that investing in a local sub shop was too risky and turned down his application.

Practicing compassion here is pretty easy because the vulnerability is so obvious. If the shop closes, people lose their jobs and the community loses a distinctive environment that encouraged civic involvement.

Clearly more was at stake than sandwiches, as deep discernment revealed. Like many small business owners, Tortoriello wanted the community as well as his business to thrive. He had roots in the region and was raising his family there. Of course, the bank wasn't against the region or against families. They were focused on their own standard procedures for measuring adequate collateral. This seemed to be a situation in which two sets of values were in conflict and one would have to be sacrificed to the other. The pivotal virtue was intentional imagination and the key question: What could count as collateral?

Or in our terminology, "What resources were not being tapped?"

As it turned out, the shop's biggest resource was its loyal customers, who were upset by the prospect of "their" shop going out of business. What if they were willing to fund the renovation? No single customer could make that investment, but what if they could band together? Tortoriello came up with the idea to issue an alternative currency called "deli dollars." The notes, which sold for $9, could be redeemed for $10 worth of subs after the store was established in its new location.

Tortoriello challenged the assumption that people needed to pay for sandwiches when they wanted to eat them. Essentially he asked his customers to lend him the money he needed for renovation, promising that they would be repaid with interest in sandwiches they could eat in the future.

Within days Tortoriello sold five hundred notes and raised the money he needed to move and renovate the shop. His example inspired other local businesses to practice imagination. Farmers began to issue Berkshire Farm Preserve notes, which gave them much-needed capital for planting crops in exchange for a share of the future harvest. Today, with help from the Schumacher Center for New Economics, "Berkshares" have become embedded in the local economy.

Of course, it takes a bit of creative courage to invest in an alternate currency.

A board of directors mitigates the risk by constantly evaluating the soundness of the hypothesis and anticipating changes that might undermine the benefits of this kind of cooperation. In addition to encouraging local business to accept Berkshares, the board offers loans to support entrepreneurs who want to use local resources to produce small-batch goods and provide local employment. The alternative currency works by confining itself to a limited area where local knowledge gives a community of people confidence about underwriting local initiatives. Again, all the virtues are being deployed, but intentional imagination led to the breakthrough.

Inclusive Integrity and Energy Innovation

On a very different scale I've watched General Electric practice inclusive integrity in the years since 2009, when I attended a presentation on Ecomagination. The company had embarked on this initiative in 2005 after an internal debate convinced top executives that climate change was creating real vulnerabilities — some of which could be mitigated by changing the way energy was consumed by GE's customers and suppliers and within the company itself. GE executives were very clear about the values at stake. The company and its suppliers had to remain profitable. Consumers had to get reliable products at reasonable prices. But the company also set a clear goal to move away from intensive use of fossil fuels.

I've read about this program. At first they encouraged teams of employees within the company to practice intentional imagination, especially about how the company could reduce its internal use of energy. Then they offered incentives to suppliers who could come up with more efficient products and processes. And in 2010 they sponsored a competition that solicited thousands of ideas from the general public.

GE offered to underwrite the best ideas. But to move from promising idea to profitable product, GE had to figure out how to coordinate new possibilities with the existing structures of a vast cooperative organization — the very essence of practicing inclusive integrity. For one thing, they had to treat every new product as a hypothesis. Would it cut energy usage as much as anticipated? Would it meet the needs of the marketplace? They made false starts, of course, but specialists in the company were encouraged to be flexible, making adaptations that resulted in a wide array of new products—and increased profits.

Ecomagination has been responsible for aggressively commercializing a variety of innovative approaches to energy generation and use. In addition to technologies that use renewables, like wind and solar energy, the company has developed fuel cells, high-efficiency gas turbines, hybrid locomotives, and lower-emission aircraft engines. Ecomagination teams have been instrumental in creating lighter, stronger construction materials as well as energy-efficient lighting and even technologies to purify and desalinate water. When my wife and I were looking for a fuel-efficient way to heat water in our home, we found a GE water heater that utilized an innovative heat pump.

There was huge risk in reconfiguring such a large company to take a new value— climate vulnerability—into account. Because of its history of pollution, especially in the Hudson River Valley, the company was initially accused of greenwashing.

In addition to taking reputational risks, GE poured capital into areas of research and development in which results weren't guaranteed. And they continue to face an energy environment that's in constant motion. When the Ecomagination program started, the United States was heavily dependent on foreign sources of oil. Then came the rapid increase in hydraulic fracturing, which has created a range of externalities, including a dramatic drop in oil prices. The market environment in which GE has to operate is constantly changing, favoring some technologies and making others marginal.

So the need to practice inclusive integrity as well as the other virtues is ongoing.

Creative Courage and a Campus in Turmoil

Practicing the virtues is always dynamic, never static, and the benefits are cumulative. In May of 1970 I witnessed a situation in which the then-president of Bowling Green State University, William Jerome, could practice creative courage because he had been practicing the other virtues for many years. That year anger about the U.S. invasion of Cambodia led to demonstrations and turmoil on campuses all over the country. In early May the governor of Ohio sent National Guard troops onto the campus of

Kent State University to restore order, and on May 4 guardsmen shot into a group of protesters, killing four students.

The next day all state universities in Ohio closed for several days—except Bowling Green, where I was teaching at the time. President Jerome was able to keep the campus open in large part because of partnerships he had created with the surrounding community, in particular with the Reverend Henry Gerner, senior pastor at the United Christian Fellowship.

Both men practiced proactive compassion in response to the events at Kent State. They recognized that, beyond the very real risk of further violence, the shootings had made many students feel highly vulnerable. Some might just as easily have attended Kent State, or they knew students at Kent State or had friends with friends there. The degrees of separation were few; students were thinking, "Yesterday I could have died!"

I vividly remember those feelings. I was an undergraduate at a private university in Ohio. Like most students in that era I'd been involved in protest, but it had never occurred to me that I could be killed because of what I was doing. Everyone was in a state of shock.

Jerome and Gerner discerned that students needed an outlet for this very justifiable agitation. Deep discernment also revealed other values in play. Students, especially those about to graduate, needed to finish their coursework and take final exams. And the town had a legitimate concern about maintaining order so it could protect the property and well-being of citizens.

Because Gerner and Jerome had been deliberate about developing healthy, constructive cooperative networks, they had access to resources not available on other campuses. Gerner had spent much of the preceding year giving peacekeeping workshops, thus building a network of people skilled in expressing grievances without violence. His ties to ministers at other local churches enabled him to enlist their help as well.

For his part Jerome had nurtured a campus climate open to nonviolent debate and protest. He had circulated catalogs of extracurricular seminars and workshops designed to raise student awareness, and encouraged campus security to cultivate cooperative relationships with the town police department and the county sheriff's office. And he had enlisted the cooperation of local officials, including the mayor. So when the governor called and asked the mayor to prevail on the university president to close the campus, the

COOPERATIVE WISDOM

mayor practiced creative courage, supporting President Jerome in finding a way to integrate the central values of student learning and civic engagement and public order.

The risks for government leaders during that era were tremendous. Martin Luther King Jr. and Robert Kennedy had been assassinated only two years earlier. There had been riots in major cities and protests on campuses across the country.

Because the passion of students was palpable, local leaders sensed that there would be risk regardless of whether the campus stayed open. Both the mayor and President Jerome practiced courage in refusing to become overwhelmed by a rapidly shifting environment. They developed a hypothesis about how students could express their understandable outrage without imperiling the mission of the university or the security of the town. Classes were suspended for a few hours. Then the campus resumed its normal schedule, with the understanding that there would be a march to protest the Kent State shootings.

The march itself must have called on the social virtues.

Absolutely. Those involved had to discern multiple values: to give students an outlet for strong emotion while protecting people and property from harm. They had to be imaginative about identifying resources and resolute about integrating them into a workable march. Gerner mobilized students to create signs and literature. People trained in peacemaking were recruited to model nonviolence and test the viability of the hypothesis by monitoring student behavior during the march. Local and regional law enforcement cordoned off streets along the parade route and stood by to minimize the risk that emotional marchers might accost innocent bystanders or damage nearby property. Only two days after the shooting at Kent State, seven thousand students and faculty members expressed their sorrow, anger, and frustration by marching peaceably through the town. So many people joined the march that the first protesters were already returning to campus as the last ones set off.

Because these leaders exercised creative courage, students had a thoughtful, nondestructive way to express their dissatisfaction and distress. The community was protected, and the university continued to function. Classes were held. Exams were given. Not only did students finish the semester, but their investment in the issues of the day infused meaning in their lessons. I

202

was teaching a Philosophy of Religion course; my syllabus topic just hours before the march was "The Meaning of Death." I've never led a more spirited or insightful discussion!

Obviously there were risks. That's why other Ohio campuses decided to cancel classes.

Jerome and Gerner could practice creative courage because they had strengthened their networks *before* any crisis emerged. They had been engaged with the social virtues all along, fortifying the cooperative structures to which they belonged, creating constructive ties with groups of professors, ministers, peacemakers, and public officials. They could rely on this established social framework to be highly responsive when those shots at Kent State suddenly changed the physical and social environment. For me that march in Bowling Green was vivid evidence that consistently practicing the social virtues—even in small ways that may seem insignificant at the time—lays the groundwork for swift, constructive response in the face of dramatic change.

Wisdom *Is* Cooperation

What all these stories have in common is a new framework for how to be good— and do good—in a complex, specialized, fast-changing world.

Our success as a species rests on caring for one another. We thrive in environments where we support each other in pursuing fulfilling lives. That's why the sense of betrayal can be so acute when cooperation breaks down. In each of the cases just described, some people could—and probably did—say, "I did my part. It's not my fault that bad things are happening." Fortunately, those committed to the social virtues recognized conflict as a call to practice a deeper, wiser understanding of goodness. When changing environments created vulnerability and significant harms threatened existing cooperative structures, people skilled in the social virtues were able to intervene constructively. They devised and integrated imaginative alternatives in response to the emerging harm, or they anticipated large-scale harms and created more resilient systems to forestall them.

When complexities started piling up, key cooperators started asking the questions that underlie the five virtues: Where is the vulnerability? What range of values defines the conflict? What hidden resources suggest novel courses of action? What kind of cooperative structure will honor all the values in play so everyone can thrive? What risks should we incur?

As these stories illustrate, problems that are fundamentally social don't respond well to the uncoordinated efforts of individuals. We cannot continue to think of goodness as a private project. For an intelligent, social species, goodness is necessarily rooted in virtues that promote, strengthen, and when necessary restore cooperation. The five virtues keep us focused on a mutual, inclusive good. And they direct us toward practices that promote cooperative wisdom, especially in trying circumstances.

It's never enough for me, or anyone else, to be good. We must create and recreate settings in which we work together so everyone can thrive.

The practices I've described require no miraculous interventions. They simply equip us to fulfill our social purpose of cooperating to produce benefits we could never achieve alone. "Good" people are those who commit themselves to cooperation, no matter how dysfunctional the social environment in which they are embedded. The right thing to do is whatever makes genuine cooperation more attainable and durable. There's nothing rigid or moralistic in this approach; the exigencies of circumstances and the evolution of norms won't allow it.

The social virtues I advocate improve our ability to navigate and strengthen any social environment. When we practice proactive compassion, we encourage trust so everyone can be candid about vulnerability. When we practice deep discernment, we open up to values beyond those encompassed by our familiar perspective and procedures. When we practice intentional imagination, we conceive alternatives to awkward, disrupted, or outmoded routines. When we practice inclusive integrity, we support and strengthen cooperative structures that embody and honor the values of all willing cooperators. When we practice creative courage, we willingly accept the risks involved in sustaining or expanding the benefits of cooperation. Taken together, these virtues affirm the social potential of the human species.

A key insight for me is that specialization — which at first we identified as a problem — in fact has the potential to strengthen human cooperation. We often start with the assumption that difficult problems could readily be resolved if only we could get people to see things our way. The virtues shift this orientation to something more respectful. Conflict is more likely to recede when we abandon blame, listen to each other's insights, and encourage novel forms of cooperation.

Using the cooperative virtues offers a new paradigm for resolving conflict. Instead of being fixated on what matters to me—my family, my profession, my business, my country — I'm led by the virtues to inquire about what matters for sustaining the human community. My own prospects are diminished if I cannot enlist the cooperation of others. If I truly believe this, I'll do everything I can to honor and protect what matters to other willing cooperators. The longer I practice the virtues, the farther I move beyond simple respect. My sense of what's important to me expands to encompass what's important to others and what enables the community to thrive.

Seen through this lens, conflicts become opportunities to create new, more robust forms of cooperation. When we recognize new vulnerabilities, discern values that were obscure, and tap resources that went unrecognized, we create cooperative systems that are more durable and less risky. Instead of a liability, differences become an asset. We benefit from paying attention to the distinctive viewpoints of all who are willing to commit themselves to our cooperative endeavors.

Another Paradigm of Leadership

A few years ago Forbes *did a survey of executives at 321 large international companies. Most agreed that diversity drives innovation and is crucial to success on a global scale. This is a very different way of thinking about leadership.*

The old model of leadership demanded deference—especially to the authority of specialists. The new paradigm understands that everyone is a specialist with a distinctive and valuable point of view based on training and experience. Today's best leaders are attentive, trying to discern what matters, especially to those who are dissatisfied with established ways of doing things. Leaders get the best results when they aspire to create cooperative systems in which everyone can thrive.

Martin Luther King Jr. is an exceptionally powerful example of this kind of leadership. He showed deep compassion for both black and white Americans and was able to discern their deepest values. Blacks wanted access to opportunities taken for granted by white Americans, yet King also understood that most whites regarded themselves as fair-minded, decent people. They wanted to safeguard their communities but recognized the vulnerabilities segregation imposed on African Americans. When peaceful marchers were attacked by police dogs, knocked down by fire hoses, and arrested, the harms implicit in exhausted forms of cooperation became vivid to every American with a television set.

That's when King stepped in with his deeply imaginative vision of a social system with genuinely mutual benefits. He practiced intentional imagination by identifying concealed resources: ministers from metropolitan churches in the North urged parishioners to join civil rights marches, and law professors from northern universities began mentoring black students. These social resources had been dormant because no one before had listened so deeply to the concerns of white as well as black Americans, scholars as well as people of faith. King discerned the values of these disparate groups and saw that they could converge in the kind of nonviolent protests pioneered by Mahatma Gandhi. He organized events across the South and eventually led a huge, peaceful march to the Lincoln Memorial, which culminated in his famous "I have a dream" speech.

And, of course, he had the courage to say, "This must change!" to people determined to defend social systems that created advantages for some at the expense of others.

We all have the opportunity to practice this kind of leadership by paying respectful attention to everyone who hopes to share in the benefits or avoid the harms generated by our cooperative efforts. The problems we face are rarely created by individuals, so they aren't likely to be resolved by an isolated agent, even one with a good idea and a captivating personality. Deploying the social virtues helps us recognize the limits of personal knowledge and power. This holds true whether the arena is business, government, education, or our own communities and families.

My point of view will always be incomplete. It *must* be supplemented. Instead of feeling antagonistic towards those with alternative viewpoints, I feel gratitude because they invite me to enlarge my vision. I've personally benefited enormously from working with people who have talents and training I lack. Colleagues have offered opportunities to cooperate that were shaped by their goodwill and by the hard work of others I never met. The students I taught and mentored brought insights that enriched and strengthened my thinking. Whatever I've been able to do has been enabled by the cooperative efforts of other people, including a host of forebears I will never know.

Humility is sometimes taken as a sign of weakness, but I've come to understand it as a source of strength. Part of wisdom is letting go of the idea that I'm supposed to be in charge and my vision should eclipse that of others. Whenever I incorporate what others know and care about, my point of view becomes more expansive, my integrations become more durable, and I can more deftly envision how to engage with willing partners to strengthen the human enterprise.

If I am alive, I am benefiting from the cooperation of other people; in appropriate gratitude I reciprocate. The social virtues and the practices that promote them give me a consistent way into complicated environments, reliably opening up new possibilities for cooperation where conflict seemed inevitable.

I won't deny that it can be discouraging to put effort into a relationship or a project only to discover that it's gone off the rails. Cooperation for mutual benefit is always provisional. None of us can ever be certain that the whole system — at least as we envision it — will work. We do, however, know that everyone is vulnerable when cooperation breaks down, so wisdom tells me that I must do my part to put things back together.

Building Community: Resilience and Response-Ability

I think your example of resilience is what drew me to these ideas in the first place. In the seminar where we met you talked about your experience of working through complex issues involving many parties with differing agendas. Instead of feeling aggravated or exasperated when things didn't go well, you did what you could and woke up the next morning eager to do it again.

Keep in mind that cooperation is never up to you alone, any more than the performance of a symphony is up to the clarinetist. When you get stuck—and you will get stuck — you may want to try a different practice, enlist partners with crucially needed skills or perspective, or make your commitment to cooperation more explicit. Each of us strengthens the cooperative community by taking every available opportunity to make our integrations more beneficial.

Here's a very simple example: the other day I was at the grocery store with my cloth bags. When the clerk started ringing up my order I was free to bag, so I did. The cashier was grateful — they were short of baggers that day — and the customer behind me got through the line faster. This kind of social adjustment may seem very small, but such everyday actions are a crucial part of strengthening the cooperative network. Much of the psychological distress people feel occurs because we don't seek out opportunities to fulfill our nature as cooperators. We stand in the grocery line fuming, rather than practicing the virtues to facilitate improved cooperation.

That's the basic theme of response-ability. Sometimes we exercise specialized abilities, but other times we step up simply because we have the resources needed in the moment.

While it's true that many roles in our cooperative networks require specialized knowledge and experience, there are countless daily opportunities to reinforce cooperation simply by recognizing a need and taking initiative. Sometimes what holds us back is a foolish investment in roles: I'm the customer, not the bagger. If I can get past that self-limitation, there are benefits for me (I'm finished with the marketing sooner) and for everyone in line behind me.

Practicing the virtues in small ways also draws us into the community of people who value the benefits that cooperation creates.

True power lies in the community of willing cooperators, so we want to engage that community whenever we can. After my wife and I built our energy-efficient home, we gave tours that got visitors thinking about how they could make modifications in their own homes. Then local building-supply stores started getting requests for setback thermometers, super-efficient hot water heaters, honeycomb blinds, and so on. If they got enough requests, they would stock the products instead of needing to place special orders.

Once energy-conserving products were on the shelves, it was easier for people to find them. And as the number of customers increased it became more profitable for companies to make these products. Our little tours weren't responsible for making this happen, but we took great satisfaction in being part of a process that generated such positive externalities.

In general I've found that fostering response-ability is one of the most gratifying ways to practice the virtues. Whenever we make it possible for others to contribute to the cooperative community, they enjoy the satisfaction of being needed and valued. As a teacher I had the opportunity to mentor and encourage young people who went on to practice the virtues in varied fields. As a consultant I've been able to help organizations expand and strengthen their cooperative efforts. The most wonderful results come from being a part of a fully enabled and cohesive community in which people routinely use the social virtues.

Such connections don't develop overnight. Strong social structures require years of virtues-based interaction. People who are part of resilient networks may not think of what they do in terms of virtue, but when we look closely we see that they regularly practice proactive compassion, deep discernment, intentional imagination, inclusive integrity, and creative courage.

The power of these principles was fully manifested for me one terrible Sunday in 2010, when my wife and I watched firefighters make their best effort—and fail—to save the home we had built for our retirement. The house embodied our lifestyle and our ideals of green living, and stored decades of memorabilia. No one died or suffered injury in the fire, but much of what we had valued up to that point literally went up in flames.

On that day I learned that, even though my physical environment had been drastically reconfigured, I was deeply embedded in a social network that provided mutual benefits. It started with my marriage. I remember having dinner that evening, looking across the table at my wife of fifty years. We knew we'd soon learn more about how the fire had started. Regardless of its cause, the fire was an unintended harm that would create potential conflict in the days ahead. It felt like a pivotal moment in our lives, and I knew we would need every one of the virtues to face it.

I remember saying, "We're going to go through God knows what in the coming months. Decision making will become intense, and we can't begin to know the pressures and feelings we'll experience." My wife nodded. She looked as numb as I felt. "Whatever happens, we're going to have to make a point of being good to each other. Getting through this will be difficult for both of us, but it will be a lot easier if we're consistently good to each other."

So we affirmed that, despite such shattering change, we retained our foundation: the loving, trusting relationship between us. And we pledged to each other, right there, that we would protect and sustain what truly mattered: the cooperative partnership that had seen us through fifty years of life together. We would practice proactive compassion by being kind to each other during a time of profound vulnerability. We would engage in deep discernment by listening carefully to each other. We would encourage each other to practice intentional imagination about how to rebuild our lives, and inclusive integrity as we divided labor to reflect our specialized talents. Even when circumstances were trying we would work hard to summon the creative courage required to avoid blame and presume goodwill.

I remember seeing you only a few days after the fire and marveling at how calm you seemed. In a situation that would have left most people in deep distress, you were already seeing opportunities for constructive and creative interaction.

By that time it was very clear that my wife and I were being supported by a cooperative environment much larger than the two of us. The fire had been reported by a young woman down the road; she didn't know how to reach us, so she called our adult granddaughter in California—who called her father, who tracked us down at church. By the time we got to the house, family members, neighbors, and friends were already on the scene. Even while the fire was still burning our neighbor to the north offered his Wi-Fi connection, and the neighbor to the south brought a duffle bag of toiletries. Church friends arrived with food, and others offered the indefinite use of a furnished apartment in their home.

Later that evening we got a phone call from a young mother whose daughter had been deeply upset when she heard about the fire. This family had suffered its own trauma earlier in the year, when a car crash claimed the life of one child. Seeing her daughter's distress, the mother asked, "What do you think we should do?" The child thought for a moment, then said, "Well, they're going to have to eat. And they don't have any dishes or silverware." Even now, when I take one of those dishes from our cupboard, I think of this family and feel heartened. Having come through an experience in which they were deeply hurt, they were moved to practice response-ability when they saw vulnerability in others.

In retrospect we can often see that social systems are healthiest when many people work together, each making unique contributions to an environment in which all can thrive. But in circumstances of chaotic change, like the fire, it can be hard to stay focused on that vision.

The virtues were in action all around us in the weeks and months after the fire. Recognizing and appreciating the cooperative efforts of others helped us get through that difficult time. Besides feeling supported by people we knew, we also benefited from a vast web of specialists trained to manage environments created by house fires. A fire inspector practiced proactive compassion by examining the rubble to find what could be learned about the cause. An insurance adjuster helped us discern what values we wanted to incorporate into the reconstruction of our home, so we could choose materials and techniques that embodied those values. It turned out that during the thirty-eight months we'd lived in the house, lots of people had practiced intentional imagination. New products and technologies allowed us to rebuild in a way that eliminated 25 percent of the energy waste of our former, already energy-efficient home.

I don't want to minimize the complexity and stress of those months. Restoring an environment in which we could thrive was a demanding and exhausting process. Yet this enforced occasion for practicing the virtues opened up opportunities we might otherwise have missed. Every day we worked to affirm and strengthen cooperative relationships, not only with each other but also with all our partners in the rebuilding project. For example, our builder was committed to constructing energy-efficient homes, so I started to jot an e-mail to him whenever I read of promising new technologies or procedures. This simple interaction, multiplied many times, produced a flexible and resilient network, responsive to the issues that inevitably arose. As conflicts emerged we had the tools to resolve them in ways that generally brought benefits to everyone involved.

A New Vision of What Makes Life Good

It's heartening to know that the virtues are effective in dealing with dramatic change as well as the problems we face day to day. Enlisting the social virtues can strengthen every social unit, from the supermarket checkout line to a committee in Congress.

Our practice of the virtues transcends the details of particular environments. Building proactive compassion, deep discernment, intentional imagination, inclusive integrity, and creative courage into your life adds value and improves every situation, as you aspire to the benefits that are possible only through cooperation. You're more likely to recognize vulnerability wherever it occurs. You're less susceptible to arguments that urge you to prefer one set of values to another. You imagine new ways of coordinating specialized practices to distribute the benefits of cooperation more widely. You seek inclusive integrations and practice the respect that makes ongoing cooperation more likely and fruitful. And you assess and accept risks that promise to expand and strengthen the cooperative system.

When you get into the groove, you are constantly engaged in mutually enriching environments that promote human flourishing. Loving the process transforms your identity; you become someone who is genuinely happy when you can facilitate mutual benefits. You feel joyful whenever you can take part in strengthening the cooperative systems that support human thriving.

Thinking about the world this way has made me a more hopeful, optimistic person. I now see healthy, cooperative social units — or the potential for them — all around me. And when breakdowns happen, I feel I have powerful tools to use as I work to restore meaningful cooperation.

Like every other living thing, human beings face the fundamental challenge of adapting to unstable, dynamic environments. As a social species our challenge is to sustain cooperation in the face of change and the conflict it provokes. Again and again I've seen how people who cultivate the practices that support our five social virtues live up to the promise of their humanity — because they engage with others to create cooperative endeavors that are protective, respectful, productive, creative, and ultimately highly rewarding.

When we internalize the virtues and practices, we understand that every form of cooperation, no matter how wonderful it may seem at the outset, will generate unanticipated problems.

The particulars may catch us by surprise, but the pattern won't. No matter how hard groups of people try, they cannot form a perfect union. And no matter how earnestly I want to be a good person, I won't live happily ever after. Things will fall apart. Environments will flourish and decay. With both the flourishing and the disintegration, new conflicts and new opportunities will arise.

For humans the viable unit has always been and continues to be we *not* me. *Like those who have gone before us and those who will follow, we have the extraordinary capacity to construct and benefit from cooperation.*

So what each of us *can* do is understand and live up to what's best in our fundamental nature. We are cooperators. Every time we choose to exercise that capability it becomes more likely that we'll transcend conflict, adapt well to change, and find benefits that are genuinely mutual. We may be enmeshed in difficulties we didn't intend, but they need not entrap us.

Just picking up one of these tools can move a person beyond despair, anger, and apathy and toward engagement, resilience, and optimism.

Building the social virtues and their practices into everything we do affirms our commitment to a good life that's available only through cooperation. We are empowered because we see opportunities to pursue compassion, discernment, imagination, integration, and courage everywhere we look. Our allies are heartened because we endorse and reciprocate their efforts. Our critics are drawn into collaboration because we're responsive to their point of view. Even our adversaries may in time become convinced that cooperation trumps antagonism.

Infusing cooperative wisdom into all our actions creates blessings for ourselves and for everyone we encounter. When things fall apart, the social virtues bring people together.

And together is the only way we can repair damage from the past, thrive in the present, and set a hopeful stage for the future.

ACKNOWLEDGMENTS

Donald Scherer: Because I have pondered, studied, taught, and written about ethics for decades, I am keenly aware of the centuries of ethical thought that have informed my work. From the American pragmatists I learned to assess human communication for its ability to improve the quality of our lives as social animals. I have been deeply influenced by a century of natural science, in which researchers have framed the regularities they observe and report within a given environment. I will always be grateful for Ludwig Wittgenstein's vision of human life and language as the communal quest of a social species to fashion environments in which people can thrive. I also wish to acknowledge the formative influence of my mentor, Norman Malcolm, as well as the scores of graduate students who stimulated my thinking as I mentored them.

Over the years I have had the honor of consulting with municipalities, government agencies, small businesses, large corporations, and faith communities. I've learned from the passion and intelligence of hundreds of people who dedicate themselves to realizing the mutual benefits that are possible only through cooperation. I regard everyone with whom I have worked to that end as family.

I have been most fundamentally molded by the enduring love I've shared with my wife, Char. In the development of this book I have benefited from the devotion of my co-author, Carolyn Jabs. I credit her and our editor, Diana Landau, with any felicity of expression we have achieved.

Like most thoughtful people, I care immensely about the quality of the world I will leave to future generations. My grandchildren have brought this general concern into sharp focus. In the hope that this work will shine light on human possibilities and offer guidance for beneficial and fruitful living, I dedicate this book to them.

Carolyn Jabs: In many ways this book draws on all the books, classes, conversations, and experiences that have been part of my life. If I tried to acknowledge all the friends and writers who have contributed to my thinking over the past six decades, I would inevitably omit important influences, so a sincere and global thank-you must suffice.

Specifically I am grateful to the Philosophy Department of Bowling Green State University. By taking a chance on a midlife student, they made it possible for me to walk into Dr. Scherer's seminar. Without that fortu-itous meeting this book would not have been possible. Over the past seven years Don has generously shared a lifetime of analysis and insight, patiently helping me master an approach to living that I wouldn't have discovered on my own. I am a different, wiser person because I was lucky enough to be his student, his collaborator, and his friend.

As an author I am indebted to three early editors: Mary McLaughlin, Andrea Linne, and Caryl Avery. Each of them pushed me to be a better writer by asking tough questions about substance and form. This book benefited tremendously from the editorial attention of Diana Landau, who introduced discipline, helping us convert meandering conversation into a polished manuscript. Don and I are also grateful to Linda Herman, who captured our concepts in her design for the cover and the interior of the book, and to Kristi Hein, whose proofreading spared us the embarrassment of inadvertent error.

Finally, I am grateful for the contributions of my family: my parents, who instilled an early and enduring interest in ethical thinking; my siblings, whose conversations deepened my understanding of the virtues; and my children, who gave me ample opportunity to put the virtues into practice. Most of all I'm grateful to my husband, David, who encouraged me to follow this project wherever it led.

APPENDIX

Five Social Virtues and
Fifteen Practices That Support Them

Proactive Compassion: Anticipating and Responding to Vulnerabilities
1. Respond to risks revealed by specialization
2. Intercept harms triggered by change
3. Address gaps between assigned responsibilities

Deep Discernment: Discovering Bedrock Values
1. Distinguish bedrock values from means
2. Be vigilant about accumulating harms
3. Honor multiple points of view

Intentional Imagination: Expanding What's Possible
1. Examine assumptions
2. Extend known resources
3. Excavate concealed resources

Inclusive Integrity: Reworking Cooperation So Everyone Can Thrive
1. Enlist flexible specialists
2. Anticipate predictable weakness
3. Treat every plan as a hypothesis

Creative Courage: Embracing the Risks of Engagement
1. Address the failing hypothesis
2. Confront imbalanced benefits without undue blame
3. Hold tight to the cooperative vision

INDEX

accumulations, 79–85, 136
air quality, 59, 82, 128
American with Disabilities Act, 98
Anderson, Ray, 166, 167
  and Interface, 166
Arab Spring, 170
assumptions, 92–103
Astor, John Jacob, 114
Bathsheba, 173
Bauer, Marybeth, 196
Bell, Alexander Graham, 115
benefits, 2, 4, 7–9, 13–19, 21–23, 26,
  28, 47–50, 61, 104, 108, 115, 120,
  130, 139, 142, 144, 148, 150–52,
  166–68, 176, 178–82, 187, 191–93,
  204, 205–13
  mixed, 68–70, 80, 83, 86, 160, 175,
  196–97, 197–99, 199–200, 200–3
  mutual (vs. exclusive), 7–9, 13,17,
  27, 28, 30–31, 32–56, 59, 61, 63,
  88, 90–92, 94–95, 107, 121, 124–26,
  135–37, 141, 147, 149, 152–56,
  157–60, 164–]68, 171–73, 174–75,
  178, 179, 182–84, 187–88, 194–96,
  196–97, 197–99, 199–200, 200–3,
  205–6, 212–13
  proportionate (vs. disproportionate),
  18, 37, 58, 63, 67, 162, 168, 169–71,
  172, 174, 176, 212
beneficiary, 48, 160, 184
Berkshares, 198–99
blame, 7–12, 18, 19, 22, 29, 30, 52–53,
  90, 151, 168–77, 205, 210
bystander(s), 29, 30, 55, 122, 159, 160,
  165, 168, 172–77, 184–88, 202
Bowling Green State University, 3, 4, 5,
  101, 200–3
CAFO (confined animal feeding operation), 118–119
Carson, Rachel, 3, 81, 175–177, 184
change, 3–10, 12, 23, 24, 26–29, 45–53,

61, 64, 67, 68, 71–73, 75–80, 86, 97,
  100, 109, 110, 113, 126, 129, 136,
  140–56, 157, 158, 160–63, 174, 176,
  180–82, 186, 187, 191, 195, 200–3,
  211–13.
cheating, 17–18
Christianity (versions of), 114
community, 8, 33, 48, 49, 50, 58–60, 63,
  64, 66, 91, 94, 100, 113, 115, 123,
  147, 158, 179–82, 185–86, 199–200
  boundaries of, 86–89, 200–03
  expanding, 86–87, 160–188, 196–97
  good of, 8, 33–34, 35–36, 48–52,
  55–60, 63–66, 88–91, 100, 104, 115,
  123, 158–59, 168–171, 175–77, 179,
  183–84, 187, 194–96, 197–99, 200–3,
  205
compassion (proactive), 32–61, 69, 77,
  140, 161, 166, 174, 175, 179,
  191, 194–96, 201, 205
  limits of, 60,61
compassionate chain reaction, 46–52
conflict, 32, 63–66, 69, 83–85, 88–92,
  100–3, 104–9, 117–19, 161, 168–71,
  174–75, 193–203
consequences, 52–53
  inadvertent, 52–53
  unintended, 28, 29, 40, 52–53, 80–83,
  121
conservation, 104–09
conservation bank, 197
cooperation, 6–10, 13–20, 28–31, 33,
  36, 37, 48–49, 100
  and mutual benefit, 21, 29–31, 37, 49,
  50, 53, 58–61, 67, 169–88, 190–209
corn, 66, 77–79, 139
cost, 69, 82, 104, 107, 116, 117–19,
  128, 139, 146, 152, 169–71
  and consent, 152
  vs. harm, 70, 82, 108, 109, 152–55
courage (creative), 157–188, 195–96,

198–99, 200–3, 204, 206, 210–213
David (King, of Israel), 173–75
deafness, 64, 98, 135
Decker, Bill, 185, 186
dementia, 39, 69, 194–196
discernment (deep), 62–92, 99, 113, 122, 128, 196, 197
  limits of, 91, 92
dispositions, 29–31. *See also* virtues
ditches, 71–74
diversity of points of view, 205
downstream effects, 71, 87, 138–41, 146
  anticipating, 138–41
Ebola, 45
Edison, Thomas, 115
efficiency, 76, 77, 127, 141
empathy, 33, 34
environment(s), 12, 13,83–85
  natural, 59, 60
  social, 59, 83, 84
  inclusive vs. exclusive, 99, 135
  unfamiliar (foreign), 43, 44, 51
  and change, 3–10, 12, 23, 24, 26–29, 45–53, 61, 64, 67, 68, 71–73, 75–80, 86, 97, 100, 109, 110, 113, 126, 136, 140–56, 157, 158, 160–63, 174, 176, 180–82, 186, 187, 191, 195, 200–3, 211–13
    and firefighters, 163, 64
    and GPS, 44
    and hospitality, 43, 44
    and service organizations, 44
Environmental Defense Fund, 196, 97
exclusion, 26–31, 99, 135. *See also* outliers
  costs of, 169–73
externalities, 22–24, 57, 69, 84, 104, 107, 108, 109, 118–19, 128, 139–41, 145–46, 149–52, 177, 192, 197, 202, 208
  of air pollution, 81–83
  of antibiotics, 171, 175–76
  of internet use, 25, 26
  of highway design 22, 23
  of intense energy use, 22–25, 105
  of pathogens, 45, 52, 175
  of power lawnmowers, 81
  of restaurant eating, 23, 24, 38, 135
  of texting, 50
facts (vs. matters of opinion), 87
fisheries, 69, 152–55
Ford, Henry, 76, 77, 117
General Electric, 199, 200
  and Ecoimagination, 199, 200
Gerner, Henry, the Reverend, 201–3
G.I. bill, 115
Glacier National Park, 85
Gladwell, Malcolm, 80
Good Samaritan, 56–58
good life, 213
Gottman, John, 124
Great Barrington, Massachusetts, 197–99
habitat, 4, 29, 61, 62, 196, 197
Hammurabi's Code, 47
Harkin, Thomas, 98
harm(s), 17–20, 33–37, 82–86
  accumulating, 79–85
  inadvertent (vs. looking for villains) 18–20
  prevented, 41–42
  proportionate (vs. disproportionate), 18, 37, 58, 63, 67, 162, 168, 169–71, 172, 174, 176, 212
  vs. hospitality, 43–45
  warned against, 43
Hawken, Paul, 166
health(care), 68–70, 82, 84, 88, 115, 128 132, 133, 141, 142, 194
  cost of, 68–70, 82, 128
Hickory Pass Ranch, 196, 197
Hirzel, Joe, 118–119
Hudson River, 138, 200
humility, 207
hypothesis, 18, 146–56, 160–64, 177–88, 193, 199, 202
  failing, 160–65
  failed, 165–68
imagination (intentional), 64–65,

93–121
learned, 94–95
insignificance, 24–25, 46, 82, 83, 104, 108, 140–141, 164, 182–88
integrity (inclusive), 122–156
and change 152–156
intentions (good), 1, 2, 11–31, 36, 46, 53, 90, 94, 194
Jerome, William, 200–03
Johnson, Ron, 162, 163
Kennedy, Robert, 202
Kent State University, 200–3
King, Martin Luther, Jr., 202, 205, 206
Kingsford, E. G. ((Kingsford Briquets), 117
knowledge (sharing), 45, 133, 137, 144–45, 199–200
risks of, 46
and its obsolescence, 46
Kroc, Ray, 23
labor, 14, 30, 210
division of, 14, 30
Lake Erie, 116, 148, 149, 151
land planning, 53, 80–82
lawns, 80–82, 101–3
leadership, 144, 205, 206
Locke, John, 114
Ma, Yo Yo, 130
and the Silk Road Ensemble, 130
Mandela, Nelson, 179
and the Truth and Reconciliation Commission, 179
margins, 27, 133–38. See also outliers, tolerance
means, 67–79
mental health (policy), 161, 194
Mill, John Stuart, 172
morbidity and mortality committees, 172
Nathan (the prophet), 174–77
New Orleans, 53
and Katrina, 182
NOAA (National Oceanic and Atmo spheric Administration), 4, 181
nutrients, 86, 116, 139, 149

Olmsted, Frederick Law, 80–81, 85–86
organization (human), 46–49
and agriculture, 73–75
and supply chain, 25–26, 77
Orwell, George, 169
outliers, 20, 26–28, 205. See also exclusion
parenthood, 34–36, 38–39, 41–42, 54
Paris accords of 2015, 186–187
partners (cooperative),15, 16, 35, 87, 90, 91, 92, 122, 124, 125, 127, 130–33, 133–134, 140, 146, 158, 170, 171
imperfect, 161, 167, 173, 177, 178, 179
Penney, JC, 162–63
perspective (point-of-view/viewpoints), 85–91, 92, 99
Pinchot, Gifford, 106–7
resilience, 144–45, 170, 207–11, 13
resources, 25, 29, 33, 47, 93–120, 208
extending, 83, 103–111, 120
excavating, 111–119, 120
reallocation of, 65
recognizing, 96–103, 120
respect, 89–91, 100
responsibility, 11, 12, 18, 19, 32, 52, 53, 100
response-ability, 52–60, 160, 164, 166, 172, 177, 183–84, 187, 191, 194, 207–11
Richards, Ellen Swallow, 138–39
risk(s), 2, 8, 15, 30, 34–36, 38–53, 94, 147–48, 153–55, 157–88, 190, 193, 196–97, 200–03, 212
and specialization, 16, 52–57, 144, 193
in faith practice, 147–48
in habitat protection, 4, 60, 196–97
in law enforcement, 161, 165, 184, 200–3
in product development, 27–28, 144–45, 145–46, 166–67, 197–99, 199–200
in human services, 26, 135–41, 161, 200–3

in affirming conflicting rights, 200–3, 205–7
of capital, 143–44, 170–71, 197–99, 199–200
Rosie the Riveter, 121
sanitation engineers vs. fisheries, 86–87
scale, 20, 23–26, 79–85, 92
and tipping points, 24–26
Schumacher Center for New Economics, 198
significance (vs. insignificance), 24
Silk Road project, 130
Sinclair Community College, 109
society (human), 36–37, 46–49, 91. *See also* parenthood *and* labor (division of)
Solomon, 63, 64
specialization(s), 20
and communication between, 21, 22, 38–41
and safety, 38–45
and silos, 21, 22, 51–60, 84, 85
sport injuries, 27
speaking truth to power, 173–77
specialists, 15, 19–23, 38–45, 48–52
flexible, 51, 126–32, 142, 199–200
specialization, 13–15, 84, 85
independence vs. interdependence and cooperation, 15
standard operating procedure, 75–77, 83–85, 108–11, 161. *See also* tradition
sustainability, 13, 60, 65, 80, 100, 130, 134, 141, 142, 153–155, 185, 190, 205, 209, 212
swamp, 71–74
and drainage, 71–72
and flooding, 72–73
and "too much" water, 73–74
Swift, Gustavus Franklin, 117-18

tai chi, 151
Ten Commandments (the), 47
3M Corporation, 144–145
thriving, 125, 147, 168, 205–12
Title IX, 115
tolerance, 28, 53, 134, 146, 191, 194
Tortoriello, Frank, 197–99
tradition, 46–49, 75, 76
limits of, 47–49
tunnel vision, 20–23
U.S. Fish and Wildlife Service, 197
upstream (vs. downstream), 20, 70–75, 86–87, 138–41, 145–46, 148–51, 185
Uriah the Hittite, 173–174
Valley Conservation Council, 60
values, 67–79, 99
bedrock, vs. means, 67–79
victim, 54, 160, 165, 172, 173, 187
villains, 12, 18
virtues, 29–31, 32–61, 62–92, 93–121, 122–156, 157–188
refined, 31
and practices, 4, 6
virtuosos, 128–31
vulnerabilities, 32–61, 68, 69, 134–38, 138–41, 146–51, 152–55, 162–64, 180–82, 205
anticipated, 35–38
at the margins, 32, 134–39
from accumulation, 32, 138–41
from differences, 32; accentuated by pace of change, 141–45
waste, 4, 29, 38, 44, 86, 108–111, 116–119, 139, 145–146, 166, 169, 185, 211
winter coats, 65, 67
wisdom, 32, 189–213

ABOUT THE AUTHORS

Dr. Donald Scherer, PhD, is Professor Emeritus in the Philosophy Department of Bowling Green State University, Ohio. For more than forty years he has thought deeply about environmental ethics and social environments in which people can thrive. *Cooperative Wisdom* distills insights gleaned from his research and writing, teaching and mentoring. Dr. Scherer has won national respect for devising innovative partnerships that respond effectively to incipient conflict. He has consulted with businesses, faith communities, volunteer organizations, and educational institutions including Georgia State University and Santa Clara University. Among other projects, he has advised the World Wildlife Fund on enlisting Fortune 500 corporations in ecological restoration, promoted interfaith dialogue through the World Council of Churches, developed ethical guidelines for responding to oil spills with the National Oceanic and Atmospheric Agency (NOAA), devised plans for exotic species management with regional park systems, and consulted with various cities on innovative design for urban corridors. Dr. Scherer served as past president of Green Energy Ohio. He is the lead author of *Upstream/Downstream: Issues in Environmental Ethics* and co-author with Dr. James Child of *Two Paths Toward Peace*. He lives with his wife, Char, in a wind-powered home in Bowling Green, Ohio.

Carolyn Jabs, MA, is an experienced professional writer with a reputation for insight and sensitivity in dealing with complex social issues. She has written hundreds of articles about families, ethics, environmental issues, and the Internet. Her work has appeared in many publications including the *New York Times, Newsweek, Working Mother,* and *Family PC.* Her award-winning column, Growing Up Online, is featured in regional parenting publications across the country. She is the author of *The Heirloom Gardener* and a contributor to *Children and Nature: Making Connections.* Carolyn and her husband, David, live in Santa Barbara, California, where she participates in the Women's Fund, serves on the board of the local chapter of the Association for Women in Communications, and practices tai chi.

PRAISE FROM EARLY READERS

"In *Cooperative Wisdom*, Don Scherer and Carolyn Jabs provide a friendly, accessible guide to tackling some of our most vexing problems. This is a book that will educate, inspire, and empower."

—Dr. Nancy Unger
Author of *Beyond Nature's Housekeepers:*
American Women in Environmental History

"A great read! *Cooperative Wisdom* helped me think more clearly about the skills I need to put together coalitions that produce benefits for everyone involved."

—Dale Arnold
Director of Energy, Utility and Local Government Policy,
Ohio Farm Bureau Federation

"Penetrating, accessible, and profoundly practical, *Cooperative Wisdom* delivers on its promise. It truly is a distillation of a lifetime of practical problem solving, a primer in how to transform unsustainable environments into sustainable ones."

—Dr. Mark Aulisio
Consultant on Medical Ethics, Case Western Reserve University

"Provides a framework for resolving conflicts by showing how the values we share dwarf the issues that divide us."

—Dr. Jeff Flagg
Program Director, Sagamore Institute of the Adirondacks

"This is a book I would like to share and discuss with trusted friends. The practices Scherer and Jabs describe open up opportunities for cooperation in situations that might otherwise seem hopelessly deadlocked."

—Dr. Angela Zimmann
Visiting Professor, Lutheran Theological Seminary at Gettysburg

NEXT STEPS

Thank you for reading *Cooperative Wisdom*. We hope you have found the ideas explored here helpful. If you think the book might be valuable to people you know, please recommend it to them.

Mastering the social virtues takes time and support from others. We are working to build an online community that will encourage people who are making efforts to restore and strengthen cooperation in a variety of settings. If you have experiences or stories about the social virtues in action, please share them on our Facebook page, facebook.com/cooperativewisdom, or on our website, cooperativewisdom.org. On the website you can also:

- Purchase additional books (discounts available for classes and book groups)
- Find out about author appearances and interactions
- Sign up for our e-mail newsletter
- Discover additional resources for cooperators, including study guides

Finally, if you think the book has merit, we would be grateful for a review on the site where you purchased it. Reviews from readers like you can make a huge difference as we work to spread the word about *Cooperative Wisdom*. Thank you.

CPSIA information can be obtained
at www.ICGtesting.com
Printed in the USA
LVOW01s0209190516
488921LV00005B/7/P